Preface

This book is mainly targeted for the exam of Modern Indian Political Thought for all Universities. It has been introduced in market after seeing the huge demand of ready to grasp material for exams with high level of quality, and its un-availability in market. We the GullyBaba Publishing House (P) Ltd. took a step ahead to publish the quality material focusing on exams at the same time giving you indepth knowledge about the subject.

GPH Book is the pioneer effort that provides a unique methodology so as to perform better in exams. If your goal is to attain higher grade use this powerful study tool independently or along with your text.

On the Web : ***www.gullybaba.com*** *is the vital resource for your exams acting as catalyst to boost up your preparation. Now you can access us on the net through* ***www.doeacconline.com, www.ignouonline.com, and www.astrologyeverywhere.com.***

We gratefully acknowledges the significant contributions of Mr. S.K. Goel, Mr. Dinesh Verma, Mr. Mahesh Chand, Mrs. Bimla Devi, Mrs. Bhawna Verma and our experts in bringing out this publication.

New Delhi

Dear Reader, You are welcome in the world of GullyBaba Publishing House.

By long, in deep study & Research, we assure / guarantee you the most reliable, latest & accurate information on the subject.

We still believe that there is always a scope for improvement.

You a reader can be our best guide in making this book more interesting & user friendly.

We welcome your valuable suggestions.

Feedback about the book can be sent at **feedback@gullybaba.com.**

Publisher.

Topics Covered

BLOCK-6 Gandhism: Evolution and Character

BLOCK-7 Nationalism and Social Revolution-I (Socialism)

BLOCK-8 Nationalism and Social Revolution II (Communists)

Contents

Question Papers

Chapter 1

Background of Social and Political Thought

Q1. Define colonialism. Discuss different stages of British colonialism in India. [Dec 09, Q 1]

Or

Examine the courses of the third stage of the British colonialism.

Ans. Colonialism is essentially the **integration** of the economy of the colony with the economy of the metropolis through **trade** and **industry**. This integration is geared to serve the interests of the metropolitan economy and to that extent, it completely subordinates the economy of the colony to the economy of the metropolis.

In other words, colonialism is a relationship between two countries, a relationship of domination and subordination, a relationship of political control exercised by one country over another.

The aim of this political control is to subordinate and control the colonial economy and this subordination takes place mainly through trade and industry, and does not remain confined to economy only but spreads to all the areas of society.

This subordination (not just economic subordination but a much larger subordination of society, polity, culture, institutions, ideas and even minds of the people) was not static but was a **process**, spread over various stages.

The First Stage: The Period of Monopoly Trade and Revenue Appropriation

During the first stage of colonialism, the basic objectives of colonialism were:

i) Monopoly of trade with the colony vis-a-vis other European merchants and the colony's traders and producers. However, handicraftmen or other producers were employed on account of the colonial state, their surplus was directly seized not in the manner of industrial capitalists, but in that of merchant-usurers.

ii) The direct appropriation of revenue or surplus through the use of the state power. The colonial state required large financial resources to wage wars in the colony and on the seas and to maintain naval forces, forts, armies and trading posts. Direct appropriation of the colony's surplus was also needed to finance purchase of colonial products. Directly appropriated surplus was also to serve as a source of profit to the merchants, corporations and the exchequer of the metropolis. The large number of Europeans employed in the colony also appropriated a large part of the colony's surplus directly through extortion and corruption or high salaries.

It is to be noted that **(i)** the element of plunder and direct seizure of surplus is very strong during this stage of colonialism: and **(ii)** there is no significant import of metropolitan manufactures into the colony.

A basic feature of colonial rule during this period was that no basic changes were introduced in the colony as regards administration, judicial system, transport and communication, methods of agricultural or industrial production, forms of business Management or economic organisation, education or intellectual fields, culture, and social organisation. The only changes made were in military organisation and technology, which contemporary independent chieftains and rulers in the colonies, were also trying to introduce, and in administration at the top of the structure of revenue collection so as to make it more efficient.

This was because the colonial mode of surplus appropriation via purchase of colony's urban handicrafts and plantation and other products through a buyer's monopoly and through control over its revenues, did not require basic socio-economic and administrative changes in the colony. It could be superimposed over its existing economic, social, cultural, ideological and political structures. Also the colonial power did not feel the need to penetrate the village deeper than their indigenous predecessors and done as long as their economic surplus was successfully sucked out.

The Second Stage: Exploitation through Trade —The Era of Foreign Investment and International Competition for Colonies

The newly developing industrial and commercial interests in the metropolis and their ideologies began to attack the existing mode of exploitation of the colony with a view to making it serve their interests. Moreover, as it became clear that colonial control was to be a long-term phenomenon, the metropolitan capitalist class as a whole demanded forms of surplus appropriation which would not destroy the golden goose. It realised that the plundering form is less capable than others of reproducing conditions for its advantage.

Industrial bourgeoisie's interest in the colony lay in satisfying the need for outlets for their ever-increasing output of manufactured goods. Linked with this was the need to promote the colony's exports. This was for several reasons: **(i)** The colony could buy more imports only if it increased its exports, which could only be of agricultural and mineral products, to pay for them. Colony's exports had also to pay for the 'drain' or to earn foreign exchange to provide for the export of business profits and the savings and pensions of Europeans working there; **(ii)** The metropolis desired to lessen dependence on non-empire sources of raw material and foodstuffs. Hence, the need to promote the production of raw materials in the colony. The colonial rulers must enable the colony to do so. The colony had to be developed as a reproductive colony in the agricultural and mineral spheres and **(iii)** As the subordinated complement of a capitalist economy; the use of the colony both as a market for goods and as a supplier of raw materials most occur within the perspective of extended reproduction.

Thus, the essence of the second stage of colonialism was the making of the colony into a subordinate trading partner which would export raw materials and import manufactures. The colony's social surplus was to be appropriated through trade on the basis of selling dear and buying cheap. This stage of colonialism could even embrace counties which retained political freedom.

The colony could not be exploited in the new way within its existing economic, political, administrative, social, cultural and ideological setting; this setting had to be shattered and transformed all along the line.

The transformation was actively undertaken under the slogan of development and modernisation. In the economic field, this meant integrating the colonial economy with the world capitalist economy and above all, the metropolitan economy. The chief instrument of this integration was the freeing of foreign trade (in the colony) of all restrictions and tariffs, especially in so far as its trade with the metropolis was concerned. For most of this period, the colony was to be far more of a free trading country than the metropolis itself. Free entry was now given to the capitalists of the metropolis to develop plantations, trade, transport, mining and in some cases industries in the colony. The colonial state gave active financial and other help to these capitalists, even when the doctrine of laissez faire reigned supreme at home. The agrarian structure of the colony was sought to be transformed with the purpose of making the colony a reproductive one by initiating capitalist agriculture.

Similarly, a major effort to improve the system of transport and communication was made.

Major changes occurred in the administrative field. Colonial administration now had to be more extensive and comprehensive, if metropolitan products were to penetrate the interior towns and villages and the agricultural produce was to be drawn out of them. The legal structure in the colony had to be overhauled. Sanctity of contract and its enforcement became essential, if transactions needed to promote imports and exports were to become viable. It was during this stage that the Western capitalist legal and judicial system was introduced in the colonies and semi-colonies. The changes, however, often related only to criminal law, law of contract, and civil law procedure; personal law, including that of marriage and inheritance, was often left untouched.

Modern education was now introduced basically with a view to man the new vastly expanded administrative machinery, but also with a view to transform the colony's society and culture.

The second stage of colonialism generated a liberal imperialist political ideology and sections of imperialist statesmen and administrators who talked of training the colonial people in the arts of democracy and self-government. It was believed that if the colonial people 'learnt' the virtues of law and order, sanctity of business contract, free trade, and economic development, the economic interest of colonialism could be perpetuated even if the metropolitan power was to withdraw direct political and administrative control.

One point needs to be stressed in this connection: The colonial authorities did not deliberately set out to underdevelop the colony. On the contrary, their entire effort was to develop it so that it could complement, though in a subordinate position, the metropolitan economy. Underdevelopment was not the desired but the inevitable consequence of the inexorable working of colonialism of trade and its inner contractions.

The earlier forms of surplus extraction continued during this stage and became a drag on its full working. Moreover, since the colony had also to pay the costs of its transformation, the burden on the colonial peasant rose steeply.

The Third Stage: The Era of Foreign Investment and International Competition for Colonies

A new stage of colonialism was ushered in as a result of several major changes in the world economy:

(i) Spread of industrialisation to several countries of Europe, North America, and Japan;

(ii) Intensification of industrialisation as a result of the application of scientific knowledge to industry, and

(iii) Further unification of the world market due to a revolution in the means of international transport. There now occurred an intense struggle for new, secure, and exclusive markets and sources of agricultural and mineral raw materials and foodstuffs. Moreover, expanded reproduction at home and extended exploitation of colonies and semi-colonies produced large accumulations of capital in the developed capitalist countries. There occurred simultaneously concentration of capital and merger of banking capital with industrial capital in several countries. This led to large-scale export of capital and search for monopolised fields and areas where it could be invested. All the three aspects namely markets, sources of raw material, and capital export, were interlinked. As struggle for the division and redivision of the world among the imperialist countries was intensified, fresh use was found for the older colonies. Their social surpluses and manpower could be used as counters in this struggle. Colonialism at this stage also served important political and ideological purpose in the metropolis. Nationalism or Chauvinism, adventure, and glorification of empire could be used to tone down the growing social divisions at home by stressing the common interests in the empire. More specifically, empire and glory were used to counter the growth of popular democracy and the introduction of adult franchise, which could have posed a danger to the political domination of the capitalist class and which increased the importance of the ideological instruments of hegemony over society. In this hegemony, the ideas of empire played an increasingly important role.

Where colonies had been acquired in the earlier stages, vigorous efforts were made to consolidate metropolitan control. Reactionary imperialist polices now replaced liberal imperialist policies of the earlier stage. To preserve direct colonial rule on a permanent basis was now seen essential on all counts, but especially, to attract metropolitan capital to the colony and to provide it security.

Once again the earlier forms of surplus appropriation continued into this stage. In fact, in some of the colonies, for example, India, the earlier two forms of surplus extraction remained more important than the third one.

Politically and administratively the third stage of colonialism meant more intensive control over the colony. Moreover, it was now even more important that colonial administration should permeate every pore of colonial society and that every port, town, and village be linked with world economy. The administration also now became more bureaucratic, detailed and efficient.

A major change now occurred in the ideology of colonialism. The talk of training the colonial people for independence died out and was revived later only under the pressure of anti-imperialist movements. Instead came the talk of benevolent despotism, of the colonial people being a permanently immature or 'child' people over whom permanent trusteeship would have to be exercised. Geography, 'race', climate, history, social organisation, culture and religion of the colonial people were cited as factors which made them permanently unfit for self-government. This was in stark contrast to second stage belief that colonial people were capable of being educated and trained into becoming carbon copies of the advanced European people and therefore, into self-governing nations.

Efforts at the transformation of the colony's economy, society, and culture continued during this stage also though once again with paltry results. However, the tendency developed to abandon social and cultural modernisation, especially as the anti-imperialist forces began to take up the task. Colonial administration increasingly assumed a neutral stance on social and cultural questions and then began to support social and cultural reaction in the name of preserving indigenous institutions.

Q2. Write a note on followings:-
(i) colonial intervention in social and cultural field in India
(ii) colonial intervention in Indian polity
(iii) colonial intervention in Indian economics [Dec 08, Q 1]

Ans. Colonial intervention in Social and Cultural field in India :
The British colonialism penetrated into every area of Indian society. Along with British rule also came a link with the West; and ideas which were developed in Western Europe made their entry into India. Through trade and travel, India had for centuries contact not only with the countries of Asia but also with Europe. Through these sources news of events and happenings in Europe and elsewhere and details of the new thinking taking place in the West were already reaching India in the 18th century. British rule not only hastened their arrival in India but the very nature of the foreign domination quickened these influences with a local meaning charged with immediacy and relevance.

The intellectual life of the Indian people were influenced by such ideas as democracy and sovereignty of the people, rationalism and humanism. These ideas helped Indians not only to take a critical look at their own society, economy, and government, but also to understand the true nature of British imperialism in India.

These ideas through many channels; education, the press, pamphlets and the public platforms. The spread of modern education, however, was very limited. If the foreign government initially neglected primary and secondary education, it turned hostile to higher education soon after 1858. As many of the educated Indians began to use their recently acquired modern knowledge to analyse and criticise the imperialist and exploitative character of British rule and to organise an anti-imperialist political movement, the British administrators began to press continuously for the curtailment of higher education. The structure and pattern, aims, methods, curricula and content of education were all designed to serve colonialism.

A few other aspects of Indian education arising out of its colonial character should be noted. One was the complete neglect of modern technical education which was a basic necessity for the rise and development of modern industry. Another was the emphasis on English as the medium of instruction in place of the Indian languages. This not only prevented the spread of education to the masses but also created a wide linguistic and cultural gulf between the educated and the masses. Government's refusal to allocate adequate funds of education gradually reduced the educational standards to an extremely low level. And because the students had to pay fees in schools and colleges, education became a virtual monopoly of the middle and upper classes and the city and town dwellers.

New ideas, a new economic and political life, and British rule produced a deep impact on the social life of the Indian people that was first felt in the urban areas and which later penetrated to the villages. Modern industries, new means of transport, growing urbanisation and increasing employment of women in factories, offices, hospital and schools promoted social change. Social exclusiveness and caste rigidities were eroded. The total disruption of old land and rural relationships upset the caste balance in the countryside. Though many of the evils persisted, the penetration of capitalism made social status dependent mainly on money and profit making became the most desirable social activity.

In the beginning the policies of the colonial state also encouraged social reform. Efforts were made to modernise Indian society in order to enable the economic penetration of the country and the consolidation of British rule. To some extent, the humanitarian instincts of some of the officials aroused by the glaring social injustices enshrined in the Indian caste system and the low status of women in society also played a role. The Christian missionaries also contributed towards the reform of Indian society at this stage. But very soon the basic conservative character and long-term interest of colonialism asserted themselves and colonial policies towards social reform were changed. The British, therefore, withdrew their support from the reformers and gradually came to side with the socially orthodox and conservative elements of society.

(ii) Colonial intervention in Indian Polity:

Ans. Besides economy and social structure, British also sought to transform the existing polity. The main objectives behind the intervention of this factor were to increase the profitability of the Indian possessions and to maintain and strengthen the British hold over India. The administrative machinery of the Government of India was designed and developed to these ends. The main emphasis in this respect was placed on the maintenance of law and order so that trade with India and the exploitation of its resources could be carried out without disturbance.

British introduced some important institutions. These are :

Civil Service

The Civil Service was brought into existence by Lord Cornwallis. The East India Company had from the beginning carried on its trade in the East through servants who were paid low wages but who were permitted to trade privately. Later, when the Company became a territorial power, the same servants assumed administrative functions. They now became extremely corrupt. By oppressing local weavers and artisans, merchants, and zamindars, by extorting bribes and 'gifts' from rajas and nawabs, and by indulging in illegal private trades, they amassed untold wealth with which they retired to England. Clive and Warren Hastings made attempts to put an end to their corruption, but were only partially successful.

Cornwallis, who came to India as Governor-General in 1786, was determined to purify the administration, but he realised that the Company's servants would not give honest and efficient service as long as they were not given adequate salaries. He therefore enforced the rules against private trade and acceptance of presents and bribes by officials with strictness. At the same time, he raised the salaries of the Company's servants. For example, the collector of a district was to be paid Rs.1500 a month and one per cent commission the revenue collection of his district. In fact, the Company, Civil Service became the highest paid service in the world. Cornwallis also laid down that promotion in the Civil Service would be by seniority so that its members would remain independent of outside influence.

In 1800, Lord Wellesley pointed out that even though civil servants often ruled vast areas, they came to India at the immature age of 18 or so and were given no regular training before starting on their jobs. They generally lacked knowledge of Indian languages. Wellesley therefore established the College of Fort William at Calcutta for the education of young recruits to the Civil Service. The Directors of the Company disapproved of his action and in 1806 replaced it by their own East Indian College at Haileybury in England.

Till 1853 all appointments to the Civil Services were made by the Directors of the East India Company, who placated the members of the Board of Control by letting them make some of the nominations. The Directors fought hard to retain this lucrative and prized privilege and refused to surrender it even when their other economic and political privileges were taken away by Parliament. They lost it finally in 1853 when the Charter Act decreed that all recruits to the Civil Service wee to be selected through a competitive examination.

A special feature of the Indian Civil Service since the days of Cornwallis was the rigid and complete exclusion of Indians from it. It was laid down officially in 1793 that all higher posts in administration worth more than $500 a year in salary were to be held by Englishmen. This policy was also applied to other branches of Government, such as the army, police, judiciary, and engineering. In the words of John shore, who succeeded Cornwallis :

The fundamental principal of the English had been to make the whole Indian nation subservient, in every possible way, to the interest and benefits of ourselves. The Indians have been excluded from every honour, dignity, or office, which the lowest Englishmen could be prevailed to accept.

There were many factors that led the British follow such a policy. For one, they were convinced that an administration based on British ideas, institutions, and practices could be firmly established only by English personnel. And, then, they did not trust the ability and integrity of the Indians. For Example, Charle Grant, Chairman of the Court of Directors, condemned the people of India as "a race of men lamentably degenerate and base; retaining but a feeble sense of moral obligation;...and sunk in misery by their vices." Similarly, Cornwallis believed that "Every native of Hindustan is corrupt." It may be noted that this criticism did apply to some extent to a small class of Indian officials and zamindars of the time. But, then, it was equally if not more true of British officials in India. In fact, Cornwallis had proposed to give them high salaries in order to help them resist temptations and to become honest and obedient. But he never thought of applying the same adequate salaries to eradicate corruption among Indian officials.

In reality, the exclusion of Indians from higher grades of services was a deliberate policy. These services were required at the time to establish and consolidate British rule in Indian. Obviously the task could not be left to Indians who did not possess the same instinctive sympathy for, and understanding of, British interests as Englishmen. Moreover, the influential classes of British society were keen to preserve the monopoly of lucrative appointments in the Indian Civil Service and other services for their sons. In fact, they fought tooth and nail among themselves over these appointments. The right to make appointment was a perpetual bone of contention between the directors of the company and the members of the British cabinet.

Indians were, however, recruited in large numbers to fill subordinate posts as they were cheaper and much more readily available than Englishmen.

The Indian Civil Service gradually developed into one of the most efficient and powerful civil services in the world. Its members exercised vast power and often participated in the making of policy. They developed certain traditions of independence, integrity, and hard work, though these qualities obviously served British and not Indian interests. At the same time they gradually came to form a rigid and exclusive and proud 'caste' with an extremely conservative and narrow outlook. They came to believe that they had an almost Divine right to rule India. The Indian Civil Service has often been called the 'steel frame' which reared and sustained British rule in India. In course of time, it became the chief opponent of all that was progressive and advanced in Indian life and one of the main targets of attack by the rising Indian national movement.

Army

The second important pillar of the British regime in India was the army. It fulfilled three important functions. It was the instrument through which the Indian powers were conquered; it defended the British Empire in India from foreign rivals; and it safeguarded British supremacy from the ever-present threat of internal revolt.

The bulk of the Company's army consisted of Indian soldiers, recruited chiefly from the area at present included in U.P. and Bihar. For instance, in 1857, the strength of the army in India was 311,400 of whom 265,900 were Indians. Its officers were, however, exclusively British, at least since the days of Cornwallis.

In 1856, only three Indians in the army received a salary of Rs. 300 per month and the highest Indian officer was a subedar. A large number of Indian troops had to be employed as British troops were far too expensive. Moreover, the population of Britain was perhaps too small to provide the large soldiery needed for the conquest of India. As a counterweight, the army was officered entirely by British officials and a certain number of British troops were maintained to keep the Indian soldiers under control. Even so, it appears surprising today that a handful of foreigners could conquer and control India with a predominantly Indian army. This was possible because of two factors. First, there was absence of nationalism in the country at the time. A soldier from Bihar or Avadh did not think, and could not have thought, that in helping the Company defeat the Marathas or the Punjabis he was being anti-India. Secondly, the Indian soldier had a long tradition of loyally serving those who paid his salary. This was popularly known as loyalty to the salt. In other words, the Indian soldier was a good mercenary, and the Company on its party was a good paymaster. It paid its soldiers regularly and well, something that the Indian rulers and chieftains were no longer doing.

Police

The third pillar of British rule was the police whose creator was once again Cornwallis. He relieved the zamindars of their police functions and established a regular police force to maintain law and order. In this respect he went back to, and modernised, the old Indian system of thanas. Interestingly, this put Indian ahead of Britain where a system of police had not developed yet. Cornwallis established a system of circles or thanas headed by a daroga, who was an Indian. Later, the post of the District Superintendent of Police was created to head the police organisation in a district. Once again, Indians were excluded from all superior posts. In the villages, the duties of the police continued to be performed by village-watchmen who were maintained by the villagers. The police gradually succeeded in reducing major crimes such as dacoity. One of its major achievements was the suppression of thugs who robbed and killed travellers on the highways, particularly in Central India. The police also prevented the organisation of a large-scale conspiracy against foreign control, and when the national movement arose, the police was used to suppress it. In its dealings with the people, the police adopted an unsympathetic attitude. A Committee of Parliament reported in 1813 that the police committed "depradations on the peaceable inhabitants, of the same nature as those practised by the dacoits whom they were employed to suppress." And William Bentinck, the Governor General, wrote in 1832:

As for the police so far from being a protection to the people, I cannot better illustrate the public feeling regarding it, than by the following act, that nothing can exceed the popularity of a recent regulation by which, if a robbery has been committed, the police are prevented from making any enquiry into it, except upon the requisition of the persons robbed: that is to say, the shepherd is a more ravenous beast of prey than the wolf.

Judicial Organisation

The British laid the foundations of a new system of dispensing justice through a hierarchy of civil and criminal courts. Though given a start by Warren Hastings, system was established by Cornwallis in 1793. In each district was established a Diwani Adalat, or civil court, presided over by the District Judge who belonged to the Civil Service. Cornwallis thus separated the posts of the Civil Judge and the collector. Appeal from the District Court lay first to four Provincial Courts of Civil Appeal and then, finally, to the Sadar Diwani Adalat. Below the District Courts were Registrars' Courts, headed by Europeans, and a number of subordinate courts headed by Indian judges known as Munsifs and Amins. To deal with criminal cases, Cornwallis divided the Presidency of Bengal into four Divisions, in each of which a Court of Circuit presided over by the civil servants was established. Below these courts came a large number of Indian magistrates to try petty cases. Appeals from the Courts of Circuit lay with the Sadar Nizamat Adalat. The criminal courts applied Muslim Criminal Law in a modified and less harsh form so that the tearing apart of limbs and such other punishment were prohibited. The civil courts applied the customary law that had prevailed in any area or among a section of the people since time immemorial. In 1831, William Bentinck abolished the Provincial Courts of Appeal and Circuit. Their work was assigned first to Commissions and later to District Judges and District Collectors. Bentinck also raised the status and powers of Indians in the judicial service and appointed them as Deputy Magistrates, Subordinate Judges and Principal Sadar Amins. In 1865, High Courts were established at Calcutta, Madras and Bombay to replace the Sadar Courts of Diwani and Nizamat.

The British also established a new system of laws through the processes of enactment and codification of old laws. The traditional system of justice in India had been largely based on customary law which arose from long tradition and practice, though many laws were based on the shastras and shariat as well as on imperial authority. Though they continued to observe customary law in general, the British gradually evolved a new system of laws. They introduced regulations, codified the existing laws, and often systematised and modernised them through judicial interpretation. Their Charter Act of 1833 conferred all law-making power on the Governor General-in-Council. All this meant that Indians were now to live increasingly under man-made laws, which might be good or bad but which were openly the products of human reason, and not under laws which had to be obeyed blindly and which could not be questioned as they were supposed to be divine and therefore sacred.

In 1833, the Government appointed a Law Commission headed by Lord Macaulay to codify Indian laws. Its labours eventually resulted in the Indian Penal Code, the Western-derived Codes of Civil and Criminal Procedure and other codes of laws. The same laws now prevailed all over the country and they were enforced by a uniform system of courts. Thus, it may be said that India was judicially unified.

The Rule of Law

The British introduced the concept of the rule of law. This meant that administration was to be carried out, at least in theory, in obedience to laws, which clearly defined the rights, privileges, and obligations of the subjects and not according to the rights, privileges, and obligations of the subjects and not according to the caprice or personal discretion of the ruler. In practice, of course, the bureaucracy and the police enjoyed arbitrary powers and interfered with the rights and liberties of the people. One important feature of the concept of the rule of law was that any official could be brought before a court of law for breaches of official duty or for acts done in excess of his official authority. The rule of law was to some extent a guarantee of the personal liberty of a person. It is true that previous rulers of India had been in general bound by tradition and custom. But they always had the legal right to take any administrative steps they wanted and there existed no other authority before whom their acts could be questioned. The Indian rulers and chiefs sometimes exercised this power to do as they wanted. Under British rule, on the other hand, administration was largely carried on according to laws as interpreted by the courts though the laws themselves were often defective, were made not by the people through a democratic process but autocratically by the foreign rulers, and left a great deal of power in the hands of the civil servants and the police. But that was perhaps inevitable in a foreign regime that could not in the very nature of things be democratic or libertarian.

Equality Before Law

The Indian legal system under the British was based on the concept of equality before law. This meant that in the eyes of law all men were equal. The same law applied to all persons irrespective of their caste, religion, or class. Previously, the judicial system had paid heed to caste distinctions and had differentiated between the so-called high-born and low-born. For the same crime lighter punishment was awarded to a Brahmin than to a non-Brahmin. Similarly, in practice zamindars and nobles were not judged as harshly as the commoner. In fact, very often they could not be brought to justice at all for their actions. Now the humble could also move the machinery of justice.

There was, however, one exception to this excellent principle of equality before law. The European and their descendants had separate courts and even laws. In criminal cases they could be tried only by European judges. Many English officials, military officers, planters, and merchants behaved with Indians in a haughty, harsh, and even brutal manner. When efforts were made to bring them to justice, they were given indirect and undue protection and consequently light or no punishment by many of the European judges before whom alone they could be tried. Consequently, miscarriage of justice occurred frequently. In practice, there emerged another type of legal inequality. Justice became quite expensive as court fees had to be paid, lawyers engaged, and the expenses of witnesses met. Courts were often situated in distant towns. Law suits dragged on for years. The complicated laws were beyond the grasp of the illiterate and ignorant peasants. Invariably, the rich could turn and twist the laws, and courts to operate in their own favour. The mere threat to take a poor persons through the long process of justice from the lower court to the highest court of appeal and thus to face him with complete ruin often sufficed to bring him to heel. Moreover, the widespread prevalence of corruption in the ranks of the police and the rest of the administrative machinery led to the denial of justice. Officials often favoured the rich. The zamindars oppressed the riots without fear of official action. In contrast, the system of justice that had prevailed in pre-British times was comparatively informal, speedy, and inexpensive. Thus, while the new judicial system marked a great step forward in so far as it was based on the laudable principles of the rule of law and equality before law and on rational and humane man-made laws, it was a retrograde step in some other respects: it was now costlier and involved long delays.

(iii) Colonial intervention in Indian economics

Ans. The exact nature of the colonial intervention in the indigenous Indian economy can be grasped by studying its influence separately in different units of the economy like agriculture, trade and industry.

Impact on Agriculture

The British brought about important transformation in India's agricultural economy but this was not with a view to improving Indian agriculture but rather to obtain for themselves in the form of land revenue, all surplus available in agriculture and to force Indian agriculture to play its assigned role in a colonial economy. Old relationships and institutions were destroyed and new ones were born. But these new features did not represent a change towards modernisation or its movement in the right direction.

The British introduced two major land revenue and tenurial systems. One was the Zamindari system. (Later, a modified version of the same Zamindari system was introduced in North India under the name of the Mahalwari system). The other was the Ryotwari system.

Whatever the name of the system, it **was** the peasant cultivators who suffered.

They were forced to pay very high rents and for all practical purposes functioned as tenants-at-will. They were compelled to pay many illegal dues and cesses and were often required to perform forced labour or begar. What is more important, whatever, the name or nature of the revenue system, in effect the Government came to occupy the position of the landlord. Much later, especially after 1901, revenue rates were gradually reduced but then the agrarian economy had been ruined to such an extent and the landlords, moneylenders, and merchants had made such deep inroads into the village that it was of no practical use to the peasant cultivators themselves.

The greatest evil that arose out the British policies with regard to Indian agricultural economy was the emergence of the moneylender as an influential economic and political force in the country. Because of the high revenue rates demanded and the rigid manner of collection, the peasant cultivator had often to borrow money to pay taxes. In addition to paying exorbitant interest, when his crops were ready he was invariably forced to sell his produce cheap. The money-lender, on the other hand could manipulate the new judicial system and the administrative machinery to his advantage. In this regard the government, in fact, actually helped him, because without him the land revenue could not be collected in time, nor could the agricultural produce be brought to the ports for export. Even to get the commercial crops for export produced in the first instance, the Government depended on the moneylender to persuade the cultivator by offering to finance him through loans. It is not surprising, therefore; that in course of time the moneylender began to occupy a dominant position in the rural economy. In both the Zamindari and the Ryotwari areas, there occurred a large-scale transfer of land from the hands of the actual cultivators to the hands of money-lenders, merchants, official and rich peasant. This led to landlordism becoming the dominant feature of land relationships all over the country. Intermediate rent receivers also grew. This process is referred to as 'Sub-infeudation'. The new landlords and zamindars had even less of a link with land than the old zamindars. Instead of taking the trouble to organise a machinery for rent collection, they merely sublet their rights to intermediate rent receivers.

The impact of British rule thus led to the evolution of a new structure of agrarian relations that was extremely regressive. The new system did not at all permit the development of agriculture. New social classes appeared at the top as well as at the bottom of the social scale. There arose landlords, intermediaries and moneylenders at the top and tenants-at-will, share-croppers and agricultural labourers at the bottom. The new pattern was neither capitalism nor feudalism, nor was it a continuation of the old Mughal arrangement. It was a new structure that colonialism evolved. It was semi-feudal and semi-colonial in character.

The most unfortunate result of all this was that absolutely no effort was made either to improve agricultural practices or develop them along modern lines for increased production. Agricultural practices remained unchanged. Better types of implements, good seeds and various types of manures and fertilisers were not introduced at all. The poverty-stricken peasant cultivators did not have the resources to improve agriculture; the landlords had no incentive to do so, and the colonial Government, behaved like a typical landlord; it was interested only in extracting high revenues and did not take any steps to modernise and improve and develop Indian agriculture.

The result was prolonged stagnation in agricultural production. Agricultural statistics as available only for the 20th century; and here the picture was quite dismal. While overall agricultural production per head fell, by 14 per cent between 1901 and 1939, the fall in the per capital production of foodgrains was over 24 per cent. Most of this decline occurred after 1918.

Impact on Trade and Industry

As with agriculture, the British Indian Government controlled trade and industry purely with a view to foster British interests. India, no doubt, underwent a commercial revolution, which integrated it with the world market, but she was forced to occupy a subordinate position. Foreign trade took big strides forward especially after 1858 and Rs. 213 crores in 1899. It reached a peak of Rs. 758 crores in 1924. But this growth did not represent a positive feature in Indian economy nor did it contribute to the welfare of the Indian people, because it was used as the chief instrument through which the Indian economy was made colonial and dependent on world capitalism. The growth of the Indian foreign trade was neither natural nor normal; it was artificially fostered to serve imperialism. The composition and character of the foreign trade was unbalanced. The country was flooded with manufactured goods from Britain and forced to produce and export the raw materials Britain and other foreign counties needed.

Last but not least, the foreign trade affected the internal distribution of Income adversely. The British policy only helped to transfer resources from peasants and craftsmen to merchants, moneylenders and foreign capitalists.

A significant feature of India's foreign trade during this period was the constant excess of exports over imports. We should not, however, imagine that it was to India's advantage. These exports did not represent the future claims of India on foreign countries, but the drain of India's wealth and resources. We must also remember that the bulk of foreign trade was in foreign hands and that almost all of it was carried on through foreign ships.

One of the most important consequences of British rule was the progressive decline and destruction of urban and rural handicraft industries. Not only did India lose its foreign markets in Asia and Europe, but even the Indian market was flooded with cheap machine-made goods produced on a mass scale. The collapse of indigenous handicrafts followed.

The ruin of the indigenous industries and the absence of other avenues of employment forced millions of craftsmen to crowd into agriculture. Thus, the pressure of population on land increased.

Thus, it will be seen that industrial development in India till 1947 was slow and stunted and did not at all present in industrial revolution or even the initiation of one. What was more important, even the limited development was not independent but was under the control of foreign capital. Secondly, the structure of industry was such as to make its further development dependent on Britain. There was almost a complete absence of heavy capital goods and chemical industrial without which rapid and autonomous industrial development could hardly occur. Machine-tool, engineering and metallurgical industries were virtually non-existent. Moreover, India was entirely dependent on the imperialist world in the field of technology. No technological research was carried out in the country.

Q3. What did the thinkers of early 19th century in India have to say by way of critique of the then society and religion?

Ans. The early thinkers of modern India were pre-occupied mainly with social and religious issues. The political questions were paid little or no attention. Rammohan Roy's first published work, Tuffat-ul-Muwahihhidin (A Gift to Deists) (1803-4) is a rational critique of religious systems in general and the role of vested interests in religion. Rammohan in his later writings exposed the irrationality of Hindu religious rituals and dogmas, and social evils such as sati, child marriage etc. He considered religious reform most essential for both social reform and political modernisation. Thus, the beginning of modern Indian thinking is marked by a critique of the existing social order. This critique was carried forward by successors with a view to create a 'modern' society. Rammohan Roy's first published work Tuffat-ul- Muwahihhidin was a comparative study of religion and a rational critique of religion and society, He attacked the belief in revolution, prophets, miracle and all kinds of superstitions like seeking salvation through bathing in a river and worshipping a tree etc., and pleaded for rational explanation and empirical verification as the only basis for truth.' Radh Kanta Deb, Henry Derozio of Hindu College, despite their criticism of Rammohan for his pro-British attitude, agreed with him on the question of rational explanations. Akshay Kumar Dutt rejected religion supernaturalism and maintained that everything could be explained on the basis of reason and rationality. Naturally, therefore Brahmo Samaj and other streams of the reform movement in Bengal fought for widespread reforms in Hindu Society. Syed Ahmed Khan, Ranaut and other thinkers too stood for a rational critique of Indian society. Jyotiba Phule challenged the legitimacy of the Hindu Social order based on caste-hierarchy and pleaded for social transformation on egalitarian grounds. Rammohan's Tuhft not only forwarded the rational explanation and reason as the basis of truth but being a study of comparative religion, also contributed to the development of the idea of religious universalism and a universal outlook based or the unit of Godhead and monotheism. Rammohan explained different religions in terms of national embodiments of one universal theism.

Q4. What is Religious Revivalism?

Ans. Religious revivalism was a trend within the reform movements which sought to reform religion, but differed in one important respect. It sought to reform by an appeal to the past—the Golden Age, as it were. It sought to restore the glory of ancient religion. Mainly emerging from within the womb of Hindu Society, they tried to dexterously combine pristine religious purity with many modern values like individual liberty and democracy. Among the major religious reform movements of 19th century India, like Brahmo Samaj, Prarthana Samaj, Arya Samaj and Ramakrishna Mission, it was the latter two that really represented this appeal to the past. The Arya Samaj with its slogan 'Back to the Vedas' and the Ramakrishna Mission with its attempt to resurrect vedantic Hinduism, though substantially different in their approaches to religion had the same essential purpose of reforming religion in terms with changing times. They sought to establish to some degree, the freedom of individual, break the stranglehold of Brahminism and reform the caste system which had birth as its solid determinant of status. Thus, Arya Samaj and its chief architect Swami Dayanand Saraswati, repudiated the authority of the Brahmins and fought against the very idea of intermediaries between God and his devotees. To that extent, they freed the individual from the tyranny of Brahmin priesthood. It opposed polytheism and associated meaningless rituals and superstitions which split people into innumerable sects. The Ramakrishna Mission which drew inspiration from saints like Chandidas and Chaitanya and was initiated by the rustic saint Ramakrishna, on the other hand idealised Hinduism, its polytheism and idol worship. Swami Vivekananda, its chief propagandist, was chiefly concerned that Indian nationalism which he said must fight the corrupting 'materialist influences' of the west. Unification and reform of Hindu society were a prerequisite to this end.

There was thus an essential unity in the religious revivalist movements, in terms of the objectives. The Arya Samaj fought against the rigid, hereditary caste system and argued for the inclusion of guna (character), Karma (action) and Swabhava (nature) as criteria for the basis of caste. Even Shudras, according to it, could study the vedas. It was this appeal of religious revivalism that drew hundreds of nationalist towards it and it thus signalled a component of India's national awakening.

Q5. Describe the thoughts of M.G. Ranade on Liberalism.

Ans. Ranade, a representative of the dominant liberal thinkers, articulated the interests of the rising Indian capitalist class. The central part of his argument was that the Indian economy should follow a capitalist path of development, if it is to solve her problems. He argued that the state must play an active role in economic development. He disagreed with the laissez-faire concept of state. He believed that India could get rid of its phenomenal poverty and dependence on agriculture through industrialisation and commercialisation of agriculture, and the state must play an active role in such transformative process.

Ranade pointed out the immense progress of agriculture in France, Germany and Russia after the liquidation of feudal agriculture and introduction of capitalist relations and peasant proprietorship.

However, Ranade's advocacy of state intervention in economic activities did not give the state unlimited sanctions, for he was a believer of individual freedom. Unlike the western liberal philosophers, however, Ranade's individual liberty was a concept that derived from his metaphysical ideas which based themselves on the Upanishads. In his view God resides in everything in this universe, and therefore, in each human being. Thus, the freedom of conscience is the real freedom and the rights of conscience must take precedence over all other considerations. Man should then submit to the voice of his inner conscience alone and not to any outside force or authority- religious or political. However, this also means that individual freedom of action is to be used in a way that is does not impose restraints on the equally free rights of other people.

Ranade, for the above-mentioned reasons, was also a critic of the caste system which imposes external restrictions on human behaviour. He supported the Bhakti movement because he thought the saints asserted the dignity of the human soul irrespective of birth.

The agency of social change and reform in Ranade's view was the elite stratum. In his opinion, "... there is always only a minority of people who monopolise all the elements of strength. They are socially and religiously in the front ranks, they possess intelligence, wealth, thrifty habits, knowledge and power. This elite group was composed of Brahmins. Banias, Zamindars and the educated middle-class." So, true to the aspirations of the capitalist class, he believed that "power must gravitate where there is intelligence and wealth." His scheme for representation to Indians contained provisions for giving political power to the rich and educated. At the municipal level, for example, the elected seats were to be divided in the ratio of two to one between property holders and the intelligent class...Though he did not consider such representation democratic, he nevertheless believed that it was necessary as the masses were still incapable of electing 'worthymen as representatives. Generations of training and education were required before they could be made capable of it.'

Q6. Write a short note on evolution of liberalism in India.

Ans. Liberalism as a political idea in India was developed by the English educated middle class, a product of the colonial education system. The colonial education was introduced with the aim of creating cultural and ideological hegemony for maintaining alien rule. It was intended to project the superiority of European values and institutions to disseminate them as the ideal for Indians. The Indian "traditional" values and institutions were not considered to be conducive to social progress.

The liberal critique of Indian society and colonial state began with Renaissance. Raja Rammohan Roy, Bankim Chandra Chattopadhyay, Devendra Nath Thakur, Akshay Kumar Dutt, Jyotiba Phule, Gopal Ganesh Agarkar, M.G. Ranade, Dada Bhai Nauroji, Surendra Nath Banerjee, Pherozshah Mehta, Sir Syed Ahmed Khan and others tried to set a liberal model for transforming Indian society and polity. The Indian liberal looked upon the colonial rulers to lead and guide the socio-political transformation. The English liberals like J.S. Mill and many others pleaded for the continuation of colonial rule as it was essential for 'civilising' the native and putting them 'on the path of progress.' The conception of colonial rule by various stands of Indian liberals was not very different from their European counterparts.

Even those who understood the exploitative character of colonialism did not go to the extent of denouncing it and were concerned only with the question of impoverishment and pauperisation of Indian masses due to the colonial drain of country's wealth. The liberals like Gopal Krishna Gokhale, Dadabhai Nauroji and others exhorted the colonial rulers, through petitions for redressal. But even this

concern eventually boiled down to the problems of the members of the educated middle class who had not found appropriate place in the administration. Dadabhai Nauroji in a memorandum submitted in 1880 appealed to the 'manliness' and the 'moral courage' of Englishmen to pay attention to "the thousands that are being sent out by the universities every year" and who "find themselves in a most anomalous position."

Similar conception of colonial rule found expression in the writings of Sir Syed Ahmed Khan who projected the colonial rule as 'emancipatory', 'democratic' and 'progressive'. Its continuance was desired to safeguard and enhance the interests of the Muslim community as Islam did not come into conflict with progress and reason symbolised by British rule. This can be compared with the logic of Renaissance thinkers who desired and justified the continuance of a representative system of government on the ground that "so long as differences of race and creed and distinction of caste form an important element in the socio-political life of India, the system of election cannot safely be adopted." This line of argument represented the interests of landed and educated Muslim middle classes and was unconcerned with the problems of lower classes of the community.

The nascent Indian capitalist class and the new intelligentsia, which drew from the traditional social elite of Indian society became the main vehicle of liberal political ideas. The Bhadraloks of Bengal, the Brahmins of Madras, and the Brahmins and Prabhus in Bombay presidency were among the earliest to be affected by the spread of liberal ideas. Raja Rammohan Roy (1772-1833), Dadabhai Nauroji (1825-1917), S.N. Banerjee (1848-1925), Pherozeshah Mehta (1845-1915), G.K. Gokhale (1866-1915), Gopal Ganesh Agarkar (1856-95) and M.G. Ranade (1842-1901) among others, evolved a liberal critique of Indian society and colonial state and underlined the importance of liberal ideas for the transformation of Indian society and polity.

Q7. Discuss about the evolution of nationalism in India during British rule.

Ans. The development of the nationalist idea right from the early days went through an intricate course. Veneration of the British empire was so strikingly articulated by Dadabhai Nauroji in 1885 at the first session of the IN Congress in the following words: "What makes us proud to be British subjects, what attaches us to this foreign rule with deeper loyalty.... is the fact that Britain is the parent of free and representative government..." As mentioned, this was a dominant idea, in varying degrees among the intellectuals and leaders of early nationalism. They realised the economic ruin and immisenisation of Indian people as a result of British rule. Indian economy according to Dadabhai Nauroji was subjected to heavy 'drain' of resources. This, he considered, the outcome of what he called "drain" theory. In fact, his critique of Indian economy was based on factors/independent of British rule: dependence on agriculture, lack of capital, antiquated credit system etc. He therefore advocated commercialisation of agriculture and industrialisation.

It was only later that Aurobindo Ghosh and S.N. Banerjee developed a case for self-government. Such an idea was never on the agenda of earlier nationalists, whose main emphasis, was on reforms. Essentially the debate was whether social reforms should precede political reforms or vice versa. Banerjee thought self-government would increase efficiency in administration. Moreover, he believed it to be India's mission to be the spiritual guide of mankind, which could not be fulfilled unless India itself was free. Aurobindo Ghosh considered that a foreign government by its very nature was bound to deny freedom to the individual to develop self-expression. He also considered self-government essential for completeness and full development of national strength. Nationalism to him was a 'religion that has come from God."

Swaraj became the clarion call of later nationalists i.e. the 'extremists', though they still defined swaraj as self-government within the Empire. Tilak took up the theme of the country's economic drain once again, which he wanted to be stopped forthwith alongwith revival of industries killed by foreign competitions. Radical nationalists led by B.G. Tilak, Aurobindo Ghosh and B.C. Pal, advocating direct methods of boycott of British goods and passive resistance denounced the colonial rule and gave the call of Swadeshi. In reaction to liberal glorification of colonial rule, they emphasised the achievements of Ancient India. To meet the challenges of nationalist political consciousness, colonial rulers introduced an elective element into the legislature through the reforms of 1892, 1909 and the Government of India Act 1919. The radical nationalists opposed the reforms, but by and large it was received well in the beginning. Gandhi, who had initially supported the idea of cooperation in working the reforms, had changed his opinions by 1921 and declared that the reforms "were only a method of further draining India of her wealth and of prolonging servitude." Anti-colonial ideas started gaining immense strength in the aftermath of the first nationalist movement of an all India character, the Non-cooperation movement in the early 1920s. The loosely connected Left-Wing of the Congress launched vigorous anti-imperialist campaign and advocated an uncompromising rule in bringing about the political and administrative unification of the country and arousal of political consciousness; recognition of Western values of knowledge and their substantiation by ancient Indian scriptures; need of a national movement across the barriers of race, castes religion and sex; and advocacy of regional and religious symbols for political mobilisation. Gandhi's concepts of 'Swarajya' (self-government), 'Swadeshi' (Indian) and Bahishkar (boycott of foreign goods) provided the future programme for the anti-colonial struggle. It can be seen therefore, that what can be called Indian nationalism comprised of innumerable streams of thought.

The first assertions of nationalism in India were mixed with a strong sense of religious revivalism -an appeal to the past, a fervent call to revive the pristine glory of the Hindu Golden Age.

This was preceded by the moderate nationalists whose main critique of colonialism was, against either the economic impact of British rule, or against the "bureaucratic aspects" of it. The methods of this school of moderate nationalists were constitutionalist, limited primarily to issuing appeals and petitions.

The militant nationalists, on the other hand, grasped fully the contradiction between the Indian people and colonial rule, and therefore, advocated a more decisive break with colonial rule. They were however, thoroughly imbued with religion, which made use of religious ceremonies for mobilisations. The student religiosity of such nationalism alienated the Muslims from the nationalist movement. The militant nationalists also drew great inspiration from the life of Mazzini and the history of the Italian Risorgimento.

The third stream of nationalists, i.e. the revolutionary nationalists were also for the most part ideologically revivalist who believed in Swaraj, and sought to achieve it through any means, including revolutionary violence. Their chief source of inspiration ranged from the Russian Narodinka to Massini.

Q8. Briefly discuss socialism in India.

Ans. The post non-cooperation period witnessed a rapid growth of socialist ideas and emergence of numerous Socialist and Communist groups. There were two factors responsible for the development of radical politics in the twenties. The increasing restlessness among Indian youth and the toiling masses who were being drawn into the national movement was coming to the fore. It was Gandhi's contribution that he made the Congress led movement a full-fledged mass movement. Yet his insistence on non-violence in the face of brutal repression by the colonial government as witnessed in the Jallianwala Bagh massacre, or his withdrawal of the non-cooperation movement in the wake of the Chauri-Chaura episode when a mob of peasants burned down a police-station manned entirely by the British led to large-scale disillusionment. Increasingly, it was being felt that non-violent methods will not do. Search for alternative forms thus became imperative.

This search was decisively influenced by another factor: the victory of the Russian Revolution and the establishment of a socialist state. The first socialist weekly, 'The Socialist', was started by .S.A. Dange in 1923 in Bombay. In Bengal a group of determined organisers led by Muzaffar Ahmed started the foundations of the Communist Party. Earlier M.N. Roy, a revolutionary nationalist, who had left India in search of arms, reached USA and became converted to socialism. Thereafter, in 1921, he along with a band of Mohajirs formed in Tashkent, the Communist Party of India, which was affiliated to the communist International. The Mohajirs were those who left the country on hijrat i.e. self-imposed exile-a concept of Islamic faith. In 1924, a number of people, including Dange and Muzaffar Ahmed, were arrested under the Kanpur conspiracy case. Workers and Peasant Parties were formed in Bombay, Bengal and Punjab. They supported the economic and political demands of the workers and peasants and organised them on class lines. They articulated and propagated the programme of national independence and stood for direct action by the workers and peasants. Trade unions were organised and a number of strikes took place. Side by side, the development of revolutionary terrorism into socialism took place. Bhagat Singh and his Hindustan Socialist Republican Association typified such developments. In 1926, a political forum by the name of Naujawan Bharat Sabha was created with the idea of educating young people in social matters, popularising swadeshi and developing a sense of brotherhood. Apart from this, it sought to cultivate a secular outlook, even atheism among the youth. This organisation was a fore-runner of the Hindustan Republic Association, which aimed at overthrowing the British rule by insurrection. It had an elabourate organisation to carry on its clandestine activities. The Sabha propagated the ideal of equality, removal of poverty and equitable redistribution of wealth. This Hindustan Republican Association (HRA) subsequently changed its name to Hindustan Socialist Republic Association (HSRA). The activities of the HSRA exemplified the transition from terrorism to radical socialist politics, as it did for finding the appropriate methods of political agitation. The first beginnings of Marxist Socialism in India were made by small groups in the Bengal, Bombay and Punjab. These groups then organised the Workers and Peasants' parties in these states, started work in the Trade Unions and also started organising the peasantry. The CPI's critique of colonialism was based on its understanding that imperialism was plundering India's raw materials. Behind the utter misery and destitution of the Indian peasantry, the communists saw the exploitation by foreign and Indian capital side by side with antiquated feudal forms of exploitation. The communists therefore derided the nationalist leadership for their implicit faith in the British rulers and their hesitation to raise the demand for complete Independence. They were also severely critical of the nationalist leaders for their use of religion in political mobilisation.

However, the communists themselves could not really join the mainstream of the national movement till the mid-1930s. After the Seventh Congress of the Comintern adopted the United front policy in 1935, two British leaders R.P. Dutt and Ben Bradley prepared a statement for Indian Communists. This document, known as the "Dutt-Bradley Thesis" constitutes a landmark, in Indian Communist history, since it brought the CPI into the mainstream of the anti-imperialist struggle. The document helped the CPI to reforge its links with the national movement. Following this, in January 1936, the Congress Socialist Party, on the recommendation of its general secretary, Jaya Prakash Narayan, decided to admit communists to its membership. Many Communists joined the CSP. From then on, till the eve of World War II, the Communists and the Congress Socialists, despite differences worked together for radicalising the Congress from within. Furthermore, the decade of the 'twenties saw a radicalisation of Indian youth and their gradual turning away from the Congress fold towards socialist ideas. As a parallel development, sections of young congressmen increasingly adopted the socialist ideal and from within the Congress sought to influence it in a Leftward direction. They formed the Congress Socialist Party in 1934. Prominent among these were Acharya Narendra Dev and Jaya Prakash Narayan. Both these leaders were profoundly influenced by Marxism and believed that socialism could be achieved only with the socialisation of the means of production. Both were for a drastic reorganisation of the agrarian economy and land to the tiller.

Q9. Write a note on the following :

(i) Revolutionary Socialism

Ans. In 1926, a political forum by the name of Naujawan Bharat Sabha was created with the idea of educating young people in social matters, popularising swadeshi and developing a sense of brotherhood. Apart from this it sought to cultivate a secular outlook, even atheism among the youth. This organisation was a fore-runner of the Hindustan Republic Association, which aimed at overthrowing the British rule by insurrection. It had an elabourate organisation to carry on its clandestine activities. The Sabha propagated the ideal of equality, removal of poverty and equitable redistributions of wealth. This Hindustan Republican Association (HRA) subsequently changed its name to Hindustan Socialist Republic Association (HSRA).

When the British Government, in its bid to suppress the working class movement, sought to introduce the Public safety Bill and the Trade Disputes Bill, the HSRA decided to protest by bombing the Assembly when the bills were placed—the action was carried out by Bhagat Singh and Batukeshwar Dutta, while many such activities carried on by the HSRA seem, on the face of it, to be conventional terrorist activities and the Naujawan Bharat Sabha functioned with a much broader perspective. Bhagat Singh clarified in his trial that revolution to him was not the cult of the bomb and pistol but a total change of society culminating in the overthrow of both Indian and foreign capitalism and the establishment of the dictatorship of the proletariat. The assembly bombs were meant to be purely demonstrative to make the authorities see reason. In a sense the activities of the HSRA exemplified the transition from terrorism to radical socialist politics, as it did for finding the appropriate methods of political agitation.

(ii) Marxist Socialism

Ans. Marxist Socialism: The first beginning of Marxist Socialism in India was made by small groups in the Bengal, Bombay and Punjab. These groups then organised the Workers and Peasants' Parties in these states, started work in the Trade Unions and also started organising the peasantry. Parallel to this development was the foundation in Tashkent of the Communist Party of India. The CPI's critique of colonialism was based on its understanding that imperialism was plundering India's raw materials. The exploitation of the Indian people, particularly the working class and peasantry by the British imperialists would remain as long as India did not fully break away from colonialism and build a society free from exploitation. Behind the utter misery and destitution of the Indian peasantry, the communists saw the exploitation by foreign and Indian capital side by side with antiquated feudal forms of exploitation.

The communists therefore derided the nationalist leadership for their implicit faith in the British rulers and their hesitation to raise the demand for complete

Independence. They were also severely critical of the nationalist leaders for their use of religion in political mobilisation.

However, the communists themselves could not really join the mainstream of the national movement till the mid-1930s.

After the Seventh Congress of the Comintern adopted the united front policy in 1935, two British leaders R.P. Dutt and Ben Bradley prepared a statement for Indian Communists. This document, known as the "Dutt-Bradley Thesis" constitutes a landmark, in Indian Communist history, since it brought the CPI into the mainstream of the anti-imperialist struggle. The document helped the CPI to reforge its links with the national movement. Following this, in January 1936, the Congress Socialist Party, on the recommendation of its general secretary, Jaya Prakash Narayan, decided to admit communists to its membership. Many communists joined the CSP. From then on, till the eve of World War II, the Communists and the Congress Socialists, despite differences worked together for radicalising the Congress from within.

An important aspect of Communist thinking has been in relation to its assessment of the leadership of the Indian National Congress, its class character and subsequently, the class character of the Indian State. They regarded the Congress as an organisation of Indian capitalists and landlords which Gandhi had transformed from an elite assembly to a mass movement. Gandhi, though he initiated the process of turning Congress into a mass movement, was in their view a compromiser determined to stem the rising militancy of national struggle. They also disapproved Gandhi's non-violent methods of struggle and the use of religious for political mobilisation.

(iii) Congress Socialism

Ans. The decade of the 'twenties saw a radicalisation of Indian youth and their gradual turning away from the Congress fold towards socialist ideas. Disenchantment with Gandhian non-violent methods, impact of the Russian Revolution and the need to evolve the masses of Indian people in the anti-colonial struggle increasingly led to this radicalisation.

As a parallel development, sections of young congressmen increasingly adopted the socialist ideal and from within the Congress sought to influence it in a Leftward direction. They formed the Congress Socialist Party in 1934. Prominent among these were Acharya Narendra Dev and Jaya Prakash Narayan. Both these leaders were profoundly influenced by Marxism and believed that socialism could be achieved only with the socialisation of the means of production. Both were for a drastic reorganisation of the agrarian economy and land to the tiller.

However, what distinguished both Narendra Dev and Jaya Prakash Narayan from the Communists was that they advocated a cooperative agriculture with a marked emphasis on decentralisation. Both believed in socialism but sought to combine it with a humanist ethics.

Ram Manohar Lohia, another member of this group pleaded for greater incorporation of Gandhian ideas in socialist thought. Lohia's insistence on Gandhian ideas was not merely at the level of incorporation of Gandhian ethics, but also in the economic performance of socialism. He advocated a decentralised economy based on a resuscitation of cottage industries. In this sense, his socialism was that of the petty producer.

Lohia believed that the interface of caste and class is the key to the understanding of historical dynamics of India. In his view, all human history has been an internal movement between castes and classes—castes loosen into classes and classes crystallize into castes. Thus, he tried to understand the caste/class dynamics—an issue that has generally been ignored in Indian politics.

Q10. Discuss briefly Mahatma Gandhi's philosophy of Sarvodaya.

Ans. Gandhi's idea of sarvodaya (welfare of all) conveys the idea of equality. Gandhi's doctrine of sarvodaya (which is often rendered as non-violent socialism) is a corrective to utilitarianism, communism and the doctrines which justify inequalities and exclusions on the basis of caste, race, colour, gender, etc. "Sarvodaya" is the title, which Gandhi gave to his paraphrase of John Ruskin's *Unto This Last*. In that book, Ruskin gave a moralistic critique of the science of political economy of self-interest. He brought out the role of "social affection" in our lives. Reading Ruskin brought about "an instantaneous and practical transformation" of Gandhi's life. He learned three lessons from Ruskin's book, namely: **(a)** that the good of the individual is contained in the good of all; **(b)** that a lawyer's work has the same value as the barber's in as much as all have the same right of earning their livelihood from their work; and **(c)** that a life of labour, i.e., the life of the tiller of the soil and the handicraftsman is the life worth living. Of these three principles, the first is the main principle of sarvodaya (welfare of all). It is also the source of the other two principles. Gandhi clarified that he had known the first principle before reading Ruskin's book, which only served to confirm it and give it a modern articulation. A good deal of Gandhi's ideas on sarvodaya were derived from the holy books of Hinduism. There are several steps in Gandhi's thinking on sarvodaya (welfare of all). They are:

i) Our aim in life is self-realisation or moksha.

ii) Self-realisation or moksha means identification of the self or atman with Brahman or God. This requires a discipline or yoga of self-purification.

iii) The way of realising our identification with Brahman or, in other words, the way

of finding God is to see God in all his creation or manifestation.

iv) Love or service of all is the way to self-realisation or moksha in this world. Conveying these ideas, Gandhi wrote as follows:

4Man's ultimate aim is the realisation of God, and all his activities, political, social
and religious, have to be guided by the ultimate aim of the vision of God... The immediate service of all human beings becomes a necessary part of the endeavour
simply because the only way to find God is to see Him in His creation and be one with it. This can only be done by the service of all.

4I am impatient to realise myself, to attain moksha in this very existence. My national service is part of my training for freeing my soul from the bondage of flesh. Thus considered, my service may be regarded as purely selfish.

For me, the road to salvation lies through incessant toil in the service of my country and there through, of humanity. Gandhi derived many of these ideas from the holy books of Hinduism. In 1926, Gandhi brought out the difference between utilitarianism and sarvodaya in the following words:

A votary of ahimsa cannot subscribe to the utilitarian formula (of the greatest good of the greatest number). He will strive for the greatest good of all and die in the attempt to realise the ideal. He will therefore be willing to die, so that the others may live. He will serve himself with the rest, by himself dying. The greatest good of all inevitably includes the good of the greatest number, and therefore, he and the utilitarian will converge in many points in their career, but there does come a time when they must part company, and even work in opposite directions. The utilitarian to be logical will never sacrifice himself. The absolutist (i.e. the universalist or the votary of ahimsa) will even sacrifice himself.

Q11. What do you understand by the term 'Anarchism'?

Ans. Anarchism is a political philosophy encompassing theories and attitudes which consider the state, to be unnecessary, harmful, or otherwise undesirable. According to *The Oxford Companion to Philosophy*, "there is no single defining position that all anarchists hold, and those considered anarchists at best share a certain family resemblance." There are many types and traditions of anarchism, not all of which are mutually exclusive. Strains of anarchism have been divided into the categories of socialist and individualist anarchism and similar dual classifications. Anarchism is often considered to be a radical left-wing ideology, and much of anarchist economics and anarchist legal philosophy reflect anti-statist interpretations of communism, collectivism, syndicalism or participatory economics; however, anarchism has always included an economic and legal individualist strain, with that strain supporting a free-market economy and private property (like classical mutualism or today's anarcho-capitalism and agorism). Others, such as panarchists and anarchists without adjectives, neither advocate nor object to any particular form of organisation as long as it is not compulsory. Some anarchist schools of thought differ fundamentally, supporting anything from extreme individualism to complete collectivism. The central tendency of anarchism as a social movement have been represented by communist anarchism, with anarcho-individualism being primarily a philosophical/literary phenomenon. Some anarchists fundamentally oppose all forms of coercion, while others have supported the use of some coercive measures, including violent revolution and terrorism, on the path to an anarchist society.

Some claim anarchist themes can be found in the works of Taoist sages Laozi and Zhuangzi. The latter has been translated, *"There has been such a thing as letting mankind alone; there has never been such a thing as governing mankind [with success],"* and *"A petty thief is put in jail. A great brigand becomes a ruler of a State."* Diogenes of Sinope and the Cynics, and their contemporary Zeno of Citium, the founder of Stoicism, also introduced similar topics. Modern anarchism, however, sprang from the secular or religious thought of the Enlightenment, particularly Jean-Jacques Rousseau's arguments for the moral centrality of freedom. Although by the turn of the 19th century the term "anarchist" had lost its initial negative connotation, it first entered the English language in 1642 during the English Civil War as a term of abuse used by Royalists to damn those who were fomenting disorder. By the time of the French Revolution some, such as the *Enragés*, began to use the term positively, in opposition to Jacobin centralisation of power, seeing "revolutionary government" as oxymoronic. From this climate William Godwin developed what many consider the first expression of modern anarchist thought. Godwin was, according to Peter Kropotkin, "the first to formulate the political and economical conceptions of anarchism, even though he did not give that name to the ideas developed in his work, while Godwin attached his anarchist ideas loan early Edmund Burke. The first to describe himself as an anarchist was Pierre-Joseph Proudhon, a French philosopher and politician, which led some to call him the founder of modern anarchist theory. Proudhon proposed spontaneous order, whereby organisation emerges without central authority, a "positive anarchy" where order arises when everybody does "what he wishes and only what he wishes" and where "business transactions alone produce the social order."

Chapter 2

Socio-Political Reform in the 19th Century India

Q1. Discuss the circumstances leading to the Social Reform Movement in India.

Ans. The 19th Century India witnessed a strong wave of reformation activities in religion and society. There were attempts made by the educated young Indians to end the evils and abuses in religion and society. Western ideas of reason, equality, liberty and humanity inspired them. They tried to remove the defects in their culture. They wanted to revive the glory of Indian culture. Hence, we call the socio-religious reform movement of the 19th century India as the Indian Renaissance movement. Raja Rammohan Roy was the pioneer of this movement.

Causes for the Social and Religious reform movement:

Political- India was politically united due to the expansion and consolidation of British rule. It led to the understanding of many common problems of the Indians. The nature of the British rule provoked many young Indians to find out the causes of their misery and degradation.

Reaction against the propaganda of Christian Missionaries:- The Christian missionaries made all possible attempts to spread Christianity particularly among the poor and the oppressed. Educational institutions, hospitals, charity services and official support were also made use for this purpose. Therefore, both the Hindus and the Muslims made efforts to protect their religions.

Contribution of foreign scholars : Many western scholars like Max Muller and William Jones rediscovered India's past. They studied the scholarly works of Indians of the ancient period. They brought to light the rich cultural heritage of India which was even superior to the western culture. They translated many literary and religious texts. These works received worldwide recognition. It made the educated Indians develop faith in their culture. They wanted to establish the superiority of Indian culture against the western culture.

Indian Press : The Europeans introduced the printing press in India. It made possible the appearance of many newspapers and magazines. Books were also published in different Indian languages. Mostly their subject matter was Indian.

It certainly helped to open the eyes of the educated Indians with regard to the national heritage and glory. Therefore, they started to work for the revival of Indian culture.

Western Education : The spread of western education led to the spread of the western concepts of democracy, liberty, equality and nationalism. The Indians who went abroad came in direct contact with the working of these concepts. After their return they were pained to see the lack of awareness among the Indians about such concepts. They did the spade work for the spread of such ideas. There is no denying the fact that Indian nationalism and modernism are largely the result of the efforts of the English educated Indians in different fields of life. The Brahmo Samaj also opposed child marriage and polygamy. It supported widow remarriage. Due to the efforts of Keshab Chandra Sen, one of the leaders of Brahmo Samaj, an Act was passed in 1872. It abolished polygamy and child-marriage. The Act also supported intercaste marriage and widow remarriage. After the death of Raja Rammohan Roy, the work of the Samaj was carried by great men like Keshab Chandra Sen and Devendranath Tagore.

The Arya Samaj (1875) : Swami Dayananda Saraswati started the Arya Samaj in 1875. He was born at a small town in Gujarat in a conservative Brahmin family. His childhood name was Mul Shankar. He met Swami Vrajanand at Mathura. He became the disciple of Vrajanand. There he studied Vedas. He devoted his life to the propagation of the Vedas. He wanted to reform the Hindu Society. According to Dayananda Saraswati the Vedas contained all the truth. His motto was "Go Back to the Vedas". His book Sathyartha Prakash contains his views about Vedas.In the field of religion Arya Samaj opposed idol worship, ritualism, animal sacrifice, the idea of heaven and hell and the concept of fatalism. Dayananda Saraswati started Suddhi movement to reconvert the Hindus who had been converted to other religions earlier. By his efforts, large number of people were taken back within the fold of Hinduism. The Arya Samaj provided useful service to Hindu society. It opposed child marriage, polygamy, purdah system, casteism and the practice of Sati. The Samaj insisted the education of the women and upliftment of the depressed classes. Intercaste marriages and interdining were encouraged. The Samaj established a number of educational institutions in India particularly in the North. Gurukulas and Swami Dayananda Saraswati Kanya Gurukulas provide education mostly on Sanskrit, the Vedas and Ayurvedas. Dayanand Anglo-Vedic (DAV) Schools and Colleges provide modern education in humanities and sciences. His followers Lala Lajpat Rai, Lala Hansraj and Pandit Guru Dutt propagated the ideas of the Arya Samaj. Many Indian national leaders like Bala Gangadhara Tilak and Gopala Krishna Gokhale were deeply influenced by the philosophy and principles of the Arya samaj.

Q2. Briefly describe the religious reforms of India.

Ans. The 19th century attempt at religious reform had two aspects. The first sought to remove idolatory and religious superstitions and the second, to present a theistic ideal.

The Attack on Idolatory and Superstitions

The early social reformers adopted almost an iconoclastic attitude towards idol worship and polytheism. The endeavour of the Brahmo Samaj, for instance, was to remove from Hinduism all idolatrous practices. They considered the proliferation of gods and goddesses as later development, unknown to vedic age. The polytheism was sought to be justified on the ground that the spirit behind it was of pure monotheism. Raja Ram Mohan Roy refused to accept this argument, as the orthodox Hindu had a distinct conception of the individuality of every deity he worships. "Neither do they (the Hindus)", Roy contended, "regard the images of these gods merely in the light of instruments for elevating the mind ...they are simply in themselves made objects of worship." The apologists of image worship argued that idolatory was a harmless practice, "calculated to do much good and no harm". The reformers in reply pointed to the quarrels among the worshippers of different gods and certain practices associated with certain forms of idol worship. Regarding the first point this is what Raja Ram Mohan Roy had to say, "So tenacious are these devotees in respect of the honour due to their chosen divinities that when they meet in such holy places as Hardwar, the adjustment of the points of precedence not only become occasions of warmest verbal altercations, but sometimes even physical blows and violence." Regarding the latter point, the Bengali reformers cited the cult of Krishna and Kali worship which were often accompanied by human and animal sacrifices and marked by 'use of wine and sexual licence'. Some critics charged the early 19th century reformers and the Brahmo Samaj in particular of being heavily influenced by Christianity and of trying to christianise Hinduism. This is not a fair charge. All that the early Bengali reformers were trying to do was to liberate and rationalise Hinduism and put it on a rational basis so that it may provide a stimulus to all-round progress without cutting the Hindus off completely from their past. These reformers can be compared to men like Bacon, Disraeli and Luther who struck hard at the roots of medieval European society. Like their European counterparts, the early Bengali reformers sought to raise their voice against blind acceptance of religious authority and against the tyranny of priests and religious dogma.

The New Theistic Ideal

The 19th century religious reform movement not only repudiated polytheism, but more importantly, stressed the theistic tendencies in Hinduism. Raja Ram Mohan Roy made common cause with Christian and Muslim Unitarianism. He thus opposed the Christian doctrine of Trinity, arguing that it was erroneous to conceive of God and his son and the Holy Spirit as if they were three distinct entities. The Brahmo Samaj claimed that only God defined as "the Eternal, Unsearchable and Immutable Being who is the author and preserver of the Universe can claim the unqualified and enthusiastic worship of all men without distinctions of caste, colour, creed or race". The Brahmo Samaj claimed that such a conception was propounded in the Upanishads written by the ancient Hindu seers and sages. It wanted to re-establish Hinduism in this pristine, pure form, freed from all superstitions and prevailing inhuman practices. It attacked the idolatrous tendency in all creeds and asked followers of all religions to return to one God.

Q3. Briefly discuss the Social reforms in India in 19th century.

Ans. Attack on the Caste System

The reformers' attack was against all custom-bound morality : but since caste typified this mentality at its worst, the reformers made it their prime target of attack. To fight caste the reformers resorted to a two-fold strategy. The firstly argued that caste was not part of the pristine and pure religion but a subsequent unhealthy development. Raja Ram Mohan Roy for instance, quoted from the Mahanirwana Tantra to show that caste was not a barrier to marriage nor essential to the organisation of society. He said "there is no discrimination of age or caste or race in the Saiva marriage as enjoyed by Siva, one should marry a woman who has no husband and who is not 'sapinda', that is, who is not within prohibited degree of marriage." Roy considered the priests as the main culprits responsible for perpetuating the myth of the sacred origins of caste. He skeptically observes that men can be truly divided into four classes : "those who deceive, those who are deceived, those who both deceive and are deceived and those who neither deceive nor are deceived".

Secondly, the reformers used rational arguments to show that caste was doing more harm than good and that caste was not promoting the political interest of the Hindus. The division into numerous castes had destroyed all feelings of oneness and patriotism, among the Hindus apart from disqualifying them from undertaking any difficult enterprise which required sustained and unified effort. In the opinion of the reformers, caste set up a tyranny greater than that of any state or foreign ruler. Expounding the Brahmo philosophy, Sittanath Tattwabhusan in his book on the Philosophy of Brahmonism observes, "whatever may have been our differences in the past, a common system of education is now happily levelling up these differences and raising us to a moral platform from which love, sympathy, co-operation and unity appear to be things higher and more valuable than all other things. When will the pernicious distinctions which are sapping the very life blood of our nation be at an end and India rise as a strong, united nation fit to fulfil the high destiny which Providence has ordained for her. There cannot be a surer truth than this that high destiny cannot be fulfilled without the utter destruction of the supreme root of all our social evils, the caste system."

The reformers not only criticised and preached, they also in their own way sought to put into practice their reforms, at times in rather extreme fashion. Debendra Nath Tagore, for instance, went to the extent of discarding his sacred thread and appointed a non-Brahmin to the ministry of the Samaj and dismissed all Brahmins from the ministry who insisted on wearing their threads. Keshub Chandra Sen openly encouraged inter-caste marriage and had his own daughter married outside his caste. The Brahmos started the practice of inter-caste dining. They opposed hereditary caste professions and gave recognition only to talent.

Education and Uplift of Women

The 19th century western educated reformers were profoundly moved by the plight of Indian women. In the 18th century, the young girls were married off at the age between 6 and 10 years, they were forced to live in purdah. However, the most pernicious custom of that century was sati and the Bengali reformers naturally concentrated on its abolition. Officially the British administration was hesitant to interfere particularly after the annexation of Peshwa's kingdom. It was only in 1812 and 1817 that the British administration sent positive instructions enjoining preventive measures such as no woman should be forcibly dragged to the pyre against her will or be forced to commit sati when pregnant or minor. It was when some citizens made petitions to the Governor General against these progressive orders of 1812 and 1817 that Raja Ram Mohan Roy came out powerfully to the rescue of Indian women and made a counter petition in 1818 narrating the gruesome practices associated with Sati and condemning it as murder.

In his petition Raja Ram Mohan Roy narrated how women were persuaded by their next heirs to commit Sati; how some women who in their first moments of grief rashly expressed the desire to perform Sati, were later forced upon the pyre and "bound down with ropes and pressed with green bamboos until consumed by the flames."

In their fight against Sati, the reformers did not hesitate to use the scriptures against their opponents. Raja Ram Mohan Roy cited Manu, Yajnavalkya and others to show that Sati was never compulsory. The very fact Manu enjoins a woman to live "voluntarily on pure flowers, roots and fruits… and not pronouncing the name of another man", meant that she was not obliged to commit Sati, he argued.

Ram Mohan Roy brought out several tracts and pamphlets in Bengali condemning Sati. The Bengali reformers refuted all the arguments forwarded by orthodox in favour of Sati viz.., **a)** failure to perform Sari would mean re-birth as an animal, **b)** its observance meant enjoyment with husband for eternity, **c)** it expiated the sins of he husband's maternal and paternal ancestors up to three generations. The reformers dismissed these arguments a metaphysical and not provable since one really did not know with certainty anything that legislation must seek to promote the greatest happiness of the greatest number on this earth. The women's happiness when alive was more important than any promise of happiness hereafter or in the next life.

The reformers also condemned various other inhuman practices such as the sale of daughters to prospective husbands and polygamy. They also sought to restore to women the rights of inheritance bestowed on her by the ancient law givers like Vajnvalkya, Narad and Vyas.

Q4. What do you understand by the term political liberalism? Discuss about the concept/idea of constitutionalism and representative government. [Dec 08, Q 2]

Or

Write a note on Political liberalism in 19th century in India.

Ans. Political liberalism or constitutional liberalism is a body of thought that attempts to provide justification for the principles of limited government, including most or all of the following: restrictions against arbitrary use of power, constitutional definition of legitimate government power, the rule of law, government that exists by consent of the people, maintenance of civil and political rights of individuals, legal toleration of a plurality of religions and moral codes, and the legal protection of private property. Liberalism is a broad class of political philosophies that considers individual liberty and equality to be the most important political goals. Liberalism emphasises individual rights and equality of opportunity. Within liberalism, there are various streams of thought which compete over the use of the term "liberal" and may propose very different policies, but they are generally united by their support for constitutional liberalism, which encompasses support for: freedom of thought and speech, limitations on the power of governments, the rule of law, an individual's right to private property, and a transparent system of government. All liberals, as well as some adherents of other political ideologies, support some variant of the form of government known as liberal democracy, with open and fair elections, where all citizens have equal rights by law. Liberalism appears in two broad forms: Classical liberalism, which emphasises the importance of individual liberty, and social liberalism which emphasises some kind of redistribution of wealth. Those who identify themselves as classical liberals, to distinguish themselves from social liberals, oppose all government regulation of business and the economy, with the exception of laws against force and fraud, and support free market laissez-faire capitalism. In Europe, the term "liberalism" is closer to the economic outlook of American economic conservatives. In the United States, "liberalism" is most often used in the sense of social liberalism, which supports some regulation of business and other economic interventionism which they believe to be in the public interest.

Constitutionalism and Representative Government

Indian liberal reformers looked to the state for doing many things. But at the same time, they were aware that absolute power corrupts and degrades the rulers. This is why they also opposed centralisation and pleaded for a constitutional structure which made government responsible to the people and ensured their participation on public affairs.

Government should be by laws and not arbitrary. It should be decentralised. The view of the reformers stemmed from their study of the philosophy of John Stuart Mill who wanted Government itself to assume responsibility for exploring avenues for increased participation of the people as a means to their political education. Gokhale testified before the Royal Commission on Decentralisation thus: "The car of administration should not merely roll over (people's) bodies… they must themselves be permitted to pull at the ropes."

The liberals also urged the bureaucracy to abandon its self-imposed unhealthy seclusion, its attitude of high caste, of super Brahmins. Bureaucracy must become sensitive to Indian public opinion and shed its veil of secrecy. Speaking on the Official Secrets Act (1903), Gokhale urged Government not to issue too many confidential circulars since official secrecy encourages rumours which can only damage the people's image of Government. Time and again the Liberals urged the bureaucracy to become more responsive and mix and interact with the people.

The liberals advocated political and administrative reforms which would make for increased people's participation. They pleased for strengthening municipal government. They urged the establishment of District Advisory Councils. Men like Surendranath Bannerjee and Dadabhai Naoroji concentrated on the question of employment of Indians in higher services and linked the issue of holding free and equal competitive examinations for recruitment to the Indian Civil Service with association of Indians with administration. The argument for the Indianisation of services was made on economic, political and moral grounds. The exclusion of Indians not only meant a drain of wealth from India by way of payment of salaries and pensions to foreign bureaucrats, it also resulted as Dadabhai pointed out, in the "Dwarfing of the race." The abilities of the people were becoming less through disuse and the people were beginning to lose confidence in the government and British rule.

To rouse political consciousness and increase political participation, the liberals established various associations. In Bengal there were the British India Association and the Indian Association. In Bombay we had the Bombay Association started by Jagannath Shanker Seth and Dadabhai Naoroji. In Poona there was the Sarvajanik Sabha under Chiplunkar and others. In 1882, Alan Octavian Hume, an Englishman and retired Secretary to the Government, took the lead in forming the National Congress. In an open letter to the graduates of the Calcutta University, he said, "constituting as you do, a large body of the most highly educated Indians, you should in the natural order of things, constitute also the most important source of all mental, social and political progress in India." The Congress from its very inception attracted Indian liberals and many great names were associated with it. Dadabhai Naoroji was its dominating figure till 1906. Gokhale, Phirozeshaw Mehta, W.C. Bonnerjie, Surendranath Bannerji, Badruddin Tyabji, K.T. Telang, R.C. Dutt and Rash Behari Ghosh were other great stalwarts associated with the Congress between 1885 and 1905. All these liberals were unanimous on two counts; One, there must be a definite though slow movement towards the ideal of self-rule; and two, the highest political development India should aspire to, should be self-rule within the framework of the British empire.

It was the political aspiration of the liberals to see the various Indian communities like the Hindus, Muslims, Christians, Sikhs, Parsis, work together in political institutions from local Boards and Municipalities to the very top in the Imperial Legislative Council. The liberal were sure of one thing: If the Indian people were not treated as equal participants in government, they would become more critics of the government and as Gokhale pointed out, once the limits of fair criticism are reached, there can be only unfair criticism.

Q5. Identify the influences that shaped Roy as a reformer.

Ans. Raja Ram Mohan Roy is known as the 'Maker of Modern India'. He was the founder of Brahmo Samaj, one of the first Indian socio-religious reform movements. He played a major role in abolishing the role of sati. He was a great scholar and an independent thinker. He advocated the study of science, western medicine and technology. Besides Bengali and Sanskrit, Roy had mastered Arabic, Persian, Hebrew, Greek, Latin and 17 other leading languages spoken in the world. Roy's familiarity with such diverse languages, exposed him to a variety of cultural, philosophical and religious experiences. He studied Islam thoroughly. The rationality and the logical consistency of Arabic literature in general and the mutajjil in particular impressed Roy greatly. The Sufi poets like Saddi and Haafiz made a deep impact on Roy's mind. The Quaranic concept of Tauhid or Unity of God fascinated Roy.

Thus, in this context, when Roy examined the Hindu religious texts and practices, he was greatly disturbed. He found polytheism, idolatory and irrational superstitions absolutely intolerable. He decided to fight against these age-old evils. A Sanskrit scholar, Ram Mohan had studied the Hindu scriptures in depth and thus he got the inspiration to free the orthodox Hinduism from its obscurantist elements. Roy also had studied the teachings of the Buddha Dhamma. It is said that in the course of his travels he reached Tibet. There he was pained to see how the principles of Buddhism were blatantly violated and how idol-worship, which had no place in the Dhamma of Lord Buddha, had come to be accepted. He strongly criticised these practices.

As a Dewan in the revenue department, when the Raja was required to go to Rangpur, he got an opportunity to study the Tantrik literature as well as the Jaina's Kalpasutras and other scriptures. He also mastered the English language and acquainted himself with political developments and ideas like rationalism and liberation in England and Europe. The knowledge of English not only facilitated Roy's contacts with Englishmen but also opened up a whole new world to him. In Roy's own words, he now gave up his initial prejudices against the British and realised that it was better to seek help from these enlightened rulers in ameliorating the condition of the ignorant and superstitious masses. He became a strong advocate of English education and a supporter of British rule.

Roy admired the Bible as much as he did the Vedanta and the Quran. Many of his critics thought that two major features of Roy's Brahmo Samaj, namely, the opposition to idol-worship and the practice of collective prayer were borrowed from Christianity. Roy was charged of Christianising Hindustan in a surreptitious manner. It is true that Roy advised Indians to imbibe Christ's ethical teachings. Roy himself admitted, 'I found the doctrine of Christ more conductive to moral principles and better adopted for the use of rational beings than any other which have come to my knowledge." He also compiled "The Precepts of Jesus" with a view to proving how the teachings of Christ could be better adapted to rational man's use. At the same time it has to be noted that he was no blind admirer of the Christian faith. He rejected the doctrine of Christ's divinity and the doctrine of Trinity preached by the missionaries.

From what has been said above, it should be clear that it is unfair to charge Roy with seeking to Christianise Hinduism. Rather it was Roy's ardent desire to revive Hinduism in its pristine, pure and universal form. He pleaded for an Advaita philosophy which rejected caste, idolatory and superstitious rites and rituals.

Thus, Roy was someone who had gone beyond narrow divisions of religious faiths. He embraced all that was the most valuable and the most inspiring in Hinduism, Christianity and Islam.

Q6. Briefly discuss Roy as a social reformer. [Dec 07, Q 2]

Or

Examine Ram Mohan Roy's views on caste, women's rights and Sati. [June 09, Q 2]

Ans. Roy as a Social Reformer

Next to religious backwardness, according to Roy, the factor responsible for the political deterioration of India was her social decadence. He had no doubts that here the social reform was an essential precondition of political liberation. He did pioneering work in the field of social reform. Roy started his public life in 1815 with the establishment of the Atmiya Sabha. This sabha vehemently protested against the prevalent practice of selling young girls to prospective husbands due to some pecuniary interests, in the name of the Kuleen tradition. It also opposed polygamy and worked for the removal of caste disabilities. Roy believed in, the progressive role of the British rule in India and sought government held in the matter of social reforms, especially in the form of socially progressive legislations. For instance, Roy was convinced that without the active support of the government it would be almost impossible to eradicate the inhuman practices of sati.

Roy's aim was the creation of a new society based on the principles of tolerance, sympathy and reason, where the principles of liberty, equality, and fraternity would be accepted by all, and where man would be free from the traditional shackles which had enslaved him for ages. He yearned for a new society which would be cosmopolitan and modern. Roy's methods of social reform were multifaceted. He combined all possible means, including even those which were commonly believed to be incompatible. He appealed to the rational faculty of his compatriots, and often quoted from the scriptures, lines and verses in support of the proposed reforms. The great scholar of Sanskrit that he was, Roy could easily counter the objections of the advocates of status quo by quoting elabourately from the original Sanskrit texts. For instance, while condemning polygamy, Roy cited Yagnavalkya who permitted a second wife only on 8 specific grounds viz. if she had the habit of drinking, suffered from incurable disease, barrenness etc. Nevertheless, he maintained that no book was a work of God and hence infallible. He wrote scholarly essays on topics of social reform and also translated and reinterpreted the important religious texts. He sent memoranda and appeals to the rulers inviting their attention to the social evils. From the platforms of the organised forums, he presented before the people the models of exemplary behaviour in religious and social matters. He took keen interest in and supported each and every movement aimed at human liberation anywhere in the world. He even had the courage of conviction to declare that he would renounce his connection with English, if a particular reform bill pending before the Parliament in England was not passed by it. He established or helped in several ways the social organisations catering to the needs of destitute widows and penniless students.

Caste system : Raja Ram Mohan Roy's strongest objection to the caste system was on the grounds that it fragmented society into many divisions and subdivisions. Caste divisions destroyed social homogeneity and the integrated texture of society and weakened it politically. Caste divisions deprived the people completely of political feeling, i.e. the feeling of commonality, of solidarity. A people so divided become incapable of undertaking any great task. Besides the divisive role of caste system, Roy was also critical about its discriminatory nature. He was against the inequities inherent in the traditional caste hierarchy. He thought it to be illogical to assess the worth of an individual on the basis of birth and not on his, merits. He was in favour of inter-caste and inter-racial marriages, which he thought, could effectively break the barriers of the caste divisions.

Sati pratha : Perhaps the greatest social reform with which Roy's name will be permanently associated is the abolition of the cruel practice of sati. Roy used all the means at his disposal to stop this inhuman practice, which forced the helpless widow to burn herself alive on the funeral pyre of her husband. In 1818, Roy wrote his first essay on sati in which he argued that the woman had an existence independent of her husband and hence, she had no reason to end her life on the demise of her husband. The society had no right over her life. Right to life of both men and women was equally important. That the practice of sati was centuries old could be no argument to make it just. All that comes through centuries need not always be right. All customs need to be adjusted to the changing circumstances, if they are to survive. According to Roy, Sati was nothing short of murder and was therefore a punishable offence under the law. Roy fought against the practice of sati on three fronts: The *first* and the most important was that of public opinion. Roy through writings, speeches, agitation and discussions prepared the minds of the people in favour of the abolition of sati and explained how the practice had no support in any of the religious texts and hence governmental action in the matter could not be an interference in religious affairs. *Secondly,* he tried to convince the rulers that it was their responsibility as civilised rulers to put an end to the cruel custom. The third front was the inquiry into the causes that led a Hindu widow to commit Sati and to make arrangements to eliminate those causes. Roy found that ignorance of the women about their legitimate rights, their illiteracy, customary denial of the property rights to the widow and the consequent helplessness, dependence, misery and humiliation were some of the causes behind this practice. Roy pleaded strongly for the restoration of property rights of the women as well as for facilities for women's education.

Women Rights: Raja Ram Mohan Roy was a champion of women's rights in India. He laid the foundations of the women's liberation movement in this country. He revolted against the subjection of women and pleaded for the restoration of their rights. The condition of the Hindu women in those days was very pitiable. They were subjected to different kinds of injustices and deprivations. According to Roy, the root cause of the all-round deterioration of Hindu women was the complete denial of their property rights. The Hindu girl was not given the traditional right to share with her brothers the property of her deceased father. The married Hindu woman was refused the right to share with her sons the property left by her deceased husband.

In 1822, Roy wrote a book entitled 'Brief Remarks Regarding Modern Encroachments on the Ancient Right of Females'. He pointed out that the ancient Hindu law givers gave the mother the right to have an equal share with her sons in the property left by her husband; and the daughter to have 114 part of the portion which a son could inherit in the property left by the father. Roy indicated how these rights were gradually taken away by the modern lawgivers. He tried to prove that all these deprivations were blatant violations of the provisions in the ancient texts written by the authorities such as Yagnyawalakya, Narad, Katyayana, Brihaspati and others.

The utter helplessness and humiliation of the Hindu widow was one of the major reasons that prompted the inhuman practice of Sati. Women completely robbed of their property rights quite naturally lost their independence and became the slaves of the male members of the family. They were thought to have less intellectual capabilities than the males. They were supposed to have an existence only at a physical level. Men were free to marry as many women as they thought fit for the satisfaction of their lust. Women however were not allowed to marry a second time. As equality of sexes was an article of faith for Roy, he could not accept that women were inferior to men in any respect. He believed that they were even superior to men in some respects. Whatever inferiority seemed to be on their part was the result, Roy argued, of keeping them away for generations from the sources of knowledge and the opportunities to shoulder different responsibilities in life. Roy vehemently opposed polygamy and with utmost vigor brought to light, its shameful evil consequences. He pleaded for an enactment allowing a Hindu male to marry second wife only after getting a clearance from the magistrate. Roy was in favour of the remarriage of women under certain circumstances. Brahmo Samaj which he founded paid special attention to women's education.

Q7. Mention the main characteristics of Roy's political liberalism.

Ans. Roy can be described as the earliest advocate of liberalism and the precursor of the liberal movement in India. Liberalism had emerged as the most valuable product of renaissance and reformation in Europe. It captured some of the best brains in the 19th century Europe and America. It became the dominant ideology of the first phase of religious and social reform in India. Liberalism, in brief, stands for the value and dignity of the individual personality; the central position of Man in the historical development; and the faith that people are the ultimate source of all power. Quite naturally liberalism insists on the inviolability of certain rights of the individual without which no human development can be thought of; it insists on human equality and also on the tenet that the individual should not be sacrificed for the sake of society. In liberalism, there is no scope for arbitrary and despotic use of authority in any field whether it be religious, social, political or economic.

Roy advocated liberal principles in all walks of life. In the religious field Roy stood for tolerance, a non-communal approach to all problems and secularism. He valued the freedom of the individual to follow the dictates of his conscience and even to defy the commands of priestly class. Politically, Roy was a supporter of the impersonal authority of law and opposed all kinds of arbitrary and despotic power. He was convinced that the existence of constitutional government is the best guarantee of human freedom. He insisted on the use of constitutional means as when required to safeguard the rights. He preferred the gradual improvements of the condition of this country because, to him, such improvements were more lasting and profound. True to the liberal principles in the economic sphere, Roy believed in the sanctity of right to property. Similarly, he believed that a strong middle class had an important role to play in socio-political dynamics. He was for the emancipation of poor peasants who were exposed to the exploitation of zamindars. He wanted the government to reduce its demands of landlords. He wanted to preserve the ryotwari system and rural basis of Indian civilisation and also establish modern scientific industry. He however differed from the other western liberal thinkers in one important respect, viz. role of state and sphere of state activities. In his scheme of things, the state is expected to bring about social reform, in protecting the rights of the tenants against the landlords etc.

On Liberty

Liberty was a pivot around which he entire religio-socio-political thought of Roy revolved. His protest against idolatory, his agitation against Sati, his demand for modern western education and his insistence on freedom of press, right of women, and his demands for "separation for powers" and for the codification of laws were all expressions of his intense love for liberty. For him, liberty was a priceless possession of mankind. He was the first to deliver the message of political freedom to India. Although Roy recognised the positive gains India would get from British rule, he was never in favour of an unending foreign rule in India. He considered the British connection necessary for India's social emancipation. Political freedom was bound to follow.

His love for liberty however was not limited to one nation or community. It was universal. He supported all struggles which aimed at human freedom. Freedom for him was indivisible. He celebrated the establishment of constitutional governments in Spain and Portugal and was pined when such a government collapsed in Naples in 1821.

Freedom was the strongest passion of Roy's mind. He believed equally in the freedom of body and mind, so also freedom of action and thought. He shunned all restrictions imposed by consideration of race, religion and customs on human freedoms.

On Rights of the Individual

Roy was the first to create an awareness for civil rights amongst the Indians. He was grateful to the Britishers because they made available to Indians all those civil rights which were enjoyed by the Queen's subjects in England. Though Roy did not specifically enlist the civil rights, he seems to include in it the following rights. Right to life and liberty, right to have opinions and freedom of expression, Right to property, Right to religion etc.

Roy gave the greatest importance to the right to freedom of opinion and expression. To him it included the freedom of creativity of mind and intellect, as well as the freedom of expressing one's opinions and thoughts through different media. According to Roy, freedom of expression was equally useful to the rulers and the ruled. Ignorant people were more likely to revolt against all that the rulers did, they could turn against authority itself. In contrast an enlightened public would be opposed only to the abuse of power by authority and not to the existence of authority itself. The free press the Raja argued, had never caused a revolution in any part of the world. But many examples could be cited where, in the absence of a free press, since the grievances of the people remained unrepresented and unredressed, the situation had become ripe for a violent 'revolutionary' change. A free and independent press alone could bring forth the best in the government as well as the people.

Roy, however, was not against the reasonable restrictions on the freedom of press. He even accepted some additional restrictions on the Indian Press, which were not imposed on the press in England. Such restrictions, he believed, might be necessary here as some Indians were likely to encourage hatred in the minds of the natives towards the British rulers. Roy also justified the restrictions imposed with a view to check the seditious attempts of creating hostilities with neighbouring friendly states. He, however, strongly objected to the restrictions imposed by the bureaucracy in India. These restrictions, in his opinion, were arbitrary and uncalled for by the circumstances in this country.

On Law and Judicial Administration

Law, Roy claimed, was the creation of passionless reason. It was the command of the sovereign. Hence, even the highest officer in the East India Company did not possess the competence for enacting the laws for India. The king-in-Parliament alone could have that authority. What is more, Roy argued that the English parliament, before finalising every piece of legislation relating to Indian should take into account the views of the economic and intellectual elites in this country.

Another important idea that Roy has contributed in the context of law relates to the codification of law. He thinks that such codification was in the interest of both the rulers and ruled. He suggested that the codification should be done on the basis of the principles common and agreeable to all groups and factions in the society. In the course of codification, the long-standing customs of this country should not be overlooked. Of course, only those customs which are reasonable and conducive to general welfare of the people should be picked up. Codified law should be simple, clear and exact. Codification would make the interpretations of laws more impersonal and its application more uniform. Roy had a clear perception of the distinction between law, custom and morality. He accepted that evolving customs were an important source of law, but the two could not be identified. He also made a distinction between law and morality. Some laws, according to Roy, might be legally valid, but morally indefensible. Conversely, some practices might be morally sound but could not be given legal force. Principles of morality are relative to the social realities and any law to be effective must take into account these ethical principles prevalent in a given society.

In his book entitled 'An Exposition of Revenue and Judicial System in Indian' Roy presented a profound discussion on urgent reforms in administrative and judicial matters. He stressed the point that the administration could not be efficient and effective unless there were official speaking in the language of the masses. There should also be several channels of communication between the administration and the people.

Roy's suggestions of reform in the judicial field are more numerous because for him an efficient, impartial and an independent judiciary was the supreme guarantee of liberty. Roy believed that the association of the natives in the judicial process had to be an essential feature of judicial administration. Other measures advocated by him included: constant supervision of the judicial proceedings by a vigilant public opinion, substitution of English for Persian as the official language to be used in the courts of law, appointment of Indian assessors in civil suits, trial by jury, separation of judicial from executive functions, and the constant consultation of the native interests before the enactment of any law that concerned them. He also suggested the revival of the age-old Panchayat system of adjudication. Roy thus urged several reforms and corrections in the Indian Judicial system in keeping with political liberalism.

On Sphere of State Action

Though Roy was a liberal thinker, he did not believe in the policy of laissez-faire. He could never accept that the sphere of state activity was limited only to the political field. He had appealed repeatedly in his writings to the state authorities to undertake many social, moral and cultural responsibilities which did not strictly come under the category of 'political'. He wanted the state to protect the tenants against the landlords, to make arrangements for the useful and liberal education, to eradicate the ugly practices like Sati and to give equal protection to the lives of both males and females, and to make efforts to create a new social order based on the principles of liberty, equality, fraternity and social justice. To Roy, the existence of any government becomes meaningful only if it performs all these functions besides the functions for which it originated.

On Education

Roy believed that unless the educational system of this country was overhauled, there was no possibility of the people coming out of the slumber of so many centuries. His ambition was to change the educational system completely. He was convinced that only a modern, science education could instill new awareness and new capabilities in the Indian people. Without this kind of education, social reform in India would be very weak and the country would always remain backward. Though Roy himself was a great scholar of Sanskrit, he always felt that the Sanskrit learning was irrelevant to modern India and hence he strongly opposed it. He appealed to the rulers that instead of perpetuating irrelevant Sanskrit learning, they should help equip the new generations of Indians with useful modern scientific knowledge. Roy wanted instruction in useful modern sciences like chemistry, mathematics, anatomy, natural philosophy and not load young minds with grammatical complexities, and speculative or imaginary knowledge. Roy's views and activities were really pioneering in giving a new turn to the educational system in India. He was the first eminent advocate of women's education.

On International Co-existence

Thoughts of Ram Mohan Roy on this subject are the expressions of his future oriented imagination and insight. He has portrayed a beautiful picture of international co-existence. He was perhaps the first thinker of the 18th century who had a clear vision of internationalism. This vision might have occurred to him in the course of his search for universal religion. Roy, the prophet of universalism, argued that all nations of the world must be placed on an equal footing in order to achieve global unity and a sense of broad fraternity. It is only then that the contradiction between nationalism and internationalism can be ended.

Roy held that the different tribes and nations were merely the branches of the same family and hence, there must be frequent give and take in all matters among the enlightened nations of the world. This, according to Roy, was the only way to make the human race happy and contented. Differences in political perspectives could be eliminated by thrashing out the differences on the common platforms composed of equal number of delegates from each of the contestant countries. Such a common forum could also be useful for the settlement of all international issues, which would enable mankind to live in peace for generations together.

Q8. Discuss the main criticism of Ranade against the popular practice of the Hindu religion. [June 09, Q 13]

Or

Write a brief note on Ranade's criticism of Religious Hindu Practice.

Ans. Ranade was a deeply religious person and he wanted to bring about basic reforms among the Hindus who he believed had degenerated considerably. This deterioration had come about due to distortions in religious beliefs and practices, hence he pleaded for their reformation.

Though Ranade was a great admirer of Indian culture and religion, he was highly critical of some of the Hindu religious beliefs and practices. What he wanted was reformation of Hindu religion. Therefore, he did not advocate conversion or the establishment of a separate sect. He felt that the basic philosophy of Hindu religion was sound and what was needed was to rid Hinduism of corrupt and perverted practices that had crept into the religion over a period of time.

Strict adherence to the letter rather than the spirit of the Hindu religious practices irked Ranade. He was critical of polytheism – i.e. worshipping of many goods. He believed in the existence of one God. He did not believe in polytheism, encouraged superstitions and corrupt practices. It also gave birth to idol worship. The temples of different gods became the centres of religious orthodoxy and vested interests. Idol worship strengthened the hands of the religious authorities and gave birth to the worst type of priestcraft. All these had succeeded in keeping the masses away from the true religious and philosophical precepts. There was, therefore, an urgent need for reform within the Hindu religious tradition.

Ranade wanted to purge Hindu religion of all its evil practices and for that purpose, he along with his friends established the Prarthana Samaj.

Q9. Discuss M.G. Ranade's ideas on social reforms. [June 06, Q 11(ii)]

Ans. Ranade on Social Reforms

Ranade believed in all-round development of the society and held that social, religious, political and economic reforms were interdependent. Reform according to Ranade had to be gradual and undertaken in such a manner that it did not break the continuity of traditions. He was opposed to revival of the old and archaic since these did not have anything positive to offer. He said, "in a living organisation as society is, no revival is possible. The dead are, buried and burnt once for all and the dead past cannot be revived. If revival is impossible, reformation is the only alternative open to sensible people". In his addresses to different social conferences and gatherings, he exhorted reformers to work for slow and gradual change. He believed that India's future was bleak if this process of reform was not undertaken. Ranade's efforts were in the backdrop of a controversy about the relative importance of social and political reforms. Lokmanya Tilak and his followers were of the opinion that political reforms were more important than social reforms because after securing political power, it was always possible to effect social reforms. But Ranade did not agree with this view and believed that social reforms were more important. In his opinion the foundations of a modern society could be established only through social reforms, which, in its turn, would facilitate the struggle for political power. Ranade was a critic of the caste system, he believed that the caste system prevented the development of individual capacities. Ranade was critical of the fact that the caste system did not permit free choice of vocation, nor did it ensure an equality of opportunity. Ranade favoured reorganisation of the Hindu society on the basis of freedom of choice and quality. He pleaded for the abolition of caste system and argued in favour of intercaste marriages. He suggested-the extension of education through the other developmental facilities to the lower castes.

M.G. Ranade

The oppression of women by the Hindu social system was yet another tradition which Ranade sought to reform. Ranade supported the age of consent bill that raised the marriageable age of women.

Education was another important subject that drew Ranade's attention. He favoured the introduction of secular education in India which would inculcate the virtues of civic life. The aim of education should be the pursuit of truth. Thus, education for him had a liberating influence. He did not like students to blindly follow their teachers. He wanted them to develop the spirit of adventure. He was of the opinion that, in the university courses, there should be judicious blending of tradition and modernity. He accorded equal importance to physical education. Ranade attached more importance to what was taught rather than to how it was taught. He set little in store by examinations and wanted the universities to be the centres of knowledge and excellence.

Ranade was a champion of Indian languages and sought their development so as to enrich the cultural life of the Indian people. Ranade wanted the British government to spend more on education especially on primary education because the latter was greatly neglected. It was not possible for the government at that time to open schools at every place; hence, he pleaded for the establishment both government aided schools and private schools. He demanded that every village should be provided with a school. Education of women and education of backward communities were subjects dear to his heart and he exhorted the government and society to carry forward educational activities for these helpless sections of the society. Ranade wanted to establish a new Indian society based upon contract and free choice. He wanted to instil among Indians a sense of human dignity and commitment to progress.

Q10. State different methods of social changes discussed by Ranade.

Ans. Ranade advocated social reforms because he knew that all-round reforms were necessary to bring about basic change in Hindu society. There were different methods of social reform and Ranade held that barring revolution all other methods should be pursued. According to him, there were four methods of social reform and they were as follows :

i) The first method was the method of tradition in which the cause of social reforms was advocated with the help of religious texts.

ii) The second method was that of appealing to the conscience of the people. Reformers could attempt to sensitise people to the corrupt, superstitious and unjust practices.

iii) The third method was enforcement of reforms by means of penalties, for instance, the government banned the practice of burning widows.

iv) The fourth method was that of rebellion which sought to change the evil and inhuman customs by force. This could, however, break the continuity and would divide the society.

Ranade, did not favour the revolutionary method because it would break the historical continuity of the community. Ranade recommended the first two methods, but he was not averse to the use of state power or enforcement of reforms. He was not averse to the idea of a foreign government legislating for Indians so long. At the same time, he knew that mere legislations would not bring about change and it had to be accompanied by popular movements of the people. Ranade was neither a revolutionary nor a revivalist; he was devoted to the evolutionary path of slow and gradual change. In his opinion, lasting progress was possible only by accommodating new ideas within the accepted way of life.

Q11. Write a note on followings :
(i) Ranade's views on rise of Maratha power
(ii) Ranade on nature and function of state
(iii) Ranade—prophet of Indian nationalism
(iv) Ranade on Indian political economy

Ans. (i) Ranade's views on rise of Maratha power

Ranade was a keen student of Maratha history and he was appalled by the distortion of Maratha history at the hands of the British historians. He was profoundly impressed by the personality of Shivaji and undertook a deep study of the historical processes involved in the Maratha uprising. He wrote his famous essay 'The Rise of Maratha Power' to show that the Maratha movement had its own philosophy and purpose.

According to Ranade, the Maratha state was the result of a great social and political movement begun by Marathi speaking people. Ranade pointed out that the Maratha state survived after Shivaji, and in fact, expanded far and wide for 140 years after his death. Ranade held that the rise of Maratha power was a national uprising, the uprising of the whole people strongly bound together by the common affinities of language, religion and literature and seeking further solidarity by a common independent political existence. Secondly, Ranade held that the rise of Maratha power was not a mere political revolution but it was essentially a social revolution. This social revolution preceded a political revolution and prepared the ground for the latter. He likened the Bhakti movement in Maharashtra to the protestant reformation movement of Europe in the 16th century. He held that the Bhakti movement was "heterodox in its spirit of protest against all forms of ceremonies and class distinctions based on birth and ethical in its preferences of a pure heart". This according to Ranade proved that every political change needed reformation. Ranade held that under the leadership of Shivaji the Marathas rose to power mainly because of Shivaji's exceptional abilities. He motivated them to fight for Swaraj by uniting and overcoming separatist tendencies. It was because the Maratha state was deeply rooted in the hearts of he people that it survived despite adversities.

But Ranade knew that the national upsurge of the Marathas could not become permanent because the Maratha state lacked solidarity and self-discipline. The

Marathas could not establish a modern state which required virtues not promoted by the prevailing caste system. Caste arrogance and pride tended to destroy social unity. They failed to develop a liberal social polity "which would help bring about the progress of different sections of society." Pointing out the moral of the story, Ranade wrote, "the attempts failed; but even the failure was itself an education in highest virtues and possibly intended to be a preparatory discipline to cement the union of Indian races under the British guidance."

(ii) Ranade on nature and function of state

Ranade differed from the British individualists regarding the role of the state in the field of political economy. He maintained that the state represented the power, wisdom, mercy and charity of its best citizens; therefore, it had to play a more positive role in human life. It was the duty of the state to protect the lives of the people and to make it nobler, happier and richer. The purpose of the state was essentially moral. It was a means to attain higher grades of civilised life.

According to Ranade, in modern times the state could not rest with its police functions. Now it had to look after the social welfare and social progress. According to Ranade, the state must perform regulative, productive and distributive functions. The state should regulate and control public life. The force of the state must be used to prevent social malpractices and exploitation of man by man. Secondly, the state should get involved in productive activities. The classical liberals held that the state should not interfere in economic matters, but Ranade argued that the state could perform productive functions by establishing industries in key areas of the economy. He did not want to substitute the state action for individual initiative but to make individual initiative more broad based and to encourage the spirit of creativity and self-help among members of the society. When individuals became capable of managing their own affairs, the state should withdraw because ultimately the state protection and control were but crutches to teach the nation to walk. Thus, he wanted to strike a right balance between individual initiative and state intervention.

Though Ranade was not a socialist, he realised the importance of the distributive functions of the state. He maintained that it was the duty of the state to provide the minimum means of betterment to the people. Ranade upheld the right to property and free individual initiative. He, however, advocated some limitations on the rights of the rich people. He suggested state intervention to reduce the gulf between the wealthy and the poor and to assure a minimum standard of living to all the citizens. Ranade argued that in a poor and backward country like India, the state had to play a positive role in the productive and distributive processes.

(iii) Ranade—prophet of Indian nationalism

Ranade was the prophet of Indian nationalism. He was the first Indian thinker to insist that national development must be based on the principles of democracy, secularism and liberalism. He emphasised the importance of religious tolerance and Hindu-Muslim unity because he believed that the Indian people were the chosen people of God and India was the true land of promise. It was their historic duty to show the patch to the world.

Ranade made it clear that Hindu or Muslim culture could not become the foundation of Indian nationalism. The composite Indian culture which had been developing since the past 3000 years was the basis of Indian nationalism. According to Ranade, the chief quality of the Indian people was their ability to absorb the best from other cultures and to give a new shape and form to their culture. Ranade expected that interaction with the British would also enrich Indian culture. "There has been no revolution, and yet old condition of things has been tending to reform itself by the slow process of assimilation. The great religions of the world took birth here and now they meet again as brothers prepared to higher dispensation, which will unite all and vivify all; India alone among all nations of the world has been so favoured."

Ranade wanted to promote the fusion of the best elements in different communities in order to develop a common Indian nationality. His ideal was national unification and for that purpose, he wanted to work in as many fields and at as many levels as possible. This would be a slow growth but he believed that short cuts to unity were dangerous.

Ranade maintained that all the major communities in India should come together to attain common objectives and fight against poverty and backwardness. Freedom and prosperity were not possible without unity. He made it clear that it was the common tenet of Indian nationalism that progress for India meant progress of all its parts and communities. He recognised the fact that through united action and progress, Indians could gather enough strength to make the transfer of power from the British to Indians inevitable. While pointing out the main characteristics of Indian nationalism, he wrote "The inner spring, the hidden purpose not consciously realised in many cases, is the sense of human dignity and freedom which is slowly asserting its supremacy over national mind. It is not confined to one sphere of family life. It invades the whole man and makes him feel that individual purity and social justice have paramount claim over us all which we can ignore long without being dragged to a lower level of existence."

Thus, in political matters Ranade advocated the cause of freedom and progress and wanted to develop such state structures that would strike the right balance between individual rights and public good. In his economic ideas, he maintained the same theoretical balance.

(iv) Ranade on Indian political economy

While studying Indian political economy, Ranade reviewed the then prevalent theories of economic development. He came to the conclusion that they could not be arbitrarily applied in a backward country like India. He made it clear that as in other social sciences in economics also, time, place, circumstances, endowments and aptitudes of men, their laws, institutions and customs should be taken into account. The laws of classical economics could not be arbitrarily applied, because history proved that they were not universal. He did not approve of the extreme individualism nor the social indifference of classical economists. He said there ought to be no theoretical limits to the action of the state even in the economic sphere and each proposal of its expansion should be considered from the practical standpoint. The countries which were late in capitalist development had to rely on the state for initial industrialisation.

Ranade thought that the problem of distribution was not properly tackled by the classical economists. It condemned the poor to poverty and helped the rich to get richer. In this situation, freedom of contract became meaningless when the two contracting parties were not evenly matched. "In such case" he wrote "all talk of equality and freedom adds insult to the injury". He supported the right to property but made it clear that the institutions of property and privileges were historical categories and products of social processes. They had no other justification for existence except moral and moral justification was always based on equity, justice and fair play. Hence, he favoured curtailing the rights of landlords in favour of tenants. He was not averse to modifying the laws concerning private property and distribution of produce if equity and fair play so demanded.

Ranade was of the view that economics was a social science and its problems should be studied through historical perspective and with social sympathy.

Q12. Briefly discuss the life of Gopal Krishna Gokhale and Development of his Political Career.

Or

Critically examine Gopal Krishna Gokhale's political thought.

[June 08, Q 3]

Ans. Born in Kothluk, a village in Maharashtra, on May 9, 1866, Gopal Krishna Gokhale was raised in the home of his maternal grandfather. This village was not too far from Tamhanmala, the native town of his father, Krishna Rao, a farmer by occupation who was forced to work as a clerk due to the poor soil of the region. His mother, Valubai, also known as Satyabhama, was a simple woman who instilled in her children the values of religion, devotion to one's family, and caring for one's fellow man.

Gopal Krishna Gokhale

Supported by his elder brother and sister-in-law, Gokhale managed an education at Rajaram High School in Kothapur. Due to his respect for his brother and recognition of the compassion with which he was treated, Gokhale learned the value of self-sacrifice to avoid asking for more material support. At times he went without meals and studied by the light of street lamps to save his elder brother as much money as possible. A hardworking student, he moved on to college and graduated from Elphinstone College, Bombay in 1884 at the age of 18, earning a scholarship of Rs. 20 per month in his final year. His education influenced Gokhale's life in many ways. Primarily, his understanding of the English language allowed him to express himself without hesitation and with utmost clarity. Also, his appreciation and knowledge of history instilled in him a respect for liberty, democracy, and the parliamentary system.

After graduation, he moved on to teaching, and took a position as an Assistant Master in the New English School in Pune. Among many achievements which testify to his talent and passion for teaching, perhaps the greatest of them all was a compilation, a book of arithmetic in collabouration with a colleague, N. J. Bapat, which became a widely used and widely translated textbook across the country. Gokhale moved on to become a founding member of Fergusson College in Pune in 1885, with colleagues in the highly honored Deccan Education Society. He pledged twenty years of his life to this college, as a teacher and board member.

The year 1886 saw the entry of Gopal Krishna Gokhale into public life. At only 20 years of age, he delivered a public address concerning "India under the British Rule" and was applauded for his expression and command of the English language. Gokhale soon moved on to managing public affairs. While contributing articles to the English weekly Mahratta, he was seduced by the idea of using education as a means to awaken patriotism among the people of India. Just as this idea was enveloping, Gokhale was promoted to Secretary of the Deccan Education Society. Once in the limelight, there was no looking back. After being given charge of the Bombay Provincial Conference in 1893, he was elected to the Senate of the Bombay University. In time, Gokhale came to devote all his spare time to the causes of the common man: famine, plague relief measures, local self- government, land reform, and communal harmony. As a member of the Pune Municipality, twice elected its president, Gokhale continued to strive to solve the problems of the poor, and those who came to him with grievances concerning water supply, drainage, etc. were pleased with the practical manner in which he dealt with the problem. Gokhale also published a daily newspaper entitled Janaprakash, which allowed him to voice his reformist views on politics and society.

In 1905, he founded the Servants of India Society, which trained people to be selfless workers so they could work for the common good of the people. So strong was the desire to make a difference, that these kindred spirits vowed a simple life of dedication to these causes. Among many things the organisation did, there were the commendable services of helping victims of floods and famines, and taking the time to educate women in society, so that they too may have a voice. Many people influenced Gokhale and gave him the strength and discipline to bring his ideas to the realm of reality, but none more than Mahadev Govind Ranade, to whom he was apprenticed in 1887. Ranade trained him for 15 years in all spheres of public life, and taught him sincerity, devotion to public service, and tolerance. These qualities, which Ranade helped instill in Gokhale, are those qualities which helped make Gokhale the man he is known today. Gokhale visited England and voiced his concerns relating to the unfair treatment of the Indian people by the British government. In one span of 49 days, he spoke in front of 47 different audiences, captivating every one of them. Before long, he was touted as the most effective pleader for India's cause. While Gokhale pleaded for gradual reform to ultimately attain Swaraj, or self-government, in India, some of his contemporaries, comprising a radical element, wished to use force as a means of persuasion. Gokhale maintained his moderate political views and worked out some reforms for the betterment of India. He was instrumental in the formation of the Minto-Morley Reforms of 1909, which eventually became law. Unfortunately, the Reforms Act became law in 1909 and it was disappointing to see that the people were not given a proper democratic system despite Gokhale's efforts. The communal harmony he had longed for was shattered when he realised that the Muslim community was steadfast in considering itself as a separate unit. On the bright side, however, Gokhale's efforts were clearly not in vain. Indians now had access to seats of the highest authority within the government, and their voices were more audible in matters of public interest. Gokhale, during his visit to South Africa in 1912, met Mohandas Karamchand Gandhi, popularly known as Mahatma Gandhi. Gokhale made him aware of the issues confronting common people back in

India. In his autobiography, Gandhi calls Gokhale his "mentor and guide". Not only Gandhi, Gokhale also guide Muhammad Ali Jinnah, the founder of Pakistan. Jinnah later aspired to become the "Muslim Gokhale". The years of hard work and devotion of Gopal Krishna Gokhale did much for the country of India, but sadly also took their toll on the health of this great leader. Excessive exertion and the resulting exhaustion only aggravated his diabetes and cardiac asthma. The end came peacefully, however, on February 19, 1915. Pointing his finger toward heaven and then folding his hands respectfully, Gopal Krishna Gokhale made his final statement to an audience, a fond farewell.

Q13. Describe the thoughts of Gokhale on Liberalism. [June 06, Q 2]

Ans. India's great Liberal Gopal Krishna Gokhale spelt out the Liberal dream when he said: "I recognise no limits to my aspiration for my motherland. I want our people to be in our country what other people are in theirs. I want our men and women, without distinction of caste or creed, to have opportunities to grow to the full height of their stature, unhampered by cramping and unnatural restrictions. I want India to take her place among the great nations of the world".

Gokhale was essentially a liberal thinker. But his liberalism was slightly different-from the classical liberalism that existed in the eighteenth and nineteenth century Europe.

Ideology of Liberalism : Liberalism as an ideology may be defined as an idea committed to individual freedom, as a method and policy in government, as an organising principle in society, and a way of life for the individual and community. Liberty is the core doctrine of liberalism and it stands against coercive interference of any kind in any walk of life. In the social sphere liberalism stands for secularism. It advocates man's freedom from the shackles of religious orthodoxy and believes in freedom of conscience. In the sphere of economy it appreciates the ideal of free trade coupled with internal freedom of production and external freedom of exportation. It stands for free competition implying no curb on import and export of goods. For this reason it stands for the exploitation of natural resources and distribution of economic dividends at the hands of the individuals.

As a liberal Gokhale cherished the idea of individual liberty. But to him, liberty did not imply the total absence of restraint; on the contrary, he felt that individual liberty could be usefully allowed only when the individuals behave with a sense of self-restraint and self-organisation. He knew that the ideal of liberty could not be realised unless the citizens are guaranteed certain rights to freedom. To him the right of free expression and the freedom of press were essential to realise the ideal of individual liberty. He, therefore, opposed the Official Secret

Bill in 1904 on the grounds that it was proposed to arm the government with a greater power to control the press.

Gokhale also favoured the right to private property and the freedom of contract. Commenting on the Land Revenue Code Amendment Bill, Gokhale said that "the ordinary citizen is as tenaciously attached to his proprietary rights over his holdings... that there is nothing he will not do if it is in his power to ward off what he regards as a direct or indirect attack on these rights. And it is not difficult to understand that a proposal to take away from his power of alienating, when necessary, his holding should appear to him to be a most serious encroachment on his rights. Thus, Gokhale defended the right to private property, individual liberty and freedom of contract which essentially constituted the core of liberal doctrine.

In order to maintain liberty and essential civil rights, Gokhale proposed the establishment of representative institutions in the country. According to him the first prerequisite for the improvement of relations between Britain and India was 'an unequivocal declaration in England to put he resolve to help forward the growth of representative institutions in India and a determination to stand by this policy." However, Gokhale did not demand universal franchise. He proposed property qualification for enfranchisement. For example, for the village Panchayat elections Gokhale wanted that only such persons should be enfranchised who a paid a minimum land revenue.

Gokhale also preferred the representation of interests along with the representation of people in the legislature. In his last testament and will be suggested that the Legislative Council in each province should constitute of 75 to 100 members. Taking Bombay as an illustration he pleaded for one seat each in the legislature for the Karachi Chamber, the Ahmedabad Mill Owners and the Deccan Sardars. He also suggested the principle of special representation for the religious minority. Recognising the communal differences between the Hindus and the Muslims, Gokhale pleaded for separate representation of the Muslims. Thus, as a liberal, Gokhale on the one hand defended the concept of individual liberty and on the other hand supported the establishment of representative institution in a limited sense.

Gokhale's ideas regarding the role of state remarkably differed from that of classical liberalism. Classical liberalism pleads for a laissez-faire state. The only functions that classical liberalism grants to the state are police functions. They believe that a government which governs the least is the best. But Gokhale following the footsteps of Justice M.G. Ranade, pleaded for state intervention to regulate the economic and social life of the country. Here Gokhale differed remarkably from J.S. Mill. Gokhale wanted the Government to intervene in the economic life for the sake of industrial development and agricultural prosperity. He wanted the government to intervene not only in the processes of distribution but also in the process of production. According to Gokhale the purpose of government was to further the moral and material interests of the people. In order to realise this purpose the government cannot remain unconcerned towards the unnatural restrictions in the path of development. According to Gokhale the government should remove these 'unnatural restrictions' and accelerate the pace of development. Gokhale said: "Indians needed a government which subordinates all other considerations to the welfare of the Indian people, which presents the indignities offered to Indians abroad as though they were offered, to Englishmen and, which endeavous by all means in its power to further the moral and material interests of the people in and outside India." Thus, to Gokhale the state should not be a 'police state' only, but it should embark upon welfare activities and intervene in the economic life of the country whenever necessary. Gokhale's liberalism was no doubt inspired by the liberalism of Mill but it significantly differed from the classical liberalism in two respects. On the one hand it did not advocate the extreme individualism, emphasising the negative meaning of liberty and on the other hand it pleaded for necessary state intervention in the economic and social life of the country.

Q14. Discuss the Gokhale's response to the British rule in India.

Ans. Like most of the liberal Indian thinkers of his time Gokhale appreciated and welcomed the British rule in India. His appreciation of the British rule and particularly his insistence on the continuation of the British rule in India were based on two premises. In the first instance, like all the moderates, Gokhale was convinced that it was because of British rule that the process of modernisation of the Indian society had set in. The British upheld the concept of equality before law, they introduced the principle of representative government (on however limited a scale it might be) they guaranteed the freedom of speech and press. All these things were certainly new. It was again the British who set in the process of political integration in India. There was much for Indians, to learn from the British and hence, Gokhale pleaded that we should bear with them for some time and make progress in the field of industry, commerce, education and politics. Gokhale was convinced that if British rule continued for some time, India would be modernised completely and eventually join the community of nations like any other independent state in Europe.

Gokhale believed that in keeping with their liberal traditions, the British would fulfill their pledges and bestow on India self-government once Indians qualified themselves for the same. This concept of 'England's pledges to India' was built upon the declarations of Thomas Munro, Macaulay, Henri Lawrence and above all Queen Victoria's Proclamation. In spite of the fact that from the end of Ripon's viceroyalty in 1884 to the August-Declaration of 1917 successive

Viceroys and Secretaries of India emphatically repudiated the feasibility of introducing English political institutions to India, Gokhale still believed that by appealing to the British sense of liberalism, by convincing them of India's genuine capabilities the British would ultimately be convinced and would introduce to India western political institutions. It was this faith in British liberalism that made Gokhale plead for the continuance of the British rule in India.

His justification for the continuance of the British rule in India did not mean that he was totally satisfied with the British administration in India. For instance, he was a bitter critic of the high handedness of the Curzonian administration. He also argued on many occasions that the British raj was more raj and less British in the sense that it was reluctant to introduce English parliamentary institutions to India, yet he believed that British rule was destined to accomplish its providential mission in India. Gokhale sincerely felt that the history of India had nothing to offer so far as the development of democratic political institutions was concerned. In a paper read before the Universal Races Congress, London, July, 1911, Gokhale admitted, "India did not develop the national idea of political freedom as developed in the west." He was convinced that the social and political institutions of the country must be reformed in the image of the west. To him the European history presented a well-marked evolution of the democratic idea and was therefore useful in shaping our ideas of liberty and democracy. The British connection would definitely serve this purpose and hence he welcomed the British rule in India. In one of his letters to his friend Gokhale wrote: "You must all realise that whatever be the shortcomings of bureaucracy, however the insolence of individual Englishman, they alone stand today in the country for order; and without continued order no real progress is possible for our people." Thus, to Gokhale British rule in Indian stood for social order which was the pre-condition of progress and hence he justified the continuance of British rule in India.

Chapter 3

Militant Nationalism

Q1. What do you understand by Militant Nationalism? What are the characteristics of Militant Nationalism?

Ans. The militant nationalist brought about a departure in the national movement by adopting more radical methods of agitation than those followed by the earlier moderates. The prominent leaders of this phase of the national movement were Bal Gangadhar Tilak, Aurobindo Ghosh, Bipan Chandra Pal and the Late Lajpat Rai. Militant nationalism represented a distinct phase in the anti-colonial struggle. It introduced new methods of political agitation, involved popular symbols for mobilisation and thus tried to broad base the movement.

In militant nationalism, each one of the factors of nationalism–population, religion, race, etc. acquire an added emotional emphasis. For example, the territory of a nation is much more than geographical entity. It is a sacred land. The motherland is considered as greater than heaven. It is a divinity in physical form and the embodiment of its philosophy of life and dharma. The mountains and rivers of the country are also more than physical objects. They are objects of worship. Sri Aurobindo wrote, "Whereas others regard the country as an inert mass and know it in terms of plains, fields, mountains and rivers, I look upon the country as the mother; I worship and adore her as the mother." Lajpat Rai in his letter to Ramsay Macdonald made this point even more explicit: "To the Indian, or India is the land of the Gods - the Deva-Bhumi of his forefathers. It is the land of knowledge, of faith, of beatitude - the Gian-Bhumi, the Dharma-Bhumi and the Punya-Bhumi of the ancient Aryas. It is the land of the Vedas and of the heroes - the Veda-Bhumi and the Vir-Bhumi of his ancestors. You may call it foolish, impractical, sentimental and unprogressive; but there it is–a mighty of life, into which no foreigner can penetrate."

Characteristics of Militant Nationalism

The adjective 'militant' gives a fair idea of its distinctive nature. While nationalism is itself a very strong feeling and sentiment, militant nationalism is an even more vehement, assertive and aggressive feeling.

There can be two ways of winning freedom for a subject country. One is to impress upon the rulers that freedom is the birthright of the people and should be granted to them gracefully. This presumes that the alien rulers are open to reason and will quit of their own accord without being forced to do so by the subjects. The other way is to attack the rulers and the government and bring their domination to an end, as it is futile to expect that colonial rulers will listen to reason and agree to surrender the gains and advantages of an empire. The first may be described as the liberal or moderate method and the second as the militant method. Liberals or moderates may well be aware of the evils of foreign rule, but they do not consider it a total or unmitigated evil. The evils can be removed by gradual stages by convincing the rulers through representations and petitions and the normal process of argument. The benefits of a modern and civilised government ought not to be lost through impatience over temporary and curable complaints. The moderates regarded the British connection as part of a divine plan for the advance of India into the modern age. The militant nationalists' attitude was entirely different. To them, the alien government was a total evil. It was the cause of political, economic, cultural and spiritual ruin of the country. The foreign ruler could never be trusted to vacate the country that he has gained by conquest. Persuasion, therefore, was futile; more forceful methods must be used and the moderates, according to them, were lacking in will and a sense of urgency. The difference between the moderates and the militant nationalist was radical, according to Lala Lajpat Rai. It was not one of speed, nor of method, but of fundamental principles. He pronounced that India would never evolve into a self-governing state, if it were to follow the methods of the moderates. He also said that unless the Congress took steps to change its nature and adopt direct methods of political action, some other movement might start with this object. The result would then be that the Congress would sink into insignificance. It was prophetic of him indeed to have said this in 1905, two years before the stormy session of the Congress at Surat in 1907.

Q2. Discuss the influence of militant nationalism. What is the significance of militant nationalism in contemporary politics?

Ans. Militant nationalism was a distinct epoch in the history of the freedom movement in our country. The background to militant nationalism was the character of the Indian National Congress at the beginning of this century. It was a political movement, which drew inspiration from the religious awakening at the end of the nineteenth century.

The Indian National Congress at the beginning, and for some years at the beginning of the present century, was dominated by the liberals and moderates. Their methods of petitioning and expressions of loyalty and trust in the British government roused the resentment of the younger generation of leaders and educated young men. They demanded that the Congress should come out openly against the rulers and act more decisively and quickly. The methods and programmes of the militant nationalists were as response to the demand. The militant nationalists, though advocated a change from the methods of the moderates were not in favour of violence. This perspective was articulated by Sri Aurobindo in his An Open Letter to My Country-men in July 1909. Thus, '.. the difficulties of our situation ask for bold yet wary walking. We must scrupulously observe the law while taking every advantage, both of the protection it gives and the latitude it still leaves for pushing forward our cause and our propaganda." The responsibility for political extremism, he argued, brought about was on the government. It was the brutality of the government which brought the violence and ruthlessness of the extremists. Let the government change its ways and there would be an end to such political madness. "With the stray assassinations which have troubled the country we have no concern, having once clearly and firmly dissociated ourselves from them, we need notice them no further. They are the rank and noxious fruit of a rank and noxious policy and until the authors of that policy turn from their errors, no human power can prevent the poison-tree from bearing according to its kind." Speaking in December 1920, Lajpat Rai stated, "1 am one of those who believe that every nation has, when the occasion arises, the inherent right of armed rebellion against a repressive, autocratic government, but I do not believe that we have either the means or even the will for such an armed rebellion at the present time." The methods of violent confrontation with the rulers might have been successful had they been used when the government was unprepared and unwary. Lightning assaults on a country-wide scale in such a situation might have brought the government down. The government had now gained the upper hand and such methods were bound to fail. Lawful but resolute protest and the development of national strength by means of Swadeshi, self-help and national efficiency attached urgent need of the time. National education and a constructive programme of national development were not to be taken up. The non-cooperation programme of the militant nationalists had come to be accepted by the Congress, though Gandhi was soon after to "prefix non-violent to non-cooperation," (Lajpat Rai) and make it a moral as well as a political programme. Those of the militant nationalist school of thought were not enthusiastic about the moral side of Gandhi's programme and regarded it as unrealistic, impractical and politically unwise. They would not object to noncooperation from a purely political point of view. In the prevailing circumstances, it was the only available method of confronting the government, and carrying on the fight for freedom. Their objection was that Gandhi had made it at the same time a moral programme too. It was, according to them, too much to expect all political workers **as** well as the common man to rise to the moral level which Gandhi demanded. Lajpat Rai was severely critical of Gandhi's sudden decision to call off the Bardoli Satyagraha because of his moral indignation over the Chauri Chaura incident. This incident, in which some policemen were burnt to death by an angry mob, angered Gandhi so much that he abruptly put a stop to the movement. Militant nationalists who were politically realistic were severely disappointed over this unexpected development. Their disappointment was shared by a large number of their countrymen also. Though militant nationalism drew inspiration from religious awakening, militant nationalists disapproved of mixing up of religion and politics. The Dharma they advocated was a wider concept than any religion or creed. It was universal in scope though outworldly it appeared like Hindu religion. They were well aware that India is a land of many religions and that these religions should learn to understand each other and coexist as different roads leading to the same goal. If, the militant nationalists were inspired by religion, how could they, at the same time object to mixing up of religion and politics? Were they not contradicting themselves particularly because some among them invoked religious symbols for political mobilisation? The answers to these questions lay in their understanding of intercommunal relations and their conception of secularism. They hold that different religions and different communities must learn to coexist in a broadly unified nation under the unifying influence of Dharma or the universal moral law of life and society. Dharma in this sense is a cohesive force, above all religions and creeds, but opposed to none. Lajpat Rai described the unifying influence of Dharma very clearly with reference to the Hindu-Muslim problem. "The expression Hindu-Muslim unity is only symbolic. It is not exclusive, but inclusive. When we speak of Hindu-Muslim unity, we do not exclude the other religious communities like the Sikhs, the Christians, the Parsis, the Buddhists, the Jains from our conception of unity or from our idea of nationhood. The Indian nation, such as it is, or such as we intend to build neither is nor will be exclusively Hindu, Muslim, Sikh, or Christian. It will be each and all. This is my ideal of Swarajya. This is my goal of nationhood." While Hindu leaders might have extolled Sanatana Dharma as more than a religion or creed, others remained suspicious and skeptical. They saw it as only the religion of the majority, seeking political ascendency over the other religious minorities. The political use of religious festivals in Maharashtra like the Ganapati festival was bound to create suspicion and fear especially in the Muslims. The Shivaji festival did so even more.

The British policy of giving representation for minorities on a communal religious basis was the beginning of separatism and its culmination in the partition of the country. The militant nationalists recognised the seriousness of the communal problem, but their approach to it was distinctive. They were of the view that religious diversity must be safeguarded while working for the unity of the country. But they were very firm that unity should be brought about through a spirit of understanding and give and take between the communities. They were totally opposed to a policy of concession and political bargaining. Concessions extended on political considerations would only strengthen the minority complex and make the minority communities more and more ambitious and aggressive. They were thus idealistic in their approach to the problem while being frank and realistic at the same time.

Q3. Give a brief life sketch of Bal Gangadhar Tilak.

Ans. Bal Gangadhar Tilak was born in a middle class family of moderate means in the Ratnagiri district of Konkan on the west coast of India on 23rd July, 1856. The family was noted for its piety, learning and adherence to ancient traditions and rituals. His father, Gangadhar Pant was a teacher by profession and a Sanskrit scholar. Young Tilak was thus brought up in an atmosphere of orthodoxy and traditions. This instilled in him a love for Sanskrit and respect for ancient Indian religion and culture. His father was transferred to Pune when he was ten years of age. This provided him with an opportunity to get higher education. After completing his graduation in 1876, he studied law. But instead of joining the government service or practising law, he decided to serve the country. Believing that the best way to serve the country was to educate the people, he and his friend Gopal Ganesh Agarkar decided to devote their lives to the cause of education.

Bal Gangadhar Tilak

They started the New English School at Pune in 1876 and started their career as school teachers. However, Tilak started feeling that educating young children was not enough and that the elderly people also needed to be exposed to the socio-political reality. Hence, in 1881 he started two weeklies, 'Maratha' in English and 'Kesari' in Marathi. In 1885 they set up the Deccan Education Society in order to start a college which was later named after the then Governor of Bombay as the Ferguson College.

Later, due to difference of opinion between Tilak and Agarkar, Tilak resigned from the society and took over the ownership of the two weeklies. His editorship of these two journals involved him directly in the social and political affairs of the Bombay Presidency. Through his writings in the Kesari, he tried to make the people conscious of their rights. In his writings, Tilak very often invoked the tradition and history of Maharashtra. These writings made him very popular among his people. It however, antagonised the government and he was imprisoned because of it on several occasions.

Tilak was recognised as one of the leading Sanskrit scholars in India. This enabled him to study the classical literature on metaphysics, religion, astronomy and other allied fields. One of his most well-known works is the "Orion: Studies in the Antiquity of Vedas." In this book, he propounded the thesis that Rigveda was composed as early as 4500 B.C. This book brought him recognition as a scholar in oriental studies. His second book was "The Arctic Home of Vedas. " On the basis of astronomical and geological data, he suggested in this book that the Aryans originally belonged to the Arctic region. However, his greatest work was the "Gita-Rahasya." It is a philosophical enquiry into the teachings of the Gita. While reinterpreting the Gita, he laid stress on the concept of Karma-Yoga, instead of renunciation (as its central message).

For longing about a radical national awakening, Tilak and his colleagues evolved the famous four-point action programme, which was disliked by the existing leadership of the Congress. The Government was alarmed and became more and more impatient and resorted to rigorous repressive measures.

Finally. at the Banaras Congress, the action programme was formally adopted. This was followed by Tilak's arrest who was tried on the charge of sedition. The charge was based on an article that he had written in the 'Kesari.' He was sentenced to six years rigorous imprisonment and was deported to Mandalay. It was here that he wrote his famous Gita Rahasya. On being released from the prison he once again threw himself into active public life. He popularised the idea of Home-Rule. He died on 2nd October 1920.

Tilak believed that the world is the field of God and is real. It is not an illusion or Maya. The individual has to live and strive in the world; it is here where he has to perform his duties. The individual will, in this way, attain spiritual freedom and promote the welfare of his fellow creatures.

Despite his belief in the Vedantic philosophy, Tilak recognised the significance of religion in the ordinary sense of the term. Symbolism and popular rituals were acceptable to Tilak because he felt that these helped in forging a sense of unity and social togetherness.

Q4. Briefly discuss the economic ideas of Tilak.

Ans. Tilak accepted Dadabhai Naoroji's 'Economic Drain Theory' and criticised the British Government for ruthlessly exploiting the resources of the country. He wrote that the foreign enterprises and investment in India have created a delusion of prosperity, while the truth was otherwise. British rule had impoverished the country. The Britishers' reckless policies had destroyed the indigenous industries, trade and art. The alien rulers had allowed a free inflow of European products and the Indian handicrafts etc. were forced to face unequal competition with them.

But Tilak realised that a foreign government cannot be expected to accord protection to the indigenous industries. The twin political programmes of 'Boycott' and 'Swadeshi' suggested by Tilak were aimed at generating indigenous and independent economic development.

Q5. Discuss the political philosophy of Tilak. **[June 06, Q 3]**

Ans. Tilak was not an armchair thinker, nor was he a political philosopher in the academic sense. He was a practical politician and his main task was the political emancipation of India.

Tilak's political philosophy was rooted in the Indian tradition but it did not reject all that was western. He was inspired by the ancient Indian spiritual and philosophical works. Thus, he imparted a spiritual connotation to his notion of Swaraj. In his view, Swaraj was more than a political or economic concept. Swaraj was more than a law and order mechanism. It was also more than an economic order providing the necessities of life or the luxuries of a pleasurable life. Swaraj, according to him, was full self-government–political, social, economic and spiritual. Thus, Swaraj was something more than mere home rule. Home rule simply indicated a political arrangement of self-rule without severing British connection. Beyond this, Swaraj also implied enlightened self-control of the individuals inspiring detached performance of their duties.

Tilak felt that materialism debases human life and reduces it to an animal level. Tilak wanted men to rise-above the level of animal pleasures through self-discipline and self-efforts and attain true happiness by sublimating their desires. Hence, he conceives the fulfilment of human life not only in enjoying rights, but also in selfless performance of duties. Man needs the rights to perform his duties not for the selfish pursuit of animal desires. Man has duties to himself, to his family, to his kith and kin and also to his fellow beings and countrymen. He has to work for the moral, spiritual and material well being of all of them. This is his duty. However, all this would be possible only if men and women were free from any kind of domination and control.

For the realisation of this Swaraj, Tilak accepted the suitability of the western liberal institutions and concepts like constitutional government, rule of law, individual freedom, dignity of the person and so on.

Thus, Tilak's political philosophy represented an interesting mix of the ancient Indian value system and western liberal institutions.

Q6. Give a brief sketch of life and work of Sri Aurobindo.

Ans. Born in Calcutta on 15th August 1872, Sri Aurobindo lived an eventful life and contributed immensely to the fields of philosophy and politics.

Sri Aurobindo

Early Life - Formative Stage

Aurobindo's upbringing was completely western. For a period of fourteen years from 1879 to 1893–he studied in England. During this period, he showed extraordinary intellectual abilities. He learned various classical and modern European languages. During his Cambridge University days, he began to take an interest in Indian politics and came in contact with some young revolutionaries from India. He was also deeply influenced by Irish nationalists and their efforts for achieving independence for Ireland. He returned to India in 1893 at the age of 21 with the fire of nationalism burning in him and a strong and resolute hill to work for it.

Preparatory Phase

On arriving in India he joined government service in the princely state of Baroda. At Baroda, he undertook a serious study of Indian history, philosophical texts and Bengali literature. He was impressed by the spiritualism underlying Indian ohilospphy and literature and this added a new dimension to his political thinking. During this period, Aurobindo wrote extensively on the then situation in the country and elabourated his ideas about nation, nationalism etc. He also remained in touch with the freedom movement generally and particularly with revolutionary activities in Bengal. His interest in revolutionary politics, however, did not keep him away from his spiritual quest.

Phase of Political Activism

In 1905 Bengal was partitioned. This event evoked strong resentment throughout the country. Aurobindo resigned from his job in Baroda (1906) and plunged into active politics which marked the beginning of the third phase of his life. This phase of political activism was very brief (1906-1910). During this period, he participated actively in politics and supported the radical group led by Tilak. He participated in the Surat session of the Congress. He also wrote extensively on various topics of national importance in this period. In 1908, he was implicated and arrested in the Maniktola Bomb Case. He was honourably acquitted in 1909. After his release, he remained involved in politics for a short while. In 1910, he withdrew from active politics and went to Chandra Nagar and later on moved to Pondicherry. His sudden withdrawal was a result .of his desire for spiritual development.

Later Phase: 1910 Onwards

During this period, Aurobindo wrote mainly in the wider context of humanity and it spiritual future. He elabourated his ideas and ideals in the context of human development and its ultimate goal of human unity. His important works like the Life Divine, Essays on Geeta, The Synthesis of Yoga and the epic poem 'Savitri' were written during this period. To sum up, we can say that his political activism and spiritual development were not separate but went together. His political thought was an extension of his yogic and spiritual vision.

Q7. Discuss the views of Aurobindo on British rule, the Indian National Congress and the Swaraj.

Or

Aurobindo's views on nature of the British rule. [Dec 09, Q 13]

Ans. Aurobindo's views on nature of the British rule

Aurobindo's first political writings in 'Indu-Prakash' - an Anglo-Marathi paper- was a direct attack on British rule. Of course, some leaders participating in the national movement were also criticising British rule at that time, but their criticism was quite indirect. His writing was a departure from this style of expression. He created such a sensation in the country that justice M.G. Ranade had to warn the editor of Indu-Prakash to be careful, and subsequently the editor had to request Aurobindo to modify his tone, which he did rather reluctantly.

The purpose of Aurobindo's criticism of the British rule was two fold. In the first instance, he wanted to strengthen the anti-British sentiments in the country and secondly, to break the myth of British superiority.

He expressed the view that the British political system was in no way the best as was widely believed by Indian intelligentsia. He was also critical of the absence of social freedom and equality. Hence, he believed that copying the British model was not in the interest of our country. Regarding the nature of the British rule in India he expressed the view that, "It is mercantile in foundation and exploitative in character". It must be, therefore, weakened from its base itself, in order to achieve freedom and independence of the country.

Aurobindo described the behaviour of the British officials as rude and arrogant. He believed that the system of administration set up by the British in India was thoroughly unsuitable to the Indian people, their socio-economic system, their mind and genius. He was also critical of the anglicised Indians who regarded the British way of life and culture worth emulating.

He, however, did not object to learning from the experience of the British, though he was against the thoughtless aping of European ideas and ideals. He objected to the growing tendency among Indians to ignore the past and of having no clear vision for the future.

His views on the Indian National Congress

When Aurobindo returned from England, he observed the political scene and expressed his views through his writings in journals like 'Bande Mataram'. He was critical of the Congress organisation and its leadership at that time. He criticised the Congress on four counts-viz. **i)** its aims and objectives, **ii)** its composition, **iii)** the motives of the leaders and **iv)** the methods adopted by them for the realisation of their aims and objectives. This does not mean that he was basically against the national Congress. On the contrary, he declared that" The Congress was to us, all that is to man most dear, most high and most sacred." But at the same time, he did not hesitate to express his disillusionment and dissatisfaction about its working. About the aims and objectives of the organisation, he thought that the Congress did not have a clearcut goal of national freedom. The leaders of the Congress were wasting time on trifles like certain administrative reforms, which were totally inadequate to meet the need of the time. Their demands, he delivered were 'shamefully modest.' About the composition of the Congress, he thought that the Congress was a middle class organisation and therefore, did not represent the Indian masses. The newly educated middle class leadership was only interested in gaining power and a place in the Indian polity. He emphasised the need for converting the national movement into a mass movement by including in it the vast numbers of the proletariat. He believed that the emergence of the Indian 'proletariat' on the horizon of the national movement would be an important key to the solution of the problem of transforming the Congress into a truly national and popular body. Thirdly, regarding the motives of the Congress leaders, his observation was that they were not sincere leaders. They were timid and afraid of displeasing their rulers. He believed that these defects in the organisation had adversely affected the national movement in the country.

He felt that the Congress leadership had not perceived the British rule correctly and therefore, instead of boldly asserting their goal, the leaders relied on the sense of justice and benevolence of the British rulers. They resorted to futile petitions and requests in the annual sessions of the Congress.

He therefore stressed the need for a broad based organisation that could channelise the entire power of the country to free it from foreign rule. Thus, his insistence on enthusing the masses with the spirit of independence was one of the first efforts to give a mass character to the freedom movement.

His views on Swaraj

India's liberation from foreign domination was the final goal for Aurobindo. 'Swaraj', i.e., self rule by Indians was not merely of economic and political nature. It was necessary for India to perform its spiritual mission dedicated to the upliftment of humanity. He advocated independence for India for the following reasons:

(i) Liberty being the first indispensable condition of rational development intellectual, moral, individual and political–is in itself a necessity of national life. Hence it was worth striving for its own sake.

(ii) Secondly, in the process of development of human beings, spiritual and moral advance is more important than material advance. Aurobindo was of the opinion that India with her spiritual development was destined to take the lead for the progress of the world and for this reason too India must be free.

(iii) India must have swaraj to live well and happily. For this Indians should not live as slaves but as free people to work for the spiritual and intellectual benefit of the human race.

The concept of nationalism which dominated his thought and activity in the early phase was just a stepping stone to move in the direction of the unity of humankind. This unity of humankind was regarded by him as a part of nature's eventual scheme and as the inevitable goal of human development.

Q8. Describe Aurobindo's concept of Nation and theory of Spiritual Nationalism.

Or

Write a note on Aurobindo's positive programme of Political Action.

[June 09, Q 5]

Or

Write a short note on Sri Aurobindo's theory of nationalism.

[Dec 08, Q 13(iii)]

Ans. During the period of 1905-1910, he articulated a coherent and powerful theory of political action. The first part of Aurobindo's message could be called spiritual nationalism that is based on two or three key concepts. The first is the concept of the nation. For Aurobindo, the nation was not only a political construct, it was in fact a divinity. It was *Bhavâni Bhârati*, Mother India and a divinity into which one had to be prepared to offer everything as a sacrifice so that one could be freed from bondage imposed by foreigners. So his fiery and flaming nationalism was because he looked upon the nation as a living goddess. In his writings, he refers to *Bhavâni Mahishamardini* and how the power of the people of India is expressed in terms of the great goddess. In the story of the goddess in the *Puranas*, all the *devas* pooled their weapons when they were overcome by the *asuras*, but could not defeat the asura individually and independently. They pooled their weapons and out of that pool of energy, the goddess arose riding on the lion with *ashtâdash bhujâ*, eighteen arms, each arm holding one weapon belonging to the different gods. In other words, she was the symbol of the collective aspiration and power of the Indian nation. That was his concept of the nation.

Aurobindo's concept of nationalism also was not merely political activity but a great and holy *yajnya*, as he put it for national emancipation. Everything that was done at that time was done as an offering to the divine. That is what made a tremendously powerful impact upon the younger generation, particularly at that time. He was the first thinker in India, who had a clear appreciation of the role of the masses, and the role of the proletariat. This was in 1893, long before the Marxist-Leninist revolution in the Soviet Union. According to him the proletariat may appear to be docile and immobile, but whoever succeeds in understanding the proletariat and arousing them will be master of India's destiny. This was a very important concept, because sometimes the freedom movement has been called "*bhadraloka* movement" or elitist movement. Among the radical group, Aurobindo was the first person to take the movement out of the drawing room and conference room on to the streets, minds and hearts of the Indian people. Previously, the moderates would draw up beautifully drafted resolutions requesting the British government to give them dominion status. That is not the way that the radicals saw it. As a radical, Aurobindo was the exponent of the ideological concept of the *poorna swarâjya* theme. As Lokmanya Tilak said, '*Swarâj* is my birthright and I will have it.'

Programme of Action

The other aspect of his strategy was an elabourate theory of boycott. The common perception is that boycott was something which Gandhi invented. This is not true. The theory of boycott was first put forward by Aurobindo in his luminous writings at the turn of the century between 1905 and 1910. He advocated economic boycott and the correlate *swadeshi*; educational boycott and the correlate national educational system. In fact, he was the principal of the National Education College, Jadavpur, now known as the Jadavpur University. He talked of judicial boycott and the setting up of national arbitration courts. At the same time he also referred to executive boycott and the setting up of a national organisation for self-government. As a sanction he talked of social boycott. In this way he evolved a whole theory. However, it did not work at that time, because he was far ahead of his times. It did not work but he had a complete theory of how to achieve independence. The theory revolved around the whole concept of boycott and the setting up of an alternative, not merely a negative boycott; with each negative boycott he had a positive plan as well. Consequently, his vision was a combination of remarkable idealism and a practical programme of action – a very rare combination. Usually people who are idealistic have very little time for the nitty-gritty of organisation, while those involved with the organisation do not have enough time to dream. Aurobindo was one of those extraordinary minds who were able to comprehend both elements of the movement.

Another point that is very important to remember is that Aurobindo always placed India's freedom in the larger context of the destiny of the human race. This fact is most remarkable because revolutionaries talk only about their own country. However, Sri Aurobindo always had a deeper vision of what India should do for humanity. In fact, he said that India has to be free in order that it can play its role in the emancipation of the human race. Sri Aurobindo was not chauvinist; he did not look upon Indian freedom as an end in itself. The remarkable coincidence is that India achieved independence on Sri Aurobindo's seventy-first birthday, that is August 15, 1947.

The first phase of Sri Aurobindo's message is one of spiritual nationalism; the message that the nation is a spiritual power, the goddess, the message that nationalism is a spiritual imperative. It is not any longer a question of choice or another career, or another thing to do; it is something that has an inner imperative, because it is only possible to fulfil one's *dharma* if one does it. It is a message of clear-cut political thinking and organisation of how to defeat the most mighty empire the world had ever known through a combination of activities, both violent underground and non-violent overground; a vision of a regenerated India, a vision that is the link between the first phase of Sri Aurobindo's life and the second phase and image of India that would play a major role in the emancipation.

Q9. Write a note on the following :
(i) Evolution of human society
(ii) Nature of Human unity
(iii) Spiritual nationalism of Aurobindo

Ans. (i) Evolution of human society

Aurobindo argues that, in the course of its development, human society has to pass through three stages. The first is the stage of spontaneity. At this stage the forms and activities of community formation, its traditions and customs and institutional setup are the result of natural organic growth. Natural instincts and environmental needs play an important part in its formation. The people believe in certain symbol which are imaginative and instinctive in nature. The people belonging to the same race or kinship follow identical symbols which become a religion for them. Thus, in this stage of development, natural instincts and religious symbols go together.

The second stage is the stage of consciousness in which people become intellectually self conscious and start thinking about his life and its problems with the help of intelligence and creative power. This stage, is predominantly psychological and ethical in nature. In this stage intellectuals get importance and come forward as the initiators of the age of reason and revolt or progress and freedom.

The third stage is that represents both the triumph and failure of reason. In this stage, human beings in collectivity begin to live more deeply and purposively. Life of human beings at this stage will be governed by a sense of unity, sympathy, spontaneous liberty and the spirit of individual and communal existence. From here humankind has to advance towards the realisation of spiritualised society. This is the ideal towards which this process of evolution of society points out.

In this spiritual society, 'nations' as a regulating mechanism will have no place. It will not be worshipped by people as their God or their larger self. There would be no clashes or conflicts on the basis of separate identities as nations. There would be unity within the nations as group but there would also be ultimate unity and oneness of the humankind. The primary responsibility of achieving this unity was entrusted by Aurobindo to India.

(ii) Nature of Human unity

It will not be a mechanical unity established under the iron law of the state or any organisation because such kind of mechanical unity will negate the diversity of various groups, individuals or races. There would be no suppression of individual life or the life of smaller community. All individuals and communities will get the fullest opportunity for the full development of their potentialities and the full expression of their multifaced diversity.

The future society will be a society of complex oneness, a world society in which present nations will be intrinsic parts of the whole. The national societies would continue to function as cultural units but their physical boundaries will have no relevance as they would look beyond them to realise the vision of the unity of mankind.

Aurobindo was aware of the problems and hurdles in the way of the emergence of such spiritual society at that time, but he was optimistic about its advent in the near future. He was not only hopeful but certain about the achievement of world unity and peace. Mankind's aspiration for peace and unity had become a reality to some extent in the form of the establishment of the League of Nations in 1920 and the United Nations in 1945. He was also aware of the practical limitations of such organisations in the face of the realities of international politics, but firmly believed in the emergence of united world. It was his belief that this was certain because it was essential for the very continuance of humanity and failure in this respect meant the failure of the human race itself. This could never be, for humanity would not, whatever be its occasional lapses, work for its own extinction.

(iii) Spiritual nationalism of Aurobindo

In the context of his theory of 'spiritual nationalism', it is argued that though it is called spiritual nationalism in reality it was religious, as we have known it, and therefore reactionary in character. It was an attempt to mobilise the masses on the emotional basis and detracting their attentions from real issues like poverty, economic exploitation, inequality which are inimical to the progress of the individual as well as the community. It was an appeal to Hindu religious sentiments in the garb of the cultural heritage of the land.

Further, it is argued that to regard nationalism as an instrument of spiritual perfection is too idealistic and visionary for the common person. To associate religion with politics, though in the name of spirituality, is a dangerous proposition in a multireligious, multicultural plural society like India. It is argued that in the ultimate analysis, this exercise has resulted in increasing the strife between the Hindus and the Muslims—two major religious communities in India, which finally resulted in the partitions of the country.

Aurobindo's defenders would, however, claim that his concept of nationalism and human unity were based on his understanding of the Hindu Sanatana Dharma, which to him meant an open and universal philosophy of life.

His concept of nationalism clearly indicates his spiritual approach to politics. Not merely his theory of nationalism but his political philosophy in its totality has spiritual overtones. Politics for him was an aspect of the broader process of personal, national and international spiritual development. He looked upon Indian independence as an essential turn in the life of this ancient land for playing the role of a spiritual guide of humanity at large. He believed this was India's predetermined role and that she could rise to that level only through the teachings of the Hindu religion. Nationalism cannot afford to neglect any one. It is therefore imperative for one to bring all the sections of the society into the mainstream of political life. In the Indian context, he believed that all the sections including tribals and communities outside of Hindu civilisations must form part of the process of national independence as nationalism excludes none. It is in this sense, Aurobindo's followers say that, his concept of spiritual nationalism should be understood.

Q10. Give a brief life sketch of Bhagat Singh.

Or

Briefly discuss the family background and life of Bhagat Singh.

Ans. Bhagat Singh was born into a Jatt Sandhu family to Sardar Kishan Singh Sandhu and Vidyavati in the Khatkar Kalan village near Banga in the Lyallpur district of Punjab. Singh's given name of Bhagat means "devotee". He came from a patriotic Sikh family, some of whom had participated in movements supporting the independence of India and others who had served in Maharaja

Ranjit Singh's army. His grandfather, Arjun Singh, was a follower of Swami Dayananda Saraswati's Hindu reformist movement, Arya Samaj, which would carry a heavy influence on Singh. His uncles, Ajit Singh and Swaran Singh, as well as his father were members of the Ghadar Party, led by Kartar Singh Sarabha Grewal and Har Dayal. Ajit Singh was forced to flee to Persia because of pending cases against him while Swaran Singh was hanged on December 19, 1927 for his involvement in the Kakori train robbery of 1925.

Shaheed Bhagat Singh

Unlike many Sikhs of his age, Singh did not attend Khalsa High School in Lahore, because his grandfather did not approve of the school officials' loyalism to the British authorities. Instead, his father enrolled him in Dayanand Anglo Vedic High School, an Arya Samaj school. At age 13, Singh began to follow Mahatma Gandhi's Non-Cooperation Movement. At this point he had openly defied the British and followed Gandhi's wishes by burning his government school books and British imported clothing. Following Gandhi's withdrawal of the movement after the violent murders of policemen by villagers from Chauri Chaura, Uttar Pradesh, Singh, disgruntled with Gandhi's nonviolence action, joined the Young Revolutionary Movement and began advocating a violent movement against the British.

In 1923, Bhagat famously won an essay competition set by the Punjab Hindi Sahitya Sammelan. This grabbed the attention of members of the Punjab Hindi Sahitya Sammelan including its General Secretary Professor Bhim Sen Vidyalankar. At this age, he quoted famous Punjabi literature and discussed the Problems of the Punjab. He read a lot of poetry and literature which was written by Punjabi writers and his favourite poet was Allama Iqbal from Sialkot.

In his teenage years, Bhagat Singh started studying at the National College in Lahore, but ran away from home to escape early marriage, and became a member of the organisation *Naujawan Bharat Sabha* (Youth Society of India).

In the Naujawan Bharat Sabha, Singh and his fellow revolutionaries grew popular amongst the youth. He also joined the Hindustan Republican Association at the request of Professor Vidyalankar, which was then headed by Ram Prasad Bismil and Ashfaqulla Khan. It is believed that he had knowledge of the Kakori train robbery. He wrote for and edited Urdu and Punjabi newspapers published from Amritsar. In September 1928, a meeting of various revolutionaries from across India was called at Delhi under the banner of the *Kirti Kissan Party*. Bhagat Singh was the secretary of the meet. His later revolutionary activities were carried out as a leader of this association. The capture and hanging of the main Hindustan Republic Association (HRA) Leaders also allowed him to be quickly promoted to higher ranks in the party, along with his fellow revolutionary Sukhdev Thapar.

Q11. State the involvement of Bhagat Singh in Lahore Conspiracy Case.

Ans. In the Lahore Conspiracy Case all the charges including the killings of Saunders and Chanan Singh, the Assembly Bomb Case and the setting up of bomb factories were put together and Bhagat Singh and his colleagues were to be tried by a Special Court to expediate the proceedings. The court's decision was to be final. The accused made it known that they did not want any counsel for their defence, that they had no belief in the justice meted out by the court, and that they would not appear before the court unless they were forced to do so. Under the leadership of Bhagat Bhagat, the prisoners resorted to hunger strike demanding the treatment of revolutionaries as political prisoners and improving the facilities in the prison. During this strike which lasted over three months, one of the revolutionaries Jatin Das died and his body was taken to Calcutta where a record crowd participated in the procession leading to cremation. Bhagat Singh and his colleagues were forcibly caught and were beaten in the presence of the magistrate. These happenings were reported in the newspaper and leaders like Jawaharlal Nehru and Subhas Bose were anxious about their condition. Mahatma Gandhi for a long time did not express any opinion and when it was asked, he disapproved of their methods and called them misguided patriots. He, however, considered Bhagat Singh and his colleagues as brave. Round Table Conference was not prepared to oblige and Gandhi did not make it a condition to observe the pact.

The Special Tribunal found Bhagat Singh and Rajguru guilty of committing the murder of Saunders and Sukhdev as the brain behind the conspiracy. A last attempt was made by Bhagat Singh's father making a petition to the Tribunal pleading that Bhagat Singh was not in Lahore when Saunders was murdered. Bhagat Singh strongly disapproved of the move and described it as the "weakness of the worst type." He rejected any move to offer defence and asked his father to publish his letter. The Tribunal gave its verdict on the 7th October, 1930 and sentenced Bhagat Singh, Rajguru and Sukhdev to death and others to transportation for life. Attempts made by various Indian leaders to save the lives of Bhagat Singh, Rajguru and Sukhdev could 'not bear fruit and they were hanged on 23rd March, 1931. Thus, when the Karachi Congress met six days after the hanging, it was in a gloomy atmosphere. Mahatma Gandhi had to defend his position which he did by paying tributes to the young martyrs for their bravery without surrendering his stand on non-violence and the path followed by Congress after Gandhi-Irwin Agreement.

Q12. Examine the thoughts of Bhagat Singh on Atheism and social revolution.

Ans. Bhagat Singh pointed out that the transition from theism to atheism that took place in him was due to the study of Bakunin, Marx, Lenin and Trotsky. A book, 'Common sense' by Nirlamba Swami in which a sort of mystic atheism was preached also influenced his ideas. When he was first arrested in 1927, the police wanted to get information from his about the Kakori Case. They threatened to hang him and asked him to say his last prayers. He found after much thought that he had no inclination to pray and thus survived the first test in atheism.

Bhagat Singh in this article did not deny that God is a strong anchor to give courage and consolation to the condemned prisoner. But he thought that it required greater courage to make greatest sacrifice without a desire for reward in this life or the life after death. He refuted the charge made by some of his colleagues that it was vanity on his part to deny the existence of God. He writes:

"The day we find a great number of men and women with this psychology who cannot devote themselves to anything else than the service of mankind and emancipation of the suffering humanity; that day shall inaugurate the era of liberty. Is the pride in their noble cause to be misinterpreted as vanity? Let us forgive him for he cannot realise the depth, the emotion, the sentiment and the noble feelings that surge in that heart... self reliance is always liable to be interpreted as vanity. It is sad and miserable but there is no help."

Bhagat Singh considered criticism and independent thinking as the "two indispensable qualities of the revolutionary." For him no man is so great as to be above criticism. He considered it as a mark of servile mentality. He was prepared to concede the use of faith and belief as a way of explaining away the environment. In the absence of direct proof, the philosophers of religion have found various ways to explain away things, contributing diversity of religious ideas and corresponding beliefs and practices.

"Where direct proofs are lacking, philosophy occupies the important place. As I have already stated, a certain revolutionary friend used to say that philosophy is the outcome of human weakness when our ancestors had leisure enough to try to solve out the mystery of this world, its past, present and the future, its whys and wherefores, they having been terribly short of direct proofs, everybody tried to solve the problem in his own way. Hence, we find the wide differences in the fundamentals of various religious creeds, which sometimes assume very antagonistic and conflicting shapes."

Bhagat Singh's argument against all faiths is that they have lost the probing and experimental attitudes which had been the hallmark of those original thinkers. Those who followed them accepted every word they uttered as revealed truth and stopped thinking for themselves. As a result of this every religion and every sect has suffered stagnation and decay. Thus, religion has come in the way of human progress.

"Any man who stands for progress has to criticise, disbelieve and challenge every item of the old faith in God as Almighty, Omnipresent, Omniscient, and Omnipotent is essentially an irrational belief. Christianity and Islam have no answers to the arguments as to why God created the world of woes and miseries. If it is to derive pleasure out of human misery, then God must be compared with such abominable figures as Nero or Changez Khan. The Hindus have attributed the sufferings in the present life as punishment of sins committed in the past life. But they have no answer as to why the Omnipotent God has not made man so perfect as to keep away from sins. Bhagat Singh's reasoning told him that there is no supreme being to control the destiny of human beings. Man has made progress by mastering nature and there is no reason to be found which "would justify the world as it exist." He wanted to recommend the study of Darwin to those curious to know the origin of mankind. It is only accidental and all the later progress of man can be answered by his constant conflict with nature and his efforts to override it.

To Bhagat Singh, the belief in God was not necessarily the invention of those who wanted to keep the people under their subjection by preaching the existence of a supreme being and then claiming an authority and sanction from him for their privileged positions. However, he accepted the argument that religion has essentially a reactionary role to play as it has always sided with tyrannical and exploiting institutions, men and classes. Originally, the idea of God was invented to give courage to man to face all adversities and also subdue his arrogance and pride. The idea of God is helpful to man in distress.

As a realist Bhagat Singh wanted to get rid of such notions.

'I do not know whether in my case belief in God and offering of daily prayers which I consider to be most selfish and degraded act on the part of man, can prove to be helpful or they make my case worse still. I have read of atheists facing all troubles quite boldly, so I am trying to stand like a man with an erect head to the last; even on the gallows.'

Thoughts on social revolution

Bhagat Singh's ideas on Socialism and the type of society he envisaged for India were influenced by Marxism and Russian Communism. Explaining what he considered the revolutions he had made it clear before the court that he understood by it reorganising society "On the Socialistic basis in which the Sovereignty of the proletariat should be recognised and a world federations should redeem humanity from the bondage of Capitalism and misery of imperial wars." Some of these ideas he further explained in his 'Introduction to the Dreamland.' Dreamland was a poetical work by Ram Saran Das who underwent transportation for life. Bhagat Singh pointed out in the introduction that the political parties had lacked any conception of the society they wanted to create after independence. They only had put freedom from foreign rule as their goals and the only exception was the Ghadar Party which wanted India to be a Republic. These parties according to him were not revolutionary. To him Revolution implied 'the programme of systematic reconstruction of society on new and adapted basis, after complete destruction of the existing state of affairs.' He rejected the contention made by the Gandhians that destruction is not the way to construction. To him 'Destruction is not only essential but indispensable for construction." From violent revolution he would propose to construct a society where violence is no more the character of social relationships. He also dismissed the idea of reconciling the ideas of various religions to avoid strife. Instead, he advocated a secular life.

Bhagat Singh also expressed himself against charity and charitable institutions which have no place in a socialist society. The social organisation would be built around the principle that 'there shall be no needy and poor, and no alms giving and alms taking.' Work would be obligatory for everyone. There is to be no superiority or inferiority attached to mental and manual labour and the payment would be equal. He, however, rejected the idea that manual labour alone is to be considered as productive labour. Compulsory manual labour for all seemed to him 'utopian and impracticable.'

Bhagat Singh also dealt with the problems like crime and punishment. Punishment should be with the view of rehabilitating the criminal. "Jails should be reformatories and not veritable hells." He considered war as an institution characteristic of a society based on exploitation. A socialist society cannot rule out war since it will have to protect itself against the capitalist society. He also seems to suggest that a revolutionary war would be necessary for the creation of the world socialist order. A peaceful revolution, through education and evolution seemed to him as utopian. After capturing power, peaceful methods shall be employed for constructive work, force shall be employed to crush the obstacles.'

Q13. Why did Bhagat Singh reject the leadership of congress?

Ans. Bhagat Singh's charge against the Congress was that it did not represent any revolutionary force. It represented the interests of the bourgeoise which did not want to lose its property in any struggle. The real revolutionary elements were to be found in the peasantry and the workers. The Congress however did not mobilise these forces. The Congress was afraid of the participation of workers and poor peasants in the struggle because it found it difficult to contain them against the interests of the Capitalists or the Landlords. Bhagat

Singh held the view that the Congress really represented the middle class and the petty bourgeoise and was not really interested in social revolution.

According to Bhagat Singh, there was nothing wrong in making compromises and adjustments, provided the goal was clear and where tactical arrangements required such compromises. He considered the strategy of Tilak as correct when he said that he would take half the loaf when it is offered but would continue to fight for the rest. The real danger is when the forces of stability gain the upper hand and block the change.

As far as the constitutional reforms were concerned, Bhagat Singh found them wanting in all the tests of responsible government. The executive used its Veto against the resolution passed by the Assembly. Was it going to be changed by making the executive elected and responsible to the legislature? He also wanted to apply the test of participation of people in elections. Whether all were allowed the right to vote or only the property holders? He would also apply the test of provincial autonomy and found that the centralised unity system would negate it.

He advised the revolutionaries to be clear about their ultimate goal, their present position and the ways and means of functioning. The goal should be socialist revolution to be preceded by political revolution. It was not only the overthrow of the British Rule that was necessary. It was not only the overthrow of the British Rule that was necessary. It would not make any difference to the workers and peasants if Lord Readings' place were to be held by Sir Purshottamdas Thakurdas or Lord Irwin's by Sir Tejbahadur Sapru. The Revolution must be for their good and they should be made to feel. It must be a proletarian Revolution for the proletariat and by the proletariat.

To this end, Bhagat Singh asked the revolutionaries to follow Lenin's views on Professional Revolutionaries' and on organised party to prepare for the revolution. To this end, he wanted the young men to join such a party to organise study groups, arrange speeches and publish books and periodicals and recruit and train political workers. He however, wanted a disciplined party not necessarily secretive. He also did not believe in violence as indispensable. What he expected of the political workers was that they should work among the masses and obtain active sympathy of peasants and workers. He also called such a party the Communist Party.

Bhagat Singh considered economic independence the ultimate goal. But he considered political freedom as the first step. He did not mind workers themselves organising themselves for small gains. But these were not be considered as the end.

In the end, Bhagat Singh asked the revolutionaries to be extremely cautions and balanced in their expectations. He warned them against utopian thinking. Revolutions could not be made by emotional and reckless men. What required was patience, sacrifice and absence on individualism. Courage, strong will and sustained hard work were to be indispensable qualities for the revolutionaries.

Chapter 4

Colonialism, Caste Order and The Tribal Societies

Q1. Examine the impact of colonialism on economy, social and cultural fields of India.

Ans. Impact of colonialism in the cultural and social fields

The integration of Indian economy with the world capitalist system was followed by changes in the social and cultural fields Colonialism facilitated India's contact with the momentous changes that the western world was undergoing and introduced Indian intellectuals to the radical and liberal ideals of democracy, popular sovereignty and rationalism. The industrial revolution, the breath-taking advance of science and technology and the great revolutionary upheavals of the 18th and 19th centuries in the west were transforming the whole face of the world—it was never to be the same again. The profound impact that this along with the introduction of modern education had on the section of Indian middle classes led to intense questioning and critical appraisal of the backward and degrading socio-religious practices prevalent in Indian society.

The socio-cultural milieu of pre-colonial India was primarily shaped by the family and kinship institutions which conditioned the mind with a religious and caste identity. All the traditional practices were through these institutions; passed on from generation to generation. Initially, modern education did not touch more than the frills of Indian society. The lack of sufficient cultural resources and ideological apparatus at the command of the colonial state eventually led the British, in the person of Lord Macaulay, to direct their efforts at producing a class from among the Indians who would be carriers of colonial culture and ideology—Indians by the colour of their skin but British in their tastes and thought. However, whatever be the case, under this influence of modern ideas there developed in India, a whole series of socio-religious reform movements.

Reformist Movements

These movements took the form of a 'struggle against the backward elements of traditional culture', an important dimension of which was opposition to caste. The movements like Brahmo Samaj and Prarthana Samaj advocated the removal of caste distinction.

Following the reform movements of the early nineteenth century which were explicitly influenced by liberal ideas, there were religious reform movements like the Arya Samaj and Ramakrishna Mission. Though different in their religious messages and concepts, these movements too, had an anti-caste edge. Arya Samaj drew its inspiration from Vedic Hinduism, rejected polytheism and idolatory, and sought to give greater role to individuality. 'Swami Dayananda Saraswati, the architect of Arya Samaj accepted that all persons including Shudras could read the Vedas. This was a remarkable innovation in traditional Hinduism, where something like Shudras having access to scriptures was considered blasphemous. Dayanand Saraswati considered caste as having had a useful function in the past. However, in his conception he introduced much greater flexibility by asserting that birth should not be the sole criterion. Guna (character), Karma (action) and Swabhav (nature), according to him must be the criteria. He, therefore, denounced untouchability as being inhuman. The Ramakrishna mission, on the other hand, preached Vedantic Hinduism and advocated universal brotherhood. Initiated by a simple village Saint Ramakrishna, this powerful revivalist movement in Bengal was subsequently carried forward by Swami Vivekananda. Vivekananda did not want to discard the caste system altogether, but attacked its rigidity. He too wanted to transform it from a system based solely on birth to one based on merit. He vigorously attacked the practice of untouchability.

Anti-Caste Movements

One of the most important aspects of these reform movements was their opposition to caste and its accompanying rigidity. The outspokenly anti-caste movements led by Ramaswami Naicker, Jyotiba Phule and Sri Narayana Guru bear testimony to this. The chief inspiration for Ambedkar's crusade came from the ideals of liberty, fraternity and equality–the slogans of the Western revolutions. The socially progressive stance of these movements on questions of sati, dowry, widow remarriage, etc. along with intense questioning of the rigidities of the caste system shows that Western ideas of liberalism had a powerful impact.

Impact on Indian Economy

Among the major changes introduced by the British in Indian economy, the far-reaching changes in agriculture were probably the most important. These changes introduced with a view to cornering the surplus in the form of land revenue and to make Indian agriculture an appendage of the British economy, greatly transformed the face of the countryside. It was precisely with this purpose that, the colonial authorities introduced two major tenurial and land revenue systems—the Zamindari and Ryotwari systems, whereby the position of peasant cultivators became quite precarious. They were forced to pay very high rents and were made to pay illegal dues and cesses and often had to perform forced labour.

High rates of revenue forced these peasant cultivators to take recourse to borrowing money—at equally high rates of interest—often forcing the peasant to resort to distress sales. Floods and famines aggravated the situation and made them more and more susceptible to the money-lenders grips, who in any case were being helped by the Government. This increasing grip of the money-lenders over the agrarian economy eventually enabled them to acquire the land of the distressed peasants whose pauperisation was becoming a growing feature of rural life. Side by side with the above, the British made conscious efforts to incorporate the Indian agricultural and tribal economy into the ever-expanding market of British colonialism. To this end, Indian agriculture was forced to cater to the needs of British Capital. Therefore, there was massive forced production of cash crops like cotton, indigo, sugar, tea and coffee. This spread of crops designed for export to Indian and foreign markets were one of the main forces which created a more homogeneous agrarian society in the early 19th century. Not only were tribal people and nomads being settled and subordinated to the discipline of producing an exportable surplus, but many of the gradations in status and function between people of the settled agricultural tracts which had obtained under indigenous rule were disappearing, giving way to simple distinctions of wealth and landholding.

Among the changes that the whole gamut of British policies brought in the agrarian set-up was a change in the social relationships too. Slow penetration of capital and of consumption into the forests (i.e. following integration of tribal economies into the market) was a very significant change. The partnership between the Company and the money-lender—trader which had facilitated the subjugation of India now proceeded in the conquest of India's internal frontiers. Monied 'settlers from the plains trickled into the central Indian tribal zone establishing landlordism and indebtedness alien to the domestic economy of the indigenous tribal systems. As late as the 18th century, there still existed an extensive pastoral and nomadic economy which had changed in a big way by mid-nineteenth century. Everywhere they (British) sought to settle and discipline groups such as the Gujars, Bhathis, Ranjar, Rajputs and Mewatis who moved around, extracting protection rent. The assessment of waste land and creation of more rigid property rights enforceable by court order restricted the nomads' mobility. Many of the herdsmen carrier people of the Deccan for instance, had already become subordinate agricultural 'Castes' before 1870. The changes in the pastoral and agrarian economy though they were a cause for much discontent and rebellions, however, affected changes in the caste structure too.

Q2. What were the features of Indian caste system? In which ways British colonialism affects the Indian caste system.

Ans. G.S. Ghurye, in his authoritative work on Caste has enumerated six such features:

a) Segmental division of society, i.e., the "quasi-sovereignty of caste" and its governing body, as a result of which members of a caste ceased to be members of a community as a whole, insofar as such caste was a groups with a separate arrangement for meeting out justice to its members. Thus, it, implied a situation where citizens owned moral allegiance to their caste first, rather than to the community as a whole.

b) Hierarchy or rigid ordering of society from top to bottom on the basis of ritual status and equally rigid definition of roles and functions that each group must perform.

c) Restrictions in interdining and social intercourse according to the detailed rules which prescribe what sort of food or drink can be accepted by a person and from what castes.

d) Civil and religious disabilities and privileges of different sections: mainly expressed through separated living and some castes not having access to certain areas, streets, temples, practices like untouchability and so on.

e) Lack of unrestricted choice of occupation

f) Endogamy or restriction of marriage

Colonialism effected the caste system mainly in two different ways. Firstly, through the various judicial and administrative practices that the British introduced. Secondly, indirectly though the influence of liberal ideas on the sections of Indian society who, thereafter took up cudgels to fight for social reforms.

Impact of British Judicial and Administrative Practices

The judicial and administrative practices introduced by the British based on the principle of equality before law, obviously made no distinction between castes. Further, introduction by the British of a uniform criminal law "removed from the purview of caste, many matters that used to be adjudicated by it earlier." No longer were caste-governing bodies to decide on matters of assault, adultery, rape and so on. Gradually, even in certain matters of civil law, like marriage and divorce, the authority of caste started getting eroded.

The second aspect was the enactment of certain laws which practically eroded the authority of castes in many respects though practically, often the impact was marginal. Despite this, legislations like the Widow Remarriage Act of 1856 or the Castes Disabilities Removal Act of 1850 did have considerable impact on the authority of caste. Regarding marriage, usually the British legal system tried to adhere to the practices laid down by local customs.

British administration also took up the question of civil equality for lower castes. The Govt. in Bombay Presidency, for example, issued a resolution in 1923 threatening to withhold grants to any school/educational institution that refused to admit students from lower castes. Also the practice of segregating students from lower castes in classes was gradually abandoned and they were made to sit with co-pupils from among the caste Hindus. The Madras Govt. in 1923 empowered Magistrates to punish offenders of lower castes and in 1925 through a special legislation threw open all public roads and streets giving access to any public office, well, tank or place of public resort to all classes of people including the depressed. The Govt. of Madras Presidency was in fact, the first to introduce protective discrimination in jobs for the lower castes, as early as in 1873.

Impact of Economic Changes

The changing economic structure led to integration of certain nomadic people into the caste structure with the expansion of agricultural activities. It also led to a changes in the status of certain caste groups within the caste hierarchy with land becoming a commodity that could be sold to anyone who could pay for it, even a 'low caste' member, provided an opportunity to many to acquire an economic status whereby they could gradually strive for upward mobility. Availability of new economic opportunities in port cities and capitals and access to new trading and employment opportunities for the lower castes resulted in relative prosperity for them. For instance, the improved communications brought about an enlargement of market for oil and pressed oilseeds, from which Telis (Oilmen) all over eastern India benefited. The Noniyas of eastern UP, Kolis of Surat coast and several other groups benefited from the new employment opportunities resulting from railway, road and canal construction. In such cases, according to M.N. Srinivas, the wealthier families or sections became possessed of a desire to move up in caste hierarchy by acquiring the symbols and rituals of higher castes. This upward mobility is known as 'Sanskritisation'. The changes from an agricultural economy to an industrial economy also brought in its wake processes like westernisation which involved a change in status based on adoption of western values.

Anti-Caste Movements under the Influence of Liberal Philosophy

The third major way in which the caste structure was affected was through powerful anti-caste and social reform movements under the Arya Samaj in Northern India, Raja Ram Mohan Roy in Bengal, Jyotiba Phule in Maharashtra, Sri Narayana Guru in Kerala, Ramaswami Naicker in Madras and so on. The major themes taken up by these movements were reform in regard to the position of women, equality for oppressed castes, general reform in religion and rituals. So, for instance, social reformers had exerted enough pressure for the enactment of the Special Marriage Act in 1872, that made inter-caste marriage possible.

Questions of widow remarriage, Sati, women's education etc. were important issues of struggle waged by the social reformers, particularly in Bengal.

The mobility of a few low castes had in Srinivas' words, a 'demonstration effect' on all others in the region. The latter felt that they were no longer condemned to a life of poverty and oppression. Provided they made the effort, they could also rise up the ladder. Perhaps this feeling significantly contributed to lending a strength to the movement of lower and backward castes. What has come to be known as the 'Backward Classes Movement' acquired a widespread character and was particularly strong in Southern parts of India. These movements, passed through two stages: in the first, the lower castes tried to acquire the symbols and rituals of high status, while in the second aspirations moved towards acquisition of political power, education and share in the new economic opportunities.

The emergence of caste sabhas or associations gave organisational impetus to the movement of backward castes. Initial activity of these sabhas were directed at trying to reform caste customs and undertake welfare activities of the benefit of their caste brethren, in the form of building hostels, houses on a co-operative basis, setting up colleges and hospitals, and provide scholarships.

An overview of the most important anti-caste movements suggests that, despite widely differing approaches and methods they had a common stand, in that they were motivated by similar issues which became the total point of reform. While the social reformers of Bengal explicitly challenged the very basis of caste oppression by advocating nationalism, the Arya Samaj and or the Ramkrishna Mission sought to modify the caste system by efforts in the direction of removal of untouchability. Phule and Naicker organised the 'lower castes' to lead an assault on the upper caste domination in all spheres of social life. However, it has been pointed out that such movements which organised the lower castes against upper caste domination, in due course got transformed into a movement of caste solidarity themselves.

Q3. Discuss the tribal movement that arouse in colonial India.

Or

Evaluate the nature of Tribal Movements during the colonial period.

[June 09, Q 3]

Ans. The tribal movements in colonial India were born out of deep dissatisfaction and often discontent against socio-economic policies of the British Government, which adversely affected their lives. Whether it be the question of encroachment of tribal lands by money-lenders backed by the Government, the acquisition of tribal forest, high taxation or enhancement of rent, everyone of these policies created among the tribes and nomadic communities extreme distrust of the authorities and turned them against the rulers—often against outsiders (Suds/

dikus) in general, since that was how the tribal mind perceived the situation to be.

The situation was further worsened by the fact that famines in the latter half of the 19th century forced the tribals into destitution. Dr. Verrier Elwin remarks that the chief cause of he decline of tribal communities "... was the loss of land and forests" which according to him, "had the effect of enervating tribal organism that it had no interior resistance against infection by a score of other evils..." It we look back over the long series of tribal rebellions against authority in other parts of tribal India, we see that the majority of them arose over this one point. Thus, the Kol insurrection of 1833 was caused by encroachment on tribal land. The Tamar rebellions repeated seven times between 1789 and 1832 were primarily due to the illegal deprivation of their rights in land, which the Hos, Mundas and Oraons suffered. The Santhal Rebellion (1855) was primarily a revolt against oppression of landlords, village money-lenders etc. The Birsa Munda Revolt (1895-1901) too was directed against the 'outsider'— namely landlords, traders and government officers. As evident, the movements were spread over large part of the country.

A noteworthy feature of these tribal movements, separated in space and time from one another, was that they occurred not in one or two pockets but were spread out across the country and had at the root, common or similar issues. Significant tribal movements took place in the beginning of the twentieth century. Most important among these was in the present Andhra Pradesh, where the tribals' forest agitation merged with Gandhi's non-cooperation movement and subsequent to its withdrawal was carried further under the leadership of Sitarama Raju. According to Prof. Summit Sarkar the spread of the movement was far beyond Andhra. "On 10 July 1921, Reading reported to the Secy. Of State that 2,50,000 out of 4,00,000 acres of forest in Kumaon Division of U.P. had been burnt down. Cavalry had to be sent to Muzaffarpur in North Bihar in Dec. 1921 to tackle an agitation over grazing rights. From Bengal, too, came reports of Santhals reasserting their lost forest right in the Jhargram region of Midnapur and widespread looting of woodlands in Banskhali land Cox's Bazar areas of Chittagone."

A study of these innumerable tribal movements reveals interesting characteristics which have parallels in similar agrarian movements elsewhere in the world. Most of these have been characterised by what has been called a negative consciousness by Ranajit Guha wherein, more than their own consciousness as a class or social group, a consciousness based on an identification of the enemy has played a vital role.

Often enemies of the people have been identified as enemies of the faithful, oppressed and disenfranchised and have been mingled with religious calls for struggle against such enemies.

Teachings of Judaism, Christianity and shia'ite Islam often had, as integral part of their teachings the promise of a paradise on earth for a thousand years through divine intervention. This has been variously described as Messianism, Millenarianism or Mahdism. Such millenarian elements can be seen in the different Mahdist movements in the Babism of mid 19th century Iran or in the vision of a Heavenly Kingdom in the Taiping Rebellion in China or in the many variants of Brasilian Cultic protest movements.

Kathleen Gough, on the basis of a study of 77 agrarian revolts has roughly classified them into five types in terms of their goals, ideology and methods of organisation: **i)** Restorative rebellions to drive out the British and to restore earlier rulers and social relations, **ii)** religious movements for the liberation of a region or an ethnic group under a new form of government, **iii)** what had been referred to as 'Social banditry' by E.J. Hobsbawm, **iv)** Terrorist vengeance, with ideas of meeting out collective justice and **v)** Mass insurrections for the redress of particular grievance.

Though Eric Hobsbawm, Norman Cohn and Peter Worsely have suggested that millenarian movements were rare or absent in India, as the widespread opinion is that they stem from Indacocuristian influences, Gough holds a different opinion. According to her, it is probably true in the 'strict sense of a belief in a thousand year period in which the evil one will be chained, in a wider sense it is not true. The belief and expectation that the present evil world will be transformed by divine intervention and bliss shall reign on earth, has permeated many a tribal movement in India. "Birsa Munda received teaching both from Lutheran missionaries and Hindu ascetics but then reverted to his Munda religion, bringing with him beliefs and images from both major faiths. He taught the Mundas first that he was divinity—appointed messenger come to deliver them from foreign rule, and later that he was an incarnation of God himself. His mission was to save the faithful from destruction in imminent flood, fire and brimstone, by leading them to the top of a mountain. Beneath them, "all the British, Hindus and Muslims would perish, after which a Munda Kingdom would be ushered in."

Some of these movements subsequently got integrated with the national movement. Particularly during the non-cooperation movement the 'forest Satyagrahas' played an important role. Gradually, they also got imbued with anti-imperialist ideology. Sumit Sarkar notes in the case of Sitarama Raju's movement that certain striking new features were visible. Sitarama Raju was not a local village muttadar unlike previous leaders but "a man without family or interest, an outsider coming from a group which claimed Kshatriya status and often some proficiency in Telugu and Sanskrit Scholarship..."

Anti-imperialist ideology was still rudimentary. Raju's anti-imperialist feeling were reflected, for instance in his statement that he was unable to shoot

Europeans as they were always surrounded by Indians whom he did not want to kill. This ideology was accompanied by primitive messianic elements. He had been wandering among the tribals since 1915 as a Sanyasi claiming astrological and medicinal powers and coming under Non-Cooperation influence in 1921. "Raju hints he is bullet-proof" reported the Malkangiri Deputy Tehsildar, while a rebel proclamation in April 1924 claimed that "God Sri Jagannadhaswami would incarnate very shortly as kalkiavatar and appear before us."

Q4. Briefly discuss about Jyotiba Phule's life and some of his writings.

Ans. Phule was born in a Mali (Gardner) family of Poona in 1827. The Malis belonged to shudra Varna and were placed immediately below peasant caste of Maratha-kunbis of Maharashtra. He was educated at a Marathi school with a three year break at a mission school in Poona. In 1848 Phule began his work as a social reformer interested in education of low caste boys and girls, when he started a school for girls of low and untouchable castes. Since no female teacher was available, Phule asked his wife Savitribai to teach in the school. He opened two more schools for girls in 1851. He was honoured by the Board of Education for the work he did for girls' education in 1852. Phule established a school for untouchables and a night school in 1852. By 1858, he gradually retired from the management of these schools and entered into a broader field of social reform. He supported the movement for widow remarriage in 1860 and in 1863 established a Home for the prevention of infanticide. Phule and his wife Savitribai adopted one orphan child from the Home because they had no child of their own. In 1865 he published a book on caste system written by one of his friends Padval.

The organisation with which Phule's name is associated and for which he is remembered even today is the Satya Shodhak Samaj. It was established in 1873 by him and his colleagues to organise the lower castes against the Hindu social order based on varna and caste system. One of his colleagues started the first newspaper of the Movement, *Din Bandhu* in 1877. The government appointed him a member of the Poona Municipality in 1876. He continued as a member till 1882 and fought for the cause of downtrodden.

Writings of Jyotiba Phule

Besides being a leader and organiser of the lower caste movement, Phule was also an original thinker and therefore, found it necessary not only to write polemical pamphlets but also to put forward his basic philosophical position. In Brahmanache Kasab(1869) Phule has exposed the exploitation of Brahmin priests. In Gulamgiri (1873) he has given a historical survey of the slavery of lower castes. In 1883 he published a collection of his speeches under the title Shetkaryancha Asud(The cultivator's whip-cord) where he has analysed how peasants were being exploited in those days. We find a text of his philosophical statement in Sarvajanik Satyadharma Pustak (A book of True Religion For All) published in 1891 a year after his death. From his writings we come to Know that his thinking on social and political issues was influenced by Christianity and the ideas of Thomas Paine (1737-1809). He was known for his religious radicalism in England. Phule himself has recorded that he was influenced by the ideas of Paine. As a recognition of his great work for the lower castes, he was felicitated and a title of 'Mahatma' was conferred on him by the people in Bombay in 1888.

Q5. Examine the attitude of Jyotiba Phule towards colonial government.

Ans. Phule's attitude towards Colonial Government

British rule had brought to an end the tyranny and chaos of the regime of the last Peshwa in Maharashtra. The colonial rulers had not only established law and order but also the principle of equality before law. The earlier regime of Brahmin Peshwas had imposed strict limitations on education, occupation and living standards of the lower castes and women. The new rulers opened the opportunities in education and mobility in occupation for the members of all castes. Missionary schools and government colleges were ready to admit any student irrespective of caste origins. New ideas of equality and liberty could reach the moderately educated sections of the lower caste. Phule was probably the best product of this process. High caste reformers and leaders also had welcomed the colonial rule. It is not surprising that Phule who was concerned with the slavery of the lower castes also favoured the British rule. He hoped that the new government which believes in equality between man and man would emancipate lower castes, from the domination of the Brahmins.

The British rule opened up new employment opportunities in the administration. The political power at local level was also being given to the Indians. Phule who had worked as a member of the Poona Municipality could visualise how lower castes would be able to acquire power at local level during the period of British rule and also enter the colonial bureaucracy. He believed in Colonialism, Cast Order and the Tribal Societies the benevolent attitude of the British rulers towards the lower castes and therefore asked for a number of things from them. He was not sure how long the British rule would continue. Therefore, he wanted lower castes to exploit the opportunity and get rid of the tyranny of Brahmins. Brahmin rulers used to collect huge wealth out of taxes levied on poor lower castes population, but never used to spend even a paisa for their welfare. On the contrary, the new regime was showing the signs of doing good things for the deprived people.

Phule assured the colonial rulers that if the Shudras were made happy and contented, they need not worry about the loyalty of the subjects. He wanted the British government to abolish Brahmin Kulkarni's position, and a post of village headman (Patil) filled on the basis of merit. In fact, Phule would have liked the British government to put an end to the balutedary system which was connected with caste specific occupations in the villages. He asked the government to make laws prohibiting customs and practices which gave subordinate status to women and untouchables. Phule wanted Brahmin bureaucracy to be replaced by non-Brahmin bureaucracy. But if the non-Brahmins were not available, the government should appoint, he thought, the British men to these posts. He believed that the British officers would take impartial view and were likely to side with lower castes.

Phule knew that education had not yet percolated to the lower castes. The masses had not yet become politically conscious. The high caste elites were claiming that they were the true representatives of the people and therefore were demanding political rights. This process, Phule thought, would re-establish the political supremacy of the high castes. Phule advised his followers from the lower castes not to participate the movement for political rights. He argued that the Indian National Congress or other political associations were not national in the true sense of the term because they represented only high castes. Phule warned his followers against the selfish and cunning motives of the Brahmins in forming these associations and advised them to keep themselves away from such associations. In his Satya Shodhak Samaj, he had made it a rule not to discuss politics. In fact, he had expressed more than once a complete and total loyalty towards the new government. He firmly believed that the almighty God had dethroned the tyrannical rulers and had established in their place a just, enlightened and peaceful British rule for the welfare of the masses. It does not mean that Phule did not understand the significance of politics. Infact, he has said at one place that the conditions of lower castes had deteriorated because they were deprived of political power. His efforts to organise lower castes under the banner of Satya Shodhak Samaj should be seen as a political activity. It is true that he gave preference to social reform rather than political reform in the 19th century. But that does not suggest that he would have continued to hold the educated, they would become conscious of their political rights vis-à-vis same views in the changed circumstances. He knew that if the lower castes were Brahmins and not only demand a share in political power, but would dethrone the Brahmins and establish their own supremacy. His writings were directed towards that.

Q6. Discuss the criticism of the Indian social order by Jyotiba Phule.

Ans. According to Jyotiba Phule, the Indian society was based on inequality between man and man and exploitation of ignorant masses by the cunning Brahmins. Phule believed that God who is the creator of the Universe has created all men and women free and capable of enjoying their rights. The creator has created all men and women as the custodians of all human rights so that a man or a group of men should not suppress an individual. The Maker has bestowed upon all men and women religious and political liberty. Therefore, no one should look down upon anyone's religious faith or political opinion. Every individual has a right to property. The Maker, Phule thought, has given all human beings the liberty of thought and expression. But the thought or opinion one is expressing should not be harmful to anybody. The creator has made all men and women capable of claiming a position in civil service or municipal administration according to their ability. No one should encroach upon the equal liberty of other human beings. Phule believed that all men and women are entitled to enjoy all the things the Maker has created. All men and women are equal before law. Phule held that the magistrates and judges of the court of law should be impartial in their judgements. Phule developed a critique of Indian society in the light of these fundamental principles.

Attack on Varna and Caste System

Indian society was founded on the Varna system. Phule challenged the view that it was god-ordained. He held that this claim was made to deceive the lower Varnas. Since this claim was made by the religious texts of the Hindus, he decided, to expose the falsehood of these texts.

Phule depended upon the contemporary theories and his own creativity to interpret these texts. Accordingly, he believed that Brahmins who were known as Aryans descended upon the plains of North India few thousand years back, possibly from Iran. They came as conquerors and defeated the original inhabitants of this land. Under the direction of the leaders such as Brahma and Parshuram, Brahmins fought protracted wars against the original inhabitants. They initially settled on the banks of the Ganges and later on spread-out over the other parts of the country. In order to keep a better hold over the masses, they devised the mythology, the Varna and caste system and also the code of cruel and inhuman laws. They founded a system of priestcraft which gave the Brahmin a prominence in all rituals. The caste system was a creation of cunning Brahmins. The highest rights and privileges were given to the Brahmins whereas Shudras and Atishudras (untouchables) were regarded with hatred and contempt. Even the commonest rights of humanity were denied to them. Their touch or even their shadow was considered as pollution. Phule reinterpreted the religious text of the Hindus to show how Aryans had conquered the original inhabitants. The nine avatars of Vishnu were seen by him as various stages of Aryan conquest. From those days, the Brahmins have enslaved the Shudras and Atishudras. For generations they have carried the chains of slavery of bondage. A number of Brahmin writers like Manu have added from time to time to the existing legends which enslave the minds of the masses. Phule compared the system of slavery fabricated by the Brahmins with slavery in America and pointed out that Shudras had to suffer greater hardships and oppression than the blacks. He thought that this system of selfish superstition and bigotry was responsible for the stagnation and all the evils from which India was suffering for centuries.

After narrating the story of Brahmin domination in the past, Phule tells us how in his times things had not changed much except for advent of the enlightened rule of Britain. The Brahmin continued to exploit the Shudra from his birth to death. Under the guise of religion, the Brahmin intervened and meddled in each and everything the Shudra did. A Brahmin tried to exploit him not only in his capacity as a priest, but did so in a number of other ways also. Due to his higher education, he had monopolised all the positions in the administration, judiciary, social, religious and political organisations. In a town or village, the Brahmin was all in all. He was the master and the ruler. The Patel of the village had become a nonentity. Instead the Brahmin village accountant known as Kulkarni had acquired power in the village. He was the temporal and spiritual adviser of the people, a money-lender and a general referee in all matters. Same was the case at tehsil level where a tehsildar used to harass to illiterate masses. Phule tells us that the story holds good at all levels of administration and in judiciary, as well as various departments of the government. The Brahmin bureaucrats used to exploit the poor and ignorant masses in each and every case by misguiding the British superiors.

It is essential at this stage to note that Phule who belonged to the gardner caste–Shudra caste–was concerned about not only Shudras but also Atishudras, i.e. the untouchables also. He advocated that these lower castes and untouchables should organise against the dominance of the Brahmins and strive for an egalitarian society.

Equality between Man and Woman

Phule always mentions women alongwith men. He did not assume that when men are mentioned, women are automatically included into that category. He makes a special reference to women when he discusses human rights. Just as Shudras were deprived of rights by the Brahmins by keeping them ignorant, Phule thought that selfish men had prohibited women from taking to education in order to continue male domination. The Hindu religious texts had given a number of concessions to men but had imposed severe restrictions on women. Phule was mainly concerned about the marriage system of those days. He attacked the customs and practices such as child marriage, marriage between young girl and old man, polygamy, objection to remarriage of women, prostitution, harassment of widows, etc, He advised Shudra peasants not to have more than one wife and not to marry their young children. He had given serious thought to the institution of marriage and had devised a simple and modern contract type ritual for the marriage ceremony of the members of Satya Shodhak Siimaj (Truth Seeking Society). It is interesting to note that

Phule did not stop at visualising equal status to women in marriage, family education and religion but claimed that woman was superior to man in many respects.

Q7. What were Jyotiba Phule's solutions to India's economic problems?

Ans. In economic terms, Phule was interested in peasantry and its problems. He was of the view to improve agriculture since he perceived Indian economy primarily as the agricultural economy. He observed that Indian agriculture was going through a crisis situation and identified the following factors as causes for the crisis.

The size of the population dependent on agriculture had increased. Earlier at least one person from a farmer's family was employed in the army or administration of the Indian states.

Farmers who owned a small piece of land used to make their living on fruits, flowers, fodder, grass and wood from nearby forest. The new government had started the department of forests which covered all hills, valleys, waste lands and grazing grounds thereby making the life of the farmers who used to depend upon them difficult.

British officers had increased the rate of land tax even though the income of the farmer had declined.

Farmers were being exploited by the money-lenders and Brahmin officers of the revenue and irrigation departments and from the judiciary.

Due to severe poverty and declining conditions of the lands, farmers could not come out of the problem of indebtedness. In these cases the lands were transferred to the money-lenders.

Another problem faced by the rural economy was that of the unfair competition by the British goods. Because of the inflow of these cheap and superior goods in large quantity, the indigenous craftsmen of the villages and towns suffered great losses and in many cases they had to close down their hereditary business. Those who worked in cottage workshops lost their jobs, thereby increasing the proportion of unemployment in the rural areas. On the basis of his in-depth knowledge of the rural economy and the agriculture sector, Phule suggested certain solutions to these problems. The first and the most important solution to the problem of the poverty of the farmers which Phule suggested was construction of bunds, tanks and dams so that sufficient water was made available to the farm. He wanted the government to take up schemes such as soil conservation, animal breeding and teaching of modern techniques of farming, holding exhibitions of agriculture annually etc. He pointed out that unless agriculture was made profitable, the agricultural banks which were talked about in those days would not succeed. He asked the government to reduce the burden of taxes on farmers in order to make agriculture profitable.

After paying land cess and local funds, each person in a farmer's family was left with less than three rupees for a month, when an ordinary Brahmin or British officer used to get fifteen rupees in a month for his miscellaneous expenses. Thus, Phule had shown a rare understanding of the economic problems of the Indian Society. Though he had welcomed, British rule he had realised how Indian economy, especially its rural sector, was being ruined by the colonial connection. The high caste elite nationalists had shown how wealth was being drained to England from India. Phule who was looking from the view point of farmers and lower castes could see another type of drain of wealth i.e. from rural sector to urban sector, from peasant economy to the Brahmin domain. It should be pointed out that Phule did not make any class differentiation within the peasantry.

Q8. Discuss the concept of universal religion of Jyotiba Phule.

Ans. The idea of the emancipation of the lower castes and the untouchables required a critique not only of the Indian social order or that of the colonial economic policy but also of Hindusim and an attempt to visualise some kind of emancipatory religion. Phule influenced by radical religious ideas of Thomas Paine could succeed in doing this kind of a theoretical exercise.

Phule believed in one God. He regarded God as a creator of this world and all men and women his children. Phule discarded idolatry, ritualism, asceticism, fatalism and the idea of incarnation. No intermediary between God and devotee was considered essential by him. Phule never believed that any book was God ordained. Apparently, it might appear that Phule's approach was similar to that of M.G. Ranade and his Prarthana Samaj. He differed from Ranade and his Prarthana Samaj. He differed from Ranade significantly and on very important issues. Ranade wanted to work within the structure of Hinduism. He was proud of the Hindu tradition and never thought of breaking from it. He looked to reformist activities as continuation of Protestantism of saints and similar efforts in the history. On the contrary, Phule visualised Sarvajanik Satya Dharma (Public True Religion) to take place of Hinduism. His true religion broke from Hindu traditions altogether. Moreover, he differed from reformers like Ranade when he severely criticised the mythology and sacred books like Smritis and Vedas of Hindus. He tried to prove that the history of Hinduisms was in fact, the history of Brahmin domination and slavery of Shudras. He found cunningness, selfishness and hypocrisy in sacred scriptures than a discussion of true religion. The elite reformers criticised the contemporary, degenerated form of Hinduism, while Phule attacked it from its very inception and showed that Brahmins had deceived lower castes throughout history. Phule interpreted Hinduism as a relation based on Varna and caste system devised by the cunning Brahmins to deceive the lower castes.

In fact, Phule accused the Prarthana Samaj and the Brahmo Samaj for their cunning motives. These Samajas, according to him, were established by the Brahmins who were educated from the revenue collected from lower castes. The activities of these associations were intended to conceal the superstructure built by their politically motivated ancestors in the name of religion. They were formed by the Brahmins for their own defence and deception of Shudras and untouchables.

But though he dismissed Hinduism altogether, he did not reject the very idea of religion or dharma. He tried to put in its place universal religion based on principles of liberty and equality. His Sarvajanik Satya Dharma put emphasis on truth seeing without the aid of any Guru or text. His religious ideas were definitely influenced by Christianity but he never advocated conversion because he was also influenced by the radical religious argument of Paine, who had shown a number of defects in Christianity.

His universal religion was liberal and in many respects very different from traditional religions. His religion was mainly and primarily concerned about secular matters. Phule had visualised a family where each member of that family might follow his own religion. In this ideal family a wife might embrace Buddhism while her husband might be a Christian and children might follow other religions because Phule believed that there might be some truth in all the religious texts and scriptures and therefore one of them could not claim the ultimate truth. He thought that the government should not close its eyes to inhuman religious customs or unjust traditions and practices of Hinduism. At one place he criticised the colonial government for its policy of continuing the practice of giving grants to temples, since he claimed that the money had been collected from lower castes in the form of tax. Thus, there was no place for any communalism or unwarranted neutralism in matters of religion so far as Phule's religious ideas were concerned.

Q9. Briefly describe the early life of E.V. Ramaswami Naicker and his political activities up to 1930.

Ans. E.V. Ramaswami Naicker was a prominent social reformer of India in the twentieth century. He was born of Balijsa Naidu parents on 28 September, 1879 at Erode in Coimbatore District in Tamil Nadu. He came from a prosperous business family in that district. But he did not have any formal education. His childhood days showed rebellious character which continued with his social and political activities. He defied all caste rules and regulations in his childhood and for that he was often taken to task by his parents.

E.V. Ramaswami Naicker

Nevertheless his home was a meeting place for pundits and religious scholars. Their discussions and discourses provided an opportunity to EVR to come to know about some rudiments of (philosophical significance) Hinduism. But soon he changed his role of a passive listener to that of an active participant. He started asking questions about inconsistencies and improbabilities in the puranic stories and ridiculed the basic concepts of Hindu religion and philosophy. More persistent questions were asked by him about the relevance of the institution of caste in society, belief in the theory of karma and the soundness of idol worship. None of the pundits, were able to give him convincing answers. In 1904 when he was twenty five years old, he went to Benares. This was a turning point in his life. Benares, he found, was no more holier than any other city. The Brahmins there ate meat and drank toddy and immoral trafficking in women was a thriving business. Disgusted with all this, he came back to join his father's business at Erode.

EVR proved himself an efficient organiser and executor of various relief measures. In 1915 when there was an outbreak of plague in Erode, he organised relief work with the help of his friends and distributed food and money to the destitute families. He served on various temple committees. He was elected as the Chairman of the Erode Municipality. During his term of office from 1917 to 1919, he executed the Cauvery water scheme which ensured a regular supply of drinking water to the citizens of Erode and thereby earned their admiration.

Political Activities up to 1930

EVR's participation in the politics of Tamil Nadu till 1920 was minimal. He participated in a protest meeting in 1916 organised against the government's action against Home Rule organ, New India. But he maintained political contact with important nationalist leaders from 1917 onwards. The non-Brahmin members of the Tamil Nadu Branch of the Congress organisation formed the Madras Presidency Association in 1917. It was formed to represent and safeguard the non-Brahmin interests in the national organisation and at the same time, to repudiate the claims of the Justice Party to be the sole representative of the non-Brahmin community in the Madras Presidency. However, the immediate aim of he Association at that time was to place before Edwin S. Montague, the Secretary of State for India, a scheme of reforms that would give non-Brahmins full communal representation in the legislature. Naicker, who attended the inaugural meeting of the Association, was in full agreement with its aims, and particularly its efforts to secure representation for non-Brahmins in public bodies. EVR viewed such efforts for representation of non-Brahmins as inspired by the need for social justice. Brahmin domination in liberal and civil services added a further sharpness to such demand for social justice in the Madras Presidency. Naicker took increasing interest in the activities of the Associations, served as one of its Vice-Presidents, participated in all its deliberations and helped to conduct its second annual conference at Erode in October 1919.

As an active member of the MPA, Naicker became familiar with the programmes and policies of the Indian National Congress. Its plans for the liberation of the country appealed to him. Especially its effort to raise the condition of the masses and do away with untouchability and prohibition impressed him. As the Congress held views similar to his on social reform, he thought by joining the political organisation he could bring about a new social order in the Presidency of Madras.

Once EVR joined the Congress in 1920, his rise was meteoric. Within the Congress, he had the support of C. Rajagopalachari and non-Brahmin politicians. He participated wholeheartedly in the non-cooperation movement, in the temperance campaign and in the campaign launched to replace foreign clothes by the progressive use of Khaddar. In 1920 itself he was elected the President of the Congress (MPCC). He fully endorsed Gandhiji's calls for boycott not only of legislatures but local taluk board elections as well. In 1921 he felled all the revenue fetching toddy trees and lost permanent income. In this he showed he would go to the extreme of keeping principle above all other considerations. In the same year he organised picketing before arrack and toddy shop. In November 1921 in order to quell the situation the Madras Government imprisoned him and the other campaigners for over a month under section 144 of the Indian Penal Code.

If Gandhiji's techniques of mass participation provided EVR a chance to have a foretaste of agitation against the colonial power, Vaikom Satyagraha gave him a chance to fight social evils within the Indian Social system. Vaikom was in the princely state of Travancore. Persons of low social status were not permitted to use the road near the temple in that place. To protest against such inequality in society and to maintain the right of untouchables to use the roads and the temples, the Congress members in Travancore launched a Satyagraha with Gandhiji's permission. But the Travancore State swiftly arrested them. Before their arrest they appealed to EVR, then the President of TNCC, to take over the leadership of the Satyagraha. EVR arrived in Travancore and made provocative speeches against the Gods and Brahmins. Fearing major clashes, the Government arrested him within 6 days of his arrival and issued a warrant to him to leave. But he defied it, was arrested and sentenced to 6 months imprisonment. However, he was released two months earlier on account of the Maharaja's death.

But the Vaikom Satyagraha revealed the positions EVR and conservative sections in the society, held on the question of untouchability. EVR launched his agitation on principle but he could not foresee the reaction of the conservatives. He could not recognise that the age old practice of untouchability could not be eradicated by one satyagraha or violent speeches against Gods. It had to be fought at every level a long period without communal rancour.

Q10. What do you know about the Gurukul controversy?

Ans. In January 1925, E.V. Ramaswami Naicker and others came to know that at the Congress funded Gurukulam at Shermadevi, in Tirunelvelly District, non-Brahmin boys were forced to eat apart from the Brahmins. This issue agitated the minds of the Congressmen but they were not able to intervene in the Gurukulam affairs. At the Tamil Nadu Congress Committee meet in Trichinopoly, a compromise resolution was agreed by which the committee recommended that all organisations partaking in the national movement should shun all gradations of merit based on birth. Ramaswamy Naicker himself agreed with the resolution. He said that if the country was not yet prepared to accept this state of thing, it was the duty of the non-Brahmins to create public opinion which was receptive to their rights.

Failure to settle the issue of the Gurukulam, in particular the refusal of the Brahmins to take a firm stand on .this question, widened the rift between the Brahmins and the non-Brahmins in the Congress. Even efforts made by EVR and another individual with the mandate from the TNCC to disperse with the communal restrictions failed to produce results. EVR whose criticisms so far were directed against the social evils and Brahmin domination in the bureaucracy now directed charges against the Congress organisation itself. At Salem in April 1925, he spoke that the Brahmin question should be settled even while the British supremacy lasted in the country. Otherwise non-Brahmins would have to suffer under "the tyranny of Brahmanocracy".

While this question opened a rift between the Congress and EVR in the Tamil Nadu Congress, two other issues completed it. They were **(i)** the question of communal representation and **(ii)** the controversy with Gandhiji on Varnashram

Dharma. On communal representation, EVR held the view that in a society marked by caste hierarchy, representation of Brahmins only in bureaucracy and other liberal professions would mean only consolidation of caste hierarchy in society. A majority of non-Brahmins denied access to economic and political power would remain low in social hierarchy. To lift them he suggested communal representation. This was in line with MPA's aims and objectives within the Congress organisation of the Madras Presidency.

At the Kanchipuram Conference of the TNPCC in November 1925, EVR sought to get a mandate from the Tamil Nadu Congress on the question of communal representation. This body accepted the demand for communal representation 'in principle', but refused to let it take a 'statutory shape' on several occasions. This EVR interpreted as a clever move to sideline the significant question. He further interpreted such a move in communal terms. He felt that Brahmins were in the national organisation only to further their own political interests rather than to strive for the independence of the country. He contended that Brahmin leaders on account of their vested interests were opposed to any measure that sought to improve the political fortunes of a majority of the non-Brahmin community.

Q11. Examine Naicker's views on the Varnashrama Dharma.

Or

Describe E.V.R. Ramswami Naicker's view on varnashrama Dharma.

[Dec 09, Q 7]

Ans. EVR held very strong views against four-fold division of caste hierarchy in the Indian society. He joined the Congress for its lofty ideals and goals, one of which was the abolition of untouchability. His fight against it at Vaikom was by itself a vigorous agitation which engaged the susceptibilities of Brahmins. Moreover, the Justice Party's formation was itself a revolt against Brahmans and Varnashrama dharma. In such a context, any attempt to reinforce such belief in Varnashrama dharma would be counterproductive in the Madras Presidency. Unfortunately, Mahatma Gandhi expressed his firm belief in Varnashrama dharma on September 1927 at Cuddalore. He appealed to the non-Brahmins that in their ire against Brahmins, non-Brahmins should not wreck the system of Varnashrama dharma, the bedrock of Hinduism. However, he stoutly rejected the notion of higher and low status attached to the system of Varnashrama dharma and suggested that neither the ban on intermarriage or that on interdining was an integral part of it.

But to many non-Brahmins in the Tamil region, Varnashrama dharma could mean the superiority of Brahmins over the rest of the population. EVR was very condemning of Varnashrama dharma. He considered that it included the relegation of all the non-Brahmin caste Hindus to the position of Shudras in the Tamil region. He felt that if each caste were to follow its own Dharma, non-

Brahmins would be forced to serve the Brahmins. "When ye think of ourselves as Shudras", said Ramaswami Naicker, "we accept ourselves as sons of prostitutes." Naicker met Gandhi in September 1927 with a view to modifying Gandhi's stand on varnashrama dharma. He expressed his deep concern over Gandhi's statements and pointed out that this only strengthen the orthodox Hindu position on the question of untouchability and child marriage, the two evils against which Gandhi himself was fighting. As the views of both of them were diametrically opposed, talks were not successful. Naicker expressed his confirmed belief in the Kudi Arasu that true freedom for India would be achieved only with the destruction of Indian National Congress, Hinduism and Brahminism.

This extreme step pushed him to support even the statutory Simon Commission which was boycotted by the Congress. He went to the extent of criticising the civil disobedience campaign in 1939. But soon seeing the public reaction against himself, he changed his own opinion and accepted the Indian National Congress as the sole organisation fighting for freedom. He urged the government to abandon its repressive measures against Congress satyagrahis and made a pointed reference to the futility of convening the Round Table Conference without Congress participation.

EVR viewed the Gandhi-Irwin Pact as a moral victory for the Congress. In that pact he saw the government conceded the Congress claims that it alone had the mandate to speak on behalf of a politically insurgent India and its views should be heard at all future conferences. In 1934 after 9 years of break with the Congress, EVR was asked to come back to the Congress fold by C. Rajagopalachari. EVR accepted the suggestion provided a common programme was agreed upon as basis for supporting the Congress. Accordingly, they jointly formulated a programme which was sent to Gandhiji for approval. The most important aspect of this programme was that the TNCC should agree to implement the principle of communal representation in all the representative bodies, in the civil and the liberal professions. As this was totally unacceptable to Gandhiji, Rajaji's efforts to bring Naicker back into the Congress fold failed.

Q12. Write a note on E.V. Ramaswami's Naicker's Self-Respect Movement. **[Dec 08, Q 4]**

Ans. E.V. Ramaswami Naicker gave a concrete shape to his ideas on social reform by founding the Suyamariyati iyakkam otherwise known as the Self-Respect Movement. It was a reform movement dedicated to the goal of giving non-Brahmins a sense of pride based on their Dravidianist past. The movement denied the superiority of the Brahmins and their implicit faith in the present system. The movement sought to turn the present social system topsy-turvy and establish a living bond of union among all the people irrespective of caste or creed, including the untouchables. One of the essential points was a denial of the mythology of Hinduism by which, it contended that, the unsuspecting were made victims of the Brahmins. Since the Brahmin was seen as a leader of the social and religious life of Tamil Nadu, he became the target of 'Self-Respect' attacks.

The tone of the movement was determined by EVR, who represented a new type of leader in Tamil Nadu. He was uneducated in English and able to speak only in Tamil in the popular idiom. The self-movement concentrated almost entirely on the Tamil Districts. It covered primarily the groups low in the social hierarchy like the Vanniya Kula Kshatriyas and the untouchables. Special efforts were also directed at women and young people. Because of the directness and simplicity of its message, the illiterate and semi-educated in the rural areas turned to the movement. This was a new development in Tamil Nadu politics. 'The Justice Party which claimed to be the sole representative of the non-Brahmins did not bother to cover these groups. In fact the leadership of the Justice Party was drawn from the landowning groups and attempted to cover the middle classes and landowning classes.

Even before the Self-Respect Movement was founded in 1925, EVR started expressing his views on the evil in the society. The Tamil language weekly Kudi Arasu (People's Government) founded in May 1924 became the organ of the Self-Respect Movement. It was specially directed at certain non-Brahmin groups that had not been reached by the Justice Party's Dravidian. Shortly after 1930, Ramaswami Naicker began a Tamil daily called Viduthalai (Freedom) and in 1935 he started a Tamil monthly called Pakkuthariuu (commonsense). But in the late 20's Kudi Arasu was the movement's propaganda weapon.

Since the Self-Respect Movement had as its target the Brahminical tradition, its symbol came under attack. On a number of occasions, the manusmriti was burned. Certain characters in the puranas were changed. For instance, Ravana in the Valmiki's Ramayana was held up as the hero and be an ideal of good Dravidian conduct. Rama was seen as a wicked and unjust Aryan.

Attack of this kind on Hindu scriptures and its symbols however were criticized even by non-Brahmin leaders apart from Brahmins. But the criticisms did not have any impact on the Self-Respect Movement's tone. The propaganda of the Self-Respect Movement continued and even grew sharper. Songs about self-respect leaders were printed and distributed and pamphlets were issued to explain the movement's aims. Some of these caricatured the characters of the Hindu pantheon. One of them was Vasittira tevarkal kortu (wonderful court of Deities) published in 1919.

The most important of the early activities of the Self-Respect Movement was the convening of the first Provincial Self-Respect Conference at Chingleput on February 17, 1929. The conference proceedings reflected its strong egalitarian bias and its determination to boycott Brahmin priests, its desire to attract young people and women and above all its commitment to what it considered to be Dravidian civilization.

At this conference many resolutions were passed. One called on members to refuse money for the construction of temples or for the employment of priests or intermediaries. Another condemned Varnashrama dharma and arbitrary division of society into Brahmins, Kshatriyas, Vaisyas and Sudras, and Panchamans, and repudiated belief in superiority based on the "accident of birth". Another resolution condemned the use of all suffixes and terminations connotative of caste. And as for women, a resolution was passed claiming for them the same rights of inheritance as men and advocating that marriage should be terminable at the will of either party. True to their spirit, self-respecters uphold a total disbelief in the religious validity of Brahmins. "Self-Respect weddings" without the use of Brahmin priests became common.

Though some Congress leader like P. Vardarajulu Naidu opposed resolutions like refusal to give 'fund to temples for renovation purpose, these resolutions remained the main plank of the Self-Respect Movement. But anti-religious tone of the management was moderated by EVR after his visit to the Soviet Union.

He toured the Soviet Union for three months as the leader of the Rationalistic Association of South India, a new name given to the Self-Respect Movement, when he was on tour in Russia, he visited other parts of Europe as well. The visit to the Soviet Union had a deeper impact on EVR. He was inspired by the "Phenomenal progress" the Russians had made in agriculture and industry and attributed this to Russian systems. He, therefore, maintained that unless India also made radical changes on the lines of the Soviet system, there would not be any meaningful system in the country. Soon after the return from the Soviet Union, EVR sought the assistance of 'Singaravelu Chetti who was a prominent communist in South India to frame a new programme. The new programme envisaged the formation of two wings within the body of Self-Respect League Samadharma (Communist) Party of South .India. Both aimed at achieving political independence for the country through constitutional methods, distribution and public transport, amelioration of the condition of the industrial and the agricultural labourers and working with redoubled vigour for the original aims of the Self-Respect Movement. These aims of the two wings of the movement were termed as the Erode Programme.

He carried on his propaganda on Socialism and Social reform through his Kudi Arasu and other organs. But his editorial in Kudi Arasu 'Why today's Government should be overthrown, forced the Government to arrest him and charge' him with inciting the people to overthrow the constituted authority by force." EVR did not challenge the charge but sent a written statement to the court to this effect: "For the last 7 or 8 years I have been propagating the principles of Socialism and in a democratic way with the aim of bringing about social and economic equality among the people. This is in no way an offence.... Followers should be prepared to face such repressive measures that might be let loose by the government."

But after his release, he did not stick to political programme of the Self-Respect Movement. He increasingly came to concentrate on the social reform question. Side by side, he carried on a political propaganda as well against the Justice Party for ignoring the interests of the non-Brahmins to defeat the Congress candidates in the municipal and legislative elections. But defeat of the Justice Party candidates in the Legislative elections in 1936 showed that the Justice Party was no longer a political force. But EVR moved closer to the Justice Party rather than to the Congress which won the elections.

Q13. What role did Naicker play in the anti-Hindi agitation/language controversy?

Ans. In the Legislative Council elections, the Congress won a sufficient number of the seats to form a government and C. Rajagopalachari became premier of the Madras Presidency. In accordance with the Congress policy, he announced (to the Press) that Hindi would be introduced as a compulsory course of study in the school curriculum for the first three forms.

The decision to introduce Hindi in the Madras Presidency ignored the linguistic differences between the North and the South and overlooked the strong currents of regionalism which were themselves an outcome of the cultural revivalism that had taken place half a century ago. Political awakening that was brought about by leaders like C. Rajagopalachari, Satyamurthi, E.V. Ramaswami Naicker and Thiru. V Kalyanasundara Mudaliar when they were all in the Congress organisation in the 20's was very much created in their mother tongue, i.e. Tamil. There were two main reasons for the Tamil scholars opposition to Hindi. First, the introduction of Hindi meant to them the revival of Sanskrit—a language which they traditionally opposed. Secondly, the mother tongue was not a compulsory subject in the curriculum in those days and many passed out of the schools without knowledge of the Dravidian tongue. Therefore, they argued that the introduction of Hindi in the schools without making the mother tongue also a compulsory subject was a deliberate attempt to relegate the Dravidian language to the background.

These genuine fears were ignored and Hindi was introduced in April 1938 in the schools. Agitations and demonstrations were launched against Hindi. Meanwhile the leaders of the Self-Respect Movement organised a march from Trichinapally to Madras in order to strengthen public opinion in favour of the anti-Hindi movement. It was sent off by EVR and other leaders at Trichinapally. It comprised one hundred and one members, took out a long route which passed through Trichinapally, Tanjore, South Arcot and Chingleput and covered 234 villages and 60 mofussil towns.

The most important feature of the anti-Hindi movement was the participation of a large number of women in the agitation. EVR also participated in the women's conference on 13th November 1938 and asked the women participants to fight against "Hindi Imperialism". And on 14th instant, he appealed to the women to protect that mother tongue 'form the onslaught of an Aryan and alien language'. After these two speeches a large number of women came to participate in the anti-Hindi movement and many of them were arrested and sentenced to imprisonment for picketing schools.

For the speeches made on the 13th and 14th November 1938, EVR also was prosecuted for inciting the women to participate in the anti-Hindi agitation and was sentenced to one year rigorous imprisonment and to a fine of Rs. 1000. Public opinion did not approve of this harsh sentence. Therefore the sentence was changed into a simple imprisonment of 6 months and he was transferred from a 'C' class to an 'A' class prison. But before the term expired EVR was released on health grounds. But Hindi was withdrawn from the schools only in 1940.

EVR because of his past experiences with the Congress which he considered as Brahmin dominated, opposed even liberal policies of the C. Rajagopalachari Ministry. Sometimes he sought alliance with any one opposed to the Congress with the sole purpose of making that party unpopular. One example was his stand on the Temple Entry Bill. The Bill made it possible for Harijans in the Malabar Districts to enter and worship in the temples. One section in the Brahmin community, the Sanatanists, started agitation against Harijan entry in Hindu temples.

In spite of the Sanatanists' opposition to the temple entry bill, EVR did not support G. Rajagopalachari's efforts to bring about social change in the Tamil society. Instead he was quite willing to compromise his own cherished and much advocated social aims like the uplift of Harijans and accommodate the Sanatanists for immediate political gains.

Naicker's opposition to the Congress did not rest with the Temple Entry Bill alone. It was extended to raise demand for a separate Tamil Nadu called Dravidianad. To some extent this demand was the culmination of a separate identity kept up over for about 50 years or so. The writings of Caldwell and G.U. Pope and other western writers, besides contributing to Tamil revivalism, also fostered a sense of new identity of Dravidianism. But EVR gave a political dimension to a nebulous identity by passing a resolution at the Executive Committee of the Justice Party in 1940. He expressed his views in the Mail of 15 November 1939 that the concept of a Tamil nation was nothing new but had been adumberated since the inception of the Justice Party. The concept had manifested itself as a political credo only in 1937 when the political Brahmins under the aegis of the Congress threatened his goal, he started a campaign. The nationalist press like the Swadesamitran criticised his demand as "mischievous" and "dangerous". Despite that he carried on his propaganda. He joined the Muslim League and supported its demand for partition. Jinnah's two nations conceded and upheld by EVR as the only solution for the Muslims to live harmoniously in a nation dominated by the Aryan Brahmins. The League's role in the politics of the nation, EVR said, was not to disrupt national unity; to defend the right and privileges of the Muslims and all the other minorities in the country.

But the demand for Dravidianad did not acquire any prominence and the Justice Party itself was a decline, EVR's leadership of it did not add up to its image. At the 1944 Salem Conference, the Justice Party was rechristened as the Dravida Kazhagam. The new name was expected to reinvigorate the party image. But the authoritarian leadership of EVR did not allow any change to take place. Again the Dravida Kazhagam under the leadership of EVR was split into two in 1949 when a considerable number of members of that body left it in protest against EVR's marriage with a woman of many years younger than himself. After 1949, EVR's role in the Tamil Nadu politics was less considerable. He carried sporadic agitations against C. Rajagopalachari's education policy in 1954. He came to support the Chief Minister of Tamil Nadu, Kamaraj as "pure Tamilian", since he hailed from the backward community of Nadars. But increasingly, the Dravida Munnetra Kazhagam a splinter group of the Dravida Kazhagam, became a major political force. The Dravida Kazhagam lost its importance as a pressure group even under his own stewardship.

Q14. Discuss the views of Ambedkar on democracy. [June 06, Q 4]

Ans. Like many other national leaders Ambedkar had complete faith in democracy. Dictatorship may be able to produce results quickly; it may be effective in maintaining discipline but cannot be one's choice as a permanent form of government. Democracy is superior because it enhances liberty. People have control over the rulers. Among the different forms of democratic government, Ambedkar's choice fell on the parliamentary form. In this case also he was in agreement with many other national leaders.

Social and Economic Democracy

Ambedkar viewed democracy as an instrument of bringing about change peacefully. Democracy does not merely mean rule by the majority or government by the representatives of the people. This is a formalistic and limited notion of democracy. We would understand the meaning of democracy in a better fashion if we view it as a way of realising drastic changes in the social and economic spheres of society. Ambedkar's idea of democracy is much more than just a scheme of government. He emphasises the need for bringing about an all-round democracy. A scheme of government does not exist in vacuum; it operates within the society. Its usefulness depends upon its relationship with the other spheres of society. Elections, parties and parliaments are, after all, formal institutions of democracy. They cannot be effective in an undemocratic atmosphere. Political democracy means the principle of 'one man one vote' which indicates political equality. But if oppression and injustice exist, the spirit of political democracy would be missing. Democratic government, therefore, should be an extension of a democratic society. In the Indian society, for instance, so long as caste barriers and caste-based inequalities exist, real democracy cannot operate. In this sense, democracy means a spirit of fraternity and equality and not merely a political arrangement. Success of democracy in India can be ensured only by establishing a truly democratic society. Along with the social foundations of democracy, Ambedkar takes into consideration the economic aspects also. It is true that he was greatly influenced by liberal thought. Still, he appreciated the limitations of liberalism. Parliamentary democracy, in which he had great faith, was also critically examined by him. He argued that parliamentary democracy was based on liberalism. It ignored economic inequalities and never concentrated upon the problems of the downtrodden. Besides, the general tendency of the western type of parliamentary democracies has been to ignore the issues of social and economic equality. In other words, parliamentary democracy emphasised only liberty whereas true democracy implies both liberty and equality. This analysis becomes very important in the Indian context. Indian society was demanding freedom from the British. But Ambedkar was afraid that freedom of the nation would not ensure real freedom for all the people. Social and economic inequalities have dehumanised the Indian society. Establishing democracy in such a society would be nothing short of a revolution. This would be a revolution in the social structure and attitudes of the people. In the place of hereditary inequality, the principles of brotherhood and equality must be established. Therefore, Ambedkar supported the idea of all-round democracy.

Factors necessary for the successful operation of Democracy

For the successful functioning of this form of government, it is necessary that certain other conditions must be fulfilled. To begin with, political parties are necessary for the effective working of parliamentary democracy. This will ensure existence of the opposition which is very important. Parliamentary government is known as responsible government mainly because the executive is constantly watched and controlled by the opposition. Respect and official status for the opposition means absence of absolute power for the executive. The other condition is a neutral and non-political civil service. A neutral civil service means that administrators would be permanent–not dependent on the fortunes of the political parties–and that they would not take sides with political parties. This will be possible only when appointments of civil servants are not made on the basis of political consideration. Success of democracy depends on many ethical and moral factors also. A country may have a constitution. But it is only a set of rules. These rules become meaningful only when people in the country develop conventions and traditions consistent with the constitution. People and politicians must follow certain norms in public life. Similarly, there must also exist a sense of morality and conscientiousness in the society. Law and legal remedies can never replace a voluntary sense of responsibility. No amount of law can enforce morality. Norms of honest and responsible behaviour must develop in the society. Democracy can be successful only when every citizen feels duty bound to fight injustice even if that injustice does not put him into any difficulty personally. This will happen when equality and brotherhood exist in the society.

To make democracy successful in India, Ambedkar suggested a few other precautions also. Democracy means rule of the majority. But this should not result into tyranny of the majority. Majority must always respect the views of the minority. In India there is a possibility that the minority community will always be a political minority also. Therefore, it is very essential that the minority must feel free, safe and secure. Otherwise, it will be very easy to convert democracy into a permanent rule against the minority. Caste system could thus become the most difficult obstacle in the successful functioning of democracy. The castes which are supposed to be of low status will never get their proper share in power. Caste will create barriers in the development of healthy democratic traditions. This means that unless we achieve the task of establishing democracy in the social field, mere political democracy cannot survive.

Q15. Critically examine Ambedkar's views on state socialism.

Ans. Ambedkar was not only a scholar with a firm intellectual grip on concepts, but he was also aware of the practical social difficulties in the way of democratic functioning. Therefore, he emphasizes that mere liberty cannot be an adequate goal. Liberty is meaningful when accompanied by equality. So Ambedkar turned to socialism.

i) Inclination to Socialism: In those days, two varieties of socialism were prominent. One was Marxist Socialism. Ambedkar studied various aspects of Marxism and favoured some Marxist principles. He generally subscribed to the material view of history and agreed to the need for a total change for bringing about equality. He also accepted the idea of public ownership of property. However, he did not become a Marxist. The other important variety of socialism was Democratic Socialism. Ambedkar's firm belief in democracy attracted him to this ideology. He felt that socialism must function within a democratic framework. Democracy and socialism need not be opposed to each other. Thus, in 1947, Ambedkar propounded the idea of 'State socialism'. Even earlier, when he established the Independent Labour Party in 1937, he had adopted a broadly socialist programme. The name of the party itself indicates that it was to be a party of all depressed classes. Its programme included state management of important industries and bringing about a just economic system. The party wanted to ensure minimum standard of living for agricultural and industrial workers.

ii) Meaning of State Socialism: In 1947, Ambedkar suggested that the Constitution of India should incorporate the principle of State Socialism. State socialism means that the state would implement a socialist programme by controlling the industrial and agricultural sectors. There are two major aspects of Ambedkar's State socialism: **(a)** Key industries and basic industries will be owned by the state. There will be no private ownership of such industries. This will help in rapid industrialisation and at the same time, benefits of industrialisation will be distributed among all the sections of the society by the state. Insurance will also be entirely under state control; **(b)** Agriculture will be treated as a state industry. This means that the state will initiate collective farming. Farmers will be allowed to enjoy part of the agricultural produce and the state will get some share in the form of levy. Foodgrains procured by way of levy will be used for distribution at fare prices. In other words, the states will actively control both the industry and the agriculture. This will ensure equitable distribution of wealth and protect the needy and the poor. Rapid industrial progress and welfare of all the sections of the society will be the responsibility of the state. However, the democratic institutions such as the parliament will also remain intact.

In the parliamentary form of government, the same party may not remain in power permanently. Different parties with different programmes may come to power. Therefore, Ambedkar suggested that the programme of State Socialism should be made an unalterable part of the constitution; so that any party which comes to power will have to implement that programme. This idea of State Socialism shows that Ambedkar was aware of the problems of poverty and economic inequality. He laid great emphasis on industrialisation. He believed that India needed rapid industrial growth. This will help to ease out the burden on agriculture. But merely of wealth, the menace of capitalism had to be avoided.

iii) Role of Government: This was possible only if the state functioned as a major partner in the field of industry. Ambedkar believed that the state operating through government will be a neutral agency looking after the interests of the entire community. Therefore, he attached much importance to the role of the government. Government, according to him, has to perform the role of a welfare agency. It has to ensure rapid progress and just distribution of the fruits of that progress. The role of the government was not restricted to industry only. It was expected to be active in the area of banking and insurance. Moreover, the government must also control the agriculture. By owning major industries and controlling agriculture, the government will curb economic injustice. In other words, changes of a revolutionary nature are to be brought about through the efforts of the government.

Q16. What role did Dr. Ambedkar play in drafting of the country's constitution?

Ans. In 1947, Ambedkar became Chairman of the Drafting Committee of the Constituent Assembly of India. His contribution in this role has become immemorable. Ambedkar's legal expertise and knowledge of constitutional laws of different countries was very helpful in framing the Indian Constitution. His deep regard for a democratic constitution and insistence upon constitutional morality also helped in this process. In this sense, he is rightly regarded as the architect of the Indian Constitution. There are many administrative details in the Indian Constitution (e.g. provisions regarding the Public Service Commission, Attorney General, Comptroller and Auditor General, etc.) which have made the constitution a very lengthy document. But Ambedkar defended inclusion of such details. He argued that we have created a democratic political structure in a traditional society. If all details are not incorporated, unscrupulous rulers in the future' may misuse the constitution without technically violating it. Thus, formally the constitution may remain in operation but its real purpose may be defeated. To avoid this, the best safeguard is to write down all necessary details and to bind future rulers to these details. In a society where the democratic tradition is weak, such safeguards become essential. This shows that Ambedkar was a staunch constitutionalist. He believed that a government must be constitutional and that constitution must be treated as a basic and sacred document. There was no room for extra-parliamentary activity in constitutional politics. He also attached much significance to the evolution of constitutional norms and public practices consistent with the constitution. Dr. Ambedkar's must important contribution to the Indian Constitution may be seen in the areas of fundamental rights, strong central government and protection of minorities. As a liberal, Ambedkar believed that fundamental rights constitute the most important part of the constitution. But mere listing of these rights is not sufficient. What makes fundamental rights really fundamental is the guarantee of constitutional protection to these rights. Ambedkar was proud of Article 32 of the Indian Constitution which guarantees judicial protection to fundamental rights. Such protection makes the rights real and meaningful. There was general agreement in the constituent assembly that India needed a strong central government. Ambedkar shared this view. But his chief reason for advocating a strong central government was slightly different from that of the others. He was aware that India was a caste-ridden society in which lower castes have always received unjust treatment from the higher castes. He was afraid that casteism would be all the more powerful at local .and provincial levels. Government at these levels would be easily subject to casteist pressures and it would fail to protect the lower castes from higher caste oppression. The national government would be less influenced by these pressures. It would be more liberal in its approach than the local governments. 'Only a strong central government, therefore, will ensure some protection to the lower castes. This was Ambedkar's most important reason for creating a strong central government. He knew that the minority communities in India were in the most vulnerable position. In India, there was a tendency of a communal or caste majority becoming a political majority also. Thus, a minority will be both a caste minority and political minority. It will be subject to political as well as social harassment. The democratic rule of 'one-man-one-vote' will not be sufficient in such a situation. What we need in India is some guarantee of share in power for the minorities. Minority communities should get an opportunity to elect their representatives. The views of these representatives must be fully respected. Ambebkar attempted to incorporate many safeguards for the minorities. Ambedkar attempted to incorporate many safeguards for the minorities, including definite representation in the executive. He was successful in creating provisions regarding political reservations in legislatures and the appointment of a special officer for Scheduled Castes and Scheduled Tribes (Commissioner) under Article 338 etc. He would have liked to create many more safeguards but for the unwillingness of the majority in the constituent assembly. What is significant here is Dr. Ambedkar's view that democracy is not merely majority rule and that caste-communal minorities must be fully protected to make democracy meaningful. He was, in other words, against the 'Majoritarianism Syndrome'.

Q17. Discuss Ambedkar's views on caste system.

Ans. Ambedkar's main battle was against the caste system. Caste had made Hindu society stagnant. Due to the caste system, Hindu society is unable to accommodate outsiders. This drawback poses permanent problems for integration. Even internally, the Hindu society fails to satisfy the test of a **homogeneous** society. It is only a conglomerate of different castes. Caste is an obstacle in the growth of national spirit. Most importantly, caste system perpetrates injustice on the lower castes. It does not allow progress of the lower castes. Lower castes receive nothing but contempt. This has resulted in moral degradation and demoralisation of the lower castes. The untouchables, in particular, are the constant object of injustice. They are denied education, good livelihood and human dignity. The caste system has dehumanised them thoroughly. The very idea that the mere touch of one human being pollutes another shows the gross level of inequality and brutality to which the caste system had sunk. Therefore, the battle for the removal of untouchability becomes the battle for human rights and justice.

The caste hierarchy and the practice of untouchability find justification in religious scriptures. The Hindus widely believed that persons belonging to the untouchable community were originally from non-Aryan races that they were of lowly origin, they have no capabilities, etc. Ambedkar wanted to refute these misunderstandings and create self-respect among the untouchables. For this purpose, he made extensive study of Hindu scriptures and the ancient Hindu society. In his books 'Who Were the Shudras?' and 'The Untouchables', he dispelled many misconceptions about untouchability. Through research and interpretation, he made scholarly attempts to prove the origins of untouchability. He argued that originally only three Varnas existed: Brahmins, Kshatriyas and Vaishyas. The Shudras were a powerful tribe belonging to the Kshatriya Varna. Conflict between the Shudras and the Brahmins resulted in the Shudras' degradation from Kshatriya status because the Brahmins denied them the rights of Upnayana, sacrifice and kingdom. Thus, the Shudras became the fourth Varna below the other three. He shows how the religious and ritual power of Brahmins caused the downfall of the Shudras. This indicates the overall supremacy of the Brahmin Varna in the ancient society. Untouchability was also partly a result of this Brahmin supremacy. Untouchability resulted from the conflict between Brahmanism and Buddhism. Ambedkar denies that untouchables were originally non-Aryans. In fact, he argues that in the Indian society, we find a mixture of various races. Therefore, the idea that the untouchables belonged to some inferior or defeated race was untenable. He provides a sociological answer. Originally there existed a number of unsettled tribes. They came into conflict with other wandering tribes. These, wandering tribes were defeated and their members scattered. These scattered people finally became attached to various settled tribes. However, their status remained subordinate to the settled tribes. Thus, the wanderers stabilised as outsiders. The next round of conflict between these outsiders and the settled tribes took place on the issue of religion and subsequently beef eating.

Ambedkar argues that to meet the challenge of Buddhism, Brahmanism adopted complete non-violence, total renunciation of meat-eating and deification of the cow. The outsiders, who were followers of Buddhism, traditionally ate meat of dead animals including cow. Since they did not suspend the practice of beef-eating, they were ex-communicated by the settled tribes under the influence of Brahmins. This ex-communication was later justified by incorporating in religious scriptures. Thus, untouchability became a permanent and sacred part of religion. Although some of Ambedkar's interpretations have been debatable, nobody denies that untouchability first came into existence and then became part of religion. Moreover, the most important task that Ambedkar's research has fulfilled is to create self-respect among the lower castes and untouchables. He convinced them that there is nothing shameful in their past, nothing inferior or inglorious in their heritage. He convinced them that their low status was not due to any disability on their part, but it was a result of social mechanism under the influence of Brahmanism. His interpretations, above all, convinced everyone that a scrutiny of the religious foundations of Hinduism was necessary.

Q18. Discuss the efforts made by Ambedkar to help remove untouchability.

Ans. Ambedkar warns that nothing worthwhile can be created on the basis of caste. We can build neither a nation nor morality on this basis. Therefore, a casteless society must be created. Intercaste marriages can effectively destroy the caste but the difficulty is that

people will not be prepared to marry outside their caste so long as casteism dominates their thinking. Ambedkar describes such methods as inter-caste dining or marriage as 'forced feeding'. What is required is a more drastic change: liberating people from the clutches of religious scriptures and traditions. Every Hindu is a slave of the Vedas and Shastras. He must be told that these scriptures perpetrate wrong and therefore need to be discarded.

Abolition of castes is dependent upon destroying the glory of the scriptures. Till the scriptures dominate the Hindus, they will not be free to act according to their conscience. In place of the unjust principle of hereditary hierarchy, we must establish the principles of equality, liberty and fraternity. They should be the foundations of any religion.

Self-respect among Untouchables

However, Ambedkar knew that all this involved a total change in Hinduism which would take a very long time. Therefore, along with this suggestion for basic change, he also insisted on many other ways for the uplift of the untouchables. Under the influence of tradition the untouchables had completely surrendered to the domination of the upper castes. They had lost all spirit to fight and assert themselves. The myth of inherent pollution also considerably influenced the minds of untouchables. Therefore, it was necessary to arouse their self-respect. Untouchables should realise that they are the equals of caste Hindus. They must throw away their bondage.

Education

Ambedkar believed that education would greatly contribute to the improvement of the untouchables. He always exhorted his followers to reach excellence in the field of knowledge. Knowledge is a liberating force. Education makes man enlightened, makes him aware of this self-respect and also helps him to lead a better life materially. One of the causes of the degradation of the untouchables was that they were denied the right to education. Ambedkar criticised the British policy on education for not adequately encouraging education among the lower castes. He felt that even under the British rule education continued mainly to be an upper caste monopoly. Therefore, he mobilised the lower castes and the untouchables and funded various centers of learning. While a labour member in the executive council of the Governor-general, he was instrumental in extending scholarships for education abroad to the untouchable students. Ambedkar wanted the untouchables to undergo both liberal education and technical education. He was particularly opposed to education under religious auspices. He warned that only secular education could instil the values of liberty and equality among the students.

Economic Progress

Another very important remedy which Ambedkar upheld was that the untouchables should free themselves of the village community and its economic bondage. In the traditional set up, the untouchables were bound to specific occupations. They were dependent upon the caste Hindus for their sustenance. Even for meagre returns they had to submit themselves to the domination of caste Hindus. Ambedkar was aware of the economic dimension of their servitude. Therefore, he always insisted that the untouchables should stop doing their traditional work. Instead, they should acquire new skills and start new professions. Education would enable them to get employment. There was no point in remaining dependent upon the village economy. With growing industrialisation, there were greater opportunities in the cities. Untouchables should quit villages, if necessary and find new jobs or engage themselves in new professions. Once their dependence on caste Hindus is over, they can easily throw away the psychological burden of being untouchables. In a realistic evaluation of the villages, Ambedkar graphically describes them as 'a sink of localism, a den of ignorance, narrow-mindedness and communalism'.

Therefore, the earlier the untouchables become free of village-bondage, the better. Even if the untouchables had to live in the villages, they should stop doing their traditional work and seek new means of livelihood. This would ensure their economic emancipation to a considerable extent. The mainstay of Ambedkar's argument was that the oppressed classes must generate self-respect among themselves. The best policy for their uplift was the policy of self-help. Only by working hard and casting off mental servitude, they can attain an equal status with the remaining Hindu society. He did not believe in social reform on the basis of humanitarianism, sympathy, philanthropy etc. Equal status and just treatment was a matter of right and not pity. The downtrodden should assert and win their rights through conflict. There was no short cut to the attainment of rights.

Political Strength

As a step in this direction, Ambedkar attaches much importance to political participation of the oppressed classes. He repeatedly emphasised that in the context of colonialism, it had become imperative that the untouchables gain political rights by organising themselves politically. He claimed that by attaining political power, untouchables would be able to protect safeguards and a sizeable share in power, so that they can force certain policies on the legislature. This was so because during the last phase of British rule, negotiations had already begun for the settlement of the question of transfer of power. Ambedkar wanted the untouchables to assert their political rights and get an adequate share in power. Therefore, he formed political organisations of untouchables.

Conversion

Throughout his life Ambedkar made efforts to reform the philosophical basis of Hinduism. But he was convinced that Hinduism will not modify its disposition towards the untouchables. So, he searched for an alternative to Hinduism. After careful consideration, he adopted Buddhism and asked his followers to do the same. His conversion to Buddhism meant reassertion of his faith in a religion based on humanism. Ambedkar argued that Buddhism was the least obscurantist religion. It appreciated the spirit of equality and liberty. Removal of injustice and exploitation was the goal of Buddhism. By adopting Buddhism, the untouchables would be able to carve out a new identity for themselves. Since Hinduism gave them nothing but sufferings, by renouncing Hinduism, the untouchables would be renouncing the stigma of untouchability and bondage attached to them. To live a new material life, a new spiritual basis consistent with the liberal spirit was essential. Buddhism would provide this basis. Therefore, at the social level, education; at the material level, new means of livelihood; at the political level, political organisation and at the spiritual level, self-assertion and conversion constituted Ambedkar's overall programme of the removal of untouchability.

Q19. What changes were brought about by the British policies in the economy of the tribals ?

Ans. Like other social groups, the tribals of India participated in the anti-colonial movement. The British policies disturbed the traditional tribal systems. The tribal land system was marked by its corporatorial ownership of land and absence of the landlords. But the British changed the land system of the tribals. They created the hitherto unknown class of zamindars (landlords) in the tribal areas. Brahmins and Rajputs were brought in the tribal areas of Chotanagpur to perform military and religious services. For their roles, they were assigned the zamindari rights in the land. The zamindars were considered outsiders by the tribals. The tribals were reduced to the position of tenants. The clan councils of the tribals were replaced by the councils of rajas consisting of their followers. The traditional land system of the British was turned into tenancy systems. The British also introduced contractors (Thekedars) in the tribal areas. The zamindars and thekedars introduced the land rent in the tribal areas. Following the introduction of market economy, a class of traders also developed in the tribal areas. The tribal tenants had to pay the rent in cash. As they did not have cash with them, they had to borrow from the money-lenders. Hence, a class of money-lenders also came into being in the tribal areas. The isolated tribal communities were connected with the outside world following the introduction of means of communication and transportation. The self-sufficient tribal economy was converted into market economy. The customary system of justice was replaced by the new legal system. The new legal system was not suitable to the tribals. The tribals could not afford to utilise the new legal system, as they were not educated and they did not have money for the fees of the lawyers. The British brought a host of petty government official and clerks in the tribal areas. All these classes—zamindars, thekedars, traders, money-lenders, government officials—were not natives of the tribal areas. Nor did they belong to the tribal communities. They were brought into the tribal areas by the British. They could be Hindus, Muslims, Christians, Sikhs or Europeans. Hence, they were considered outsiders - dikus - by the tribals. These classes collabourated with the British administration in the process of exploitation and oppression of the tribals. The landlords extracted exorbitant amount of Lent from the tribals, evicted them from their land and extracted begar (forcible labour) from the tribals. In case of defiance, the tribals were physically assaulted by the zamindars. They were deprived of their belongings. The money-lenders exploited the tribals by charging exorbitant amount of interests from them. Many a time the tribals were forced to sell out their belongings and children and wives to meet the requirements of the landlords and money-lenders. The government officials took advantage of their innocence. They were the ally of landlords, money-lenders, contractors and traders in the exploitation of the tribals.

Forest Policy

Till the middle of the nineteenth century, the tribals had customary rights in the forest. Their right to use the forest products was recognised. But the forest policy (1884) of the British curtailed the tribal rights to use the forest produce. Moreover, the development of the communication system i.e. telegraphic, roadways and railway services and the introduction of the common administrative system ruined the natural economy of the forests. These developments affected the tribals all over the country. The dikus were benefited from the British forest policies. The British policies were detrimental to the tribal interests. The government sometimes paid compensation to the tribals for the loss caused by the encroachment of the forests. But the compensation could not trickle down to them. It was usurped by the clerks, the pleaders and the munshis in between. In addition to the devastation caused to the tribal communities, the famines in the later half of the 19th century worsened the conditions of the tribals. The continuous increase in the prices of the essential commodities made their conditions unbearable. The land formed for the tribals, not only a source of livelihood, but a spiritual source as well given to them by their ancestors. They were being alienated from their land due to distress. The rights of the outsiders - money-lenders and landlords – were recognised over their land. The attack on the tribal system was a threat to their existence.

Q20. Discuss the silent features of tribal movement of India.

Ans. The tribals responded to their exploitation and oppression in the form of revolts and movements. They identified their enemies in the outsiders (dikus) - landlords, money-lenders, thekedars and missionaries and European government officials. They launched movements against their oppressors in their respective regions. Their agitations against the outsiders could be called anti-colonial. They revolted against them because of their exploitation in the form of encroachment on their land, eviction from their land, annulment of their traditional legal and social rights and customs, against enhancement of rent, for transfer of land to the tiller, abolition of feudal and semi-feudal form of land ownership. On the whole, these movements had social and religious overtone. But they were directed against the issues related to their existence. These movements were launched under the leadership of their respective chiefs. Although the movements initially began on social and religious issues and against the oppression of outsiders, in course of time, they merged with the National movement and with the no-tax campaign. The tribals fought against their enemies with their traditional weapons i.e. bows, arrows, lathis and axe! Their movement often took a violent turn resulting in the murder of oppressors and the burning of their houses. Most of the movements were ruthlessly suppressed by the government. The tribals had to comply with British policies which were detrimental to their interests. The government introduced protective administration in tribal areas. The government thought that the normal laws could not be applied in the tribal areas. The government passed the Scheduled District Act (1874) and categorised the tribal areas as excluded areas in the Govt. of India Act of 1935.

Q21. Write a note on the followings :
(i) Birsa Munda Revolt (1895-1901)
(ii) Santhal Revolt of 1855 **[June 09, Q 14]**
(iii) Tribals and National Movement in Orissa (1921-36)

Ans. (i) Birsa Munda Revolt (1895-1901)- The life history of Birsa Munda will go down in the history of the tribals as a story of emancipation of his own people, who were subjected to prolonged suppression by the Britishers. He was a visionary. He realised that the Britishers have come to this land to torture the masses and carry wealth abroad. He is reckoned as a freedom fighter who led the tribals essentially to prevent land grabbing by the non-tribals ending them up as bonded labourers in their own land.

He had organised his first protest march for remission of forest dues. It was at this time the great famine of 1895 broke out. Birsa Munda presently is being worshipped as 'Bhagaban' in the newly created State of Jharkhand. Birsa was born in the year 1874. Though lived a very short span of 25 years, he aroused the tribal mind-set and mobilised them in a little town of Chhotanagpur and was a terror for the British Rulers. True to his greatness and achievements to free the tribals, he was called 'Dharti Abba'. A visitor is overwhelmed to see his statue erected in the steel city of Rourkela as a befitting tribute to this great tribal leader who had fulfilled his mission by compelling the Britishers for the promulgation of the Chhotanagpur Tenancy Act, 1908. This legislation being an offshoot of his struggle prohibited alienation of tribal land and also provision for restoration of the alienated land. He invoked the tribals to take pride of their ancestor's patriotism and to maintain their cultural ethos. The tribals were suppressed for long by the Dikus (nontribals) and the intermediaries like Thikadars and money lenders including Zamindars tried to exploit the tribals constantly. The tribals who were for centuries the owners of the land and engaged in cultivation could not stand the trials before the British Court and the primitive practice of verbal agreement on land ownership could not be recognised by law. Finally the tribals ended themselves up as bonded labourers in their own land of origin. The level of discontentment which grew out of sustained discontentment struck at the very root of their age-old customs and practices and against this background Birsa organised his struggle to free the tribal folk from the brink of survival and he commenced his protest march on 1st October 1894 for remission of forest dues. He gave his clarion call to the tribals in his own language "*Maharani raj tundu jana oro abua raj ete Jana*". In otherwords he wanted the tribals to end the rule of the queen and re-establish their own kingdom. Birsa accordingly spearheaded the tribal movement in the region of Chhotanagpur and brought the tribal community under a single umbrella. He instigated the masses by putting examples of their ancestors and their burning patriotism which now spread like wild fire. Birsa saw to it that a gallant struggle was to be fought reawakening patriotism among his masses, which was almost at the waning state. His organisational skill, motivating the masses to regain freedom from the power grabbers like the Thikadars, Zamindars and money-lenders and restoration of full ownership rights as tillers of the soil are exemplary in the history of the tribals. After our Constitution coming into force a lot of safeguards have been bestowed upon the tribals to save them from exploitation from the affluent class. Many a legislations have been passed both by the Parliament and the State Legislatures to protect them from the land grabbing by the non-tribals. Their inherent indebtedness and alcoholism which continued to be endemic, and of late considerable tribal land has been acquired for various development projects for industrial, power and irrigation purposes leading to large scale displacement and alienation of their tenancy rights. In return the little that is given to the tribals as compensation package is grossly inadequate. This has given rise to discontentment. Birsa Munda's dream can be realised only if the tribals are restored with their land within a limited time frame by suitable enactment. It is high time that the oppression of the private money lenders should be stopped. Govt. plans such as tribal sub-plan and Integrated Tribal Development Projects (ITDP) and Modified Area Development Approach (MADA) should be implemented in right earnest under single window administration. In the words of Pandit Jawaharlal Nehru tribal people should develop along the lines of their own genius and we should avoid imposing anything on them forcibly. We should try to encourage in every way their traditional arts and culture." Then only Birsa Munda's revolt to save the tribals from the age-long repression by awakening them from the deep slumber both as a prophet and saviour can be fully realised. Birsa died in jail in 1900 at the budding age of twentyfive.

(ii) Santhal Revolt of 1855- Before the the British came to India the Santhals resided peacefully in the hilly districts of Cuttack, Dhalbhum, Manbhum, Barabhum, Chhotanagpur, Palamau, Hazaribagh, Midnapur, Bankura and Birbhum.They leaded a peaceful life by clearing the forest and also engaged themselves in hunting for subsistence. But when the British claimed their rights on the lands of the Santhals, they peacefully went to reside in the hills of Rajamahal. After some few years the Britishers and their counterparts started claiming as this new Santhal owned land theirs. The British were helped by the local Zamnidars, who were with them for their own selfish needs. The simple and honest Santhals were cheated and turned into slaves by the zamindars the money lenders who first appeared to them as mere business men who gave them loans. These loans however hard a santhal tried to repay never ended in fact through corrupt measures of the money lenders it multiplied to an amount for which a generation of the santhal family had to work as slaves. Furthermore the santhali women who worked under labour contractors were disgraced and used. This loss of freedom that once which they enjoyed turned them into rebels and finally they took oath to launch a rebellion on these axis of evil, which was done on 30th June, 1855. The attack against the British was launched by two rebel leaders, Sidhu and Kanhu Murmu. Although the rebellion was brutally suppressed, it marked a great change in the colonial rule and policy. The day is still celebrated among the Santhel community with great respect and spirit for the thousands of the Santhel martyrs who sacrificed their lives along with their two celebrated leaders to win freedom from the rule of the Jamindars and the British operatives.

Today, the government is trying to preserve forests, so cultivation shifting is limited. There is also an increase in the amount of irrigated land. As a result, other sources of income have been developed. They include such jobs as working in the tea plantations of the Northeast, working in the steel industry, or working as day labourers for local Hindu landowners. Since the Chotanagpur Plateau is the richest mineral belt in India, some of the Santhals earn wages by mining. Both men and women work to bring home adequate income for their families.

(iii) Tribals and National Movement in Orissa (1921-36)- The movement covered the Orissa Division of Orissa and Bihar which was composed of Cuttack, Puri, Balasore, Angul and Khondmals. The tribals along with the other peasants participated in the national movement in 1920s and 1930s. With the efforts of Satyavadi School which was established by Gopabandhu in 1909, the peasants and tribals of Orissa were drawn into the national movement. The peasants and tribals participated in non-cooperation movement. They implemented the "no-rent" aspect of the non-cooperation Movement. By February 1922, the peasants and tribals made inroads into the jungles and violated the forest laws. The peasants decided to stop payment of the taxes. Those who paid taxes were socially boycotted. In May 1921, the authorities promulgated Section 144 in the area and arrested the tribals. This agitated the Bhuyan tribals and about 500 of them gheraoed the Superintendent's bungalow. They demanded release of the prisoners. The arrested were tried and imprisoned and the movement gradually subsided. The Rampa rebellion of Alluri Sitaram, which was also directed against the forest rules inspired the tribals of Orissa. In 1920-30, the tribals of Gunpur launched a no-rent struggle. They violated the forest laws. The authorities found it difficult to control them. The Khonds also stopped paying rent. They attacked the police which came to arrest them. They refused to pay 'kists' (instalments) to the Maharaja of Jeypore. In the Koraput and Ganjam tracts, popular responses of the tribals to the Civil Disobedience movement grew out of the oppression and exploitation of the tribals by the landlords, money-lenders and the faulty forest laws.

Chapter 5

Politics and Religion in Modern India: The Interface

Q1. What were the main features of Indian response to British Colonialism?

Ans. British colonial rule and the impact of western culture and civilisation brought forward several categories of response among educated and concerned Indians. These responses were in evidence from 1860 onwards when British policy in India began to undergo drastic changes. Suspicion, repression, systematic exploitation of existing social distance among communities to foster divisive tendencies for political ends and strict surveillance quickly replaced pre-1858 laxity in these matters. For our purpose, however, we take up these strands of responses from 1885 when the Indian National Congress was formally established for the simple reason that some form of organised politics appeared in support of one or the other category of response.

Various Responses

These responses are as follows:

a) Modernisation of politics and social reform on the basis of rational principles of the west and through a process of gradual adaptation; loyalist, peaceful and constitutionalist in approach;

b) Radicalisation/Spiritualisation of politics, its goals and methods; mobilisation using Hindu religious symbols and emotive appeals to the virtues of self-reliance and past glory; opposition to British rule; traditional approach to social reform;

c) Loyalist, constitutionalist in political approach; mobilisation based on appeal to Muslim religion and protection of Muslim interests;

d) A political outlook in which preference for western principles of government was combined with innovative, peaceful and active methods of protest; mobilisation and action; freedom as a primary goal.

In addition, there were attempts by ***Scheduled Castes*** and ***Tribes*** to share seats and power in the emerging political order. The Marxian left forces, most prominent in the thirties, also represented an important trend of opinion and action in response to colonial subjection; a significant influence on Indian politics.

These trends found early expression in organisations and movements associated with the Brahmo Samaj, Prarthana Samaj, Arya Samaj, the Aligarh College and Sir Syed Ahmed Khan, the Ramakrishna Mission, the Theosophical Society, and Social Reform Congress. These organisations and corresponding movements stood for reform and regeneration of society or a particular community through religious or rationalist ideas. The movements were limited in scale, and were not overtly political in character. But they did underline directly or indirectly, the crucial role of religion subject of discourse or a means of social mobilisation. The lesson was not lost on the militant nationalist and the 'extremists' as they were called in Congress parlance; they represented the second strand of political response of western impact.

Moderates' Response

As long as liberal moderate leaders were in charge of the Congress (1885-1906) the effective emphasis was on western liberal principles of reason, rights, loyalty, freedom from prejudice and discrimination, national unity, gradualism and an element of elitism. Religion was considered a matter of personal concern. The liberals were democratic in their principles, but their politics never came down to the level of the people nor did they ever feel the necessity to deliberately blend religion and politics to advance political causes. As some of the Congress leaders (Tilak in Maharashtra and Aurobindo Ghosh, Surendranath Banerjee, Bipin Pal in Bengal and Lala Lajpat Rai in Punjab) entered the era of mass politics, though on a limited scale, and virtually without the approval of the liberal leadership, soon after the government proposed to partition the province of Bengal on grounds of administrative convenience in 1903, the politics of extremists and the militant nationalists could be said to have arrived on the scene.

Militant Nationalists

It was a new brand of politics—active and impatient—growing out of accumulated grievances, new developments in India, as well as a sense of disgust with the existing state of affairs. There was a new found confidence among India's industrial entrepreneurs which prompted them to demand more room for expansion. Growing volume of educated unemployment, the economic distress of the people, the combined effect of Dadabhai Naoroji's 'Poverty and the British Rule in India', R.C.Dutt's 'Economic History of British India', and William Digby's 'Prosperous British India' all contributed to increasing militancy.

Most of the militants of Bengal could be divided into strands: There were believers in the mother cult; that is, those who extolled shakti which according to them symbolised India of the past, present and future. The other group was called Vedantists who followed the preaching of Swami Vivekananda and the message of Lord Krishna. Both groups believed in the use of force or violence though it cannot be said that that was their only programme of action. An interesting comment on both these groups comes from Lajpat Rai. He said "They are neither nihilist nor anarchist. They are patriots who have raised their patriotism to the pitch of a religion. Their religion remarkably fits in with their patriotism and makes the latter indescribably intense and alive."

Again in the words of K.S. Shelvankar, Indian nationalism in the first decade of the 20th century was "romantic, mystical, aggressive riddled with fallacies but sound enough to restore the self-respect of the middle classes." It was a self-confident militancy fortified by all that was heroic and splendid in India's past."

Tilak and Aurobindo were of the belief that a quasi-religious appeal would strengthen Indian nationalism. In the second and third decades of the century, militants in Bengal broadly followed two types of activities. One was concerned with bomb throwing terrorisation and destabilisation through creating scare among army and creating the grounds for revolt and guerilla warfare. They did not believe in individual assassinations or looting.

Tilak represented another and an earlier strand of radical nationalism in Maharashtra concentrating on the systematic use of scriptural interpretations, religious festivals and festivals celebrating the heroic historical figures of the past, like Shivaji to arouse consciousness among people and to ensure enthusiastic participation in the cause of the struggle for freedom from colonial subjection and helplessness. In the words of Aurobindo "Mr. Tilak was the first political leader to break through the routine of its (Congress) somewhat academical methods, to bridge the gulf between the present and the past and to restore continuity to the political life of the nation… he used methods which Indianised the movement and brought it to the masses."

Q2. Briefly discuss the main features of Muslim separatist thought.

Ans. Many authors have pointed out that nationalism of the Maharashtra and Bengal school antagonised the Muslims of India and was a potent cause behind the rise of Muslim communal separatism. It should be pointed out here that neither of these two schools of aggressive, popular and uncompromisingly anticolonial nationalism was by intent directly against the Muslim interest or meant to hurt their sentiments. As a matter of fact, in the early stages of militant nationalism in Bengal Muslims could be found in the ranks of the militants though not in large numbers. They were also appreciative of the uncompromising hostility towards British rule and did not oppose the swadeshi movement at its inception. It is true, however, that the intense religious symbolism of both the schools was bolstered by references to Shivaji who fought against Muslim rule as well as by Bankim Chandra's novel 'Ananda Math' which hinted at a revolt and the missionary zeal which the author of the novel lent to this effort did provide grounds for uneasiness and a sense of alienation in the minds of the Muslims. Of equal importance was certainly the desperate and concerted efforts on the part of the British Indian Government to bring about a rift in the nationalist forces, by pulling back sixty two million Muslims from the fold of nationalism. Under the instructions of Lord who was the Viceroy, and Minto and egged on by the bureaucracy, a representative delegation of the Muslim upper classes was invited to be entertained by the Viceroy in his garden at Simla on October 1, 1906 to press on him the urgent need to protect the interests of the Muslim community, ostensibly against the possible onslaught of the Hindu majority. The Muslim upper classes that were to a large extent dependent on the colonial government readily obliged. The Viceroy sympathised with the claims made by the delegation for state patronage, Referring to the event, an official wrote to the Viceroy that it was "A work of statesmanship that will affect India and Indian history for many a long year." Similar views were expressed by both Morley and Minto. The same year on December 30 the All India Muslim League was founded to promote feeling of loyalty to the British government and to protect the political and other rights of Indian Muslims. In 1908 and in the following year, the League demanded the extension of representation on communal basis. In the year 1909, the Morley-Minto Reforms brought forward the divisive doctrine of minority representation on the basis of religion. The efforts of the British to divide Indians and to use one against another was given another expression through the doctrine of communal representation. It was designed to strengthen communalism, introduce political discrimination and create endless complication, especially for the Congress subjection. The Congress promptly protested against the principle of communal representations as well as disproportionate representation given to the Muslims. The Congress also pointed out in its Lahore session of 1909 that the distinctions to be brought about were "unjust, invidious, and humiliating."

In the analysis of this highly regrettable and regressive development in the struggle for freedom, proper weightage should be given to the religious symbolism of militant mischievous polices of the British government.

Main Trends of Muslim Political Thinking

If we analyse Muslim political thinking of the first two decades of the twentieth century, it will be seen that the main trends in their thinking during this period were:

a) that the Congress does not adequately represent all the nationalities and races of India;

b) that the Muslims are backward educationally and in economic standing, and constitute a minority compared to the Hindus. Therefore, in any future system of representative government and administration in India the Muslims will be swamped by the Hindus;

c) that the Muslims are different from the Hindus in their culture, moral code, social organisation, religion and therefore constitute a separate entity or nationality. In addition to the above, there were other trends of thought each of which had its ascendance and decline among the Muslims, e.g., it is the duty of Muslims to be loyal to the government, seek protection including political rights. Another trend stood for joining the fight against the British government. There was a small, though occasionally influential, nationalist group which held the opinion that the two communities should co-operate in as many spheres of actions as possible including the nationalist struggle and that Hindus should show more generosity to the requirements and sentiments of the minority community. Apart from these trends of thinking, the pan-Islamic sensitivity always played an important role in prompting the Indian Muslims to unite their ranks for action.

It will be seen that as India's political struggle unfolded, the Muslim League, which claimed to represent the entire community, and succeeded in substantially establishing its claim only after 1937, pitched its political demand on the basis of one or more of the trends of thought listed above. Sir Syed Ahamed Khan's plea for considering the Muslims as a distinct and separate nationality on grounds of "race, culture, religion, physique, social organisation, moral code, political outlook and historical associations" was a substantive formulation on which M.A. Jinnah based his 'Two Nation Theory' and the demand for partition of India in 1940. Loyalty to and dependence on the British colonial government for special favours and protection of Muslim interests resulted in separate electorates, job reservation and demand for parity of status with the majority community in political representation. From the assumed incompatibility of Muslim interests with those of the Hindus, possible intolerance and communal flare-ups that compromised the temper and strength of the anti-colonial struggle of Gandhian Congress and the Marxist parties appears to be a logical development. Similarly, pan-Islamic sentiment and religious affinity with the Muslim cause everywhere, of which Iqbal theorised so eloquently, rallied the Indian Muslims for Khilafat Non-Co-operation struggle against the government by the All India Khilafat Committee and the Indian National Congress during 1920-22. The nationalist trend of thought among the Muslims saw its ascendancy in years of the First World War. It was a trend subscribed to by some of the eminent scholars and professional men like M.A.N. Hydari, R.M. Sayani, Mohammad Ali, M.A. Ansari, Maulana Abul Kalam Azad and M.A. Jinnah. It is evident that in the thought pattern of the Muslims, the desire for peace, amity and co-operative action was present and attained temporary dominance at difference periods of the anti-colonial struggle in India. But it could not become the effective pattern for the entire period under consideration. In the following passages, we take a look at Hindu religion based political thinking as well as nationalist discourse in an attempt to ascertain the nature of the problem that existed.

Religious Imagery and Symbolism

The frequent recourse to religious imagery and symbolism to explain social and economic conditions of a people or to bring into focus political ideas and goals could come about as a result of the high degree of religious orientation of a person or a community, or more deliberately to get quick political results by motivating a people to action on the basis of emotive fervour, a sense of mission, and allegiance to a cause. To individuals or communities having such orientation, no other frame of reference except that which is based on one's religion is valid for understanding and evaluation of larger reality. This is so because to them religion is the only source of relevant knowledge. It is obvious that political discourse based on such frameworks of reference gives rise to channels of communication that are exclusive to a set of believers among whom each word / symbol having a religious connotation assumes a meaning which is unfamiliar to others. It follows that in a country with a social composition such as India's, the use of religious symbolism is bound to be seen as relevant for only one community of co-religionists. For others, it will be alienating. Such alienation is independent of secular, nationalist intentions of those who speak, write and act to produce a nationalist discourse. That is why in colonial India whenever religious ideas were linked with an essentially political discourse it resulted in Hindu or Muslim nationalism.

Q3. Briefly discuss the various aspects of the Hindu-Muslim problem.

Ans. Nehru says that the petty-bourgeois leadership of the Congress sought those remedies that suited its interests and outlooks. What Nehru said about Congress leadership was equally applicable to the leadership of the Muslim League. The Muslim League leadership was composed of rich landlords and the middle class which was scared of competition from Hindu petty-bourgeois counterparts. It has been pointed out that one of the biggest mistakes of the Congress leadership was that Congress approached only the Muslim leadership and not the Muslim people.

Another fact of the Hindu-Muslim problem comes into focus, when we consider the developments from 1920 onwards. Between 1914 and 1922 Hindu-Muslim relationship appeared to have touched a peak insofar as cordiality is concerned. International political developments, and the misery of the common people at home India, because of high prices and famines affected Muslim and Hindu feelings alike. The Lucknow Pact between the Congress and the League in 1916, and the joint participation of the Hindus and Muslims in the Khilafat Non-Co-operation Movement during 1919-22 appeared to be a real breakthrough. In retrospect, however, all this would appear to be nothing but a chance co-ordination of ideas, with no basic understanding.

The Bardoli directive by Gandhi suspending the movement quickly laid bare the lack of mutual confidence. There was an almost immediate and sharp deterioration in the communal situation which continued until 1928. The widespread sense of insult following the announcement of the white Simon Commission (1927), the prospects of another dose of constitutional reforms, and perhaps the failure of the post-Bardoli phase of politics of both sides promoted relatively simple proposals from nationalist Muslims for a more viable unity of purpose and actions between the two communities. These proposals fell through because of various objections from the Congress representatives in the All Parties Committee which was deliberating them to frame a constitution which be-acceptable to all.

In the civil disobedience movements of 1930-32, Muslim participation was not as much as it was in the Khilafat Non-Co-operation Movement. Any hope of communal amity that this may have generated quickly evaporated in the Second Round Table Conference of 1931 which Gandhi attended. The Conference deliberations did not go well for Gandhi and the Congress. The conservatives, the sectarians of both sides, encouraged by the government representatives, took charge of the proceedings at the Second Round Table Conference. Separate electorates could not be prevented, not could the Congress prevent the fragmentation of the political community it so desired for the nationalist movement and for a free India of the future. For the Congress, Gandhi, and perhaps also Nehru, this was perhaps the point where the hope of Hindu-Muslim unity was given up. There appeared to be a somewhat unexpected reluctance or a lack of enthusiasm on the part of Congress to carry on dialogues with Muslim leaders for any length of time. After the 1937 elections to provincial legislatures, the League's request for a coalition ministry in U.P. was not accepted by the Congress. At about the same time, the Muslim Mass Contact resolution of the Congress which had the important support of Gandhi and Nehru also languished for want of zealous implementation which such a proposal deserved. Soon after the demand for partition was heard, and a formal resolution demanding partition was accepted by the League in 1940.

Why this apparent resignation on the part of the congress? Why this extreme demand for partitioning the country on the part of League? Too often the Congress in blamed directly or indirectly for this failure. What appears to be more probable is that there was a mutual lack of trust which resulted in either trivial objections or demand for too many guarantees. Neither was likely to succeed in bringing about unity of purpose and action.

Q4. Briefly discuss Swami Dayanand Saraswati's political ideas. [June 06, Q 6]

Ans. Swami Dayanand Saraswati was one of those influential thinkers who drew upon traditions for the formulation of his social ideas. His main contention was that it was necessary for Indians to go back to the ideas of the Vedas.

When Dayanand was formulating his ideas and thoughts Hinduism in practice had already degenerated. It was also a time when British rule in India was consolidating itself. His basic effort was therefore directed to attaining the three objectives of Vedic revivalism, rationalism and social reform of considerable contemporary import. He was heavily critical of the West and Islam. He was equally severe on those who advocated the path of modernisation through western ideas and attitudes.

The problem India faced and their solutions, according to Dayanand, lay at the levels of philosophy, politics and society. He thought that it was necessary to inculcate a spirit of self-reliance and self-confidence in the minds of the people. Central to his thought was his attitude towards the Vedas, which he considered to be the repository of all human knowledge and wisdom. He highlighted the following aspects of the Vedas:

i) A man could communicate with God directly by rendering obedience to the divine law. He was free to obey other laws so long as they were in line with the divine laws. Dayanand felt that man can attain his pure self after examining and reviewing his position on this matter. Only after that will he be able to realise the discrepancy, thereby dissociating himself from such temporal laws which are not worthy of obedience and organise support against those laws.

ii) The freedom enjoyed by a man was equal to that enjoyed by his fellowmen.

iii) The Varnashram system provided for the full enjoyment of freedom for all, irrespective of their functional location within the social structure.

According to Dayanand, India could attain its lost glory only when the existing social weaknesses were overcome. Full of remorse, he lamented that despite the rich heritage of Indian culture, the Hindus were aping and imitating the civilisation of the west which in turn was degenerating them. He justified it by saying that India during the Vedic times had reached a level of civilisation which the west was able to attain only centuries later.

He suggested that those who had come under the influence of Islam and Christianity and had become converts, must be taken back into the Hindu fold. His prescription was that it could be done through a process of 'Shuddhi' (purification), as Dayanand felt that their unification was essential as it would inspire them to accept the Vedas and hence provide a strong and self-reliant bastion for the country. To cement the cultural homogeneity he encouraged Hindi. Only when this unification was achieved and cemented by the common bond of Hindi, would India be in a position to throw off the yoke of foreign rule. One of the biggest obstacles to national progress, however, came from within the Hindu society itself. A section of the upper caste Hindus manipulated the Varna system followed by the Hindus. As a result merit as a qualification was replaced by that of birth which in turn led to inequality and subordination of a lower occupational group (caste) to its next higher one. The Brahmins became the unchallenged and unquestioned masters of the society and Shudras were reduced to a pitiful state. The Hindus became enmeshed in elabourate rites, ceremonies, superstitions, dogmas along with idolatry, casteism, child marriage and polytheism.

Dayanand prescribed a return to the basic principles of the Varna system where birth would no longer be the sole criterion of caste status. Rather, 'Guna' (character), Karma(action) and Swabhava (nature) would be the basis of caste. He thought that caste, thus reformed could still act as a way of social reorganisation. He thus somewhat 'Secularised' the idea of caste. It naturally went a long way in challenging the domination of the hereditary upper castes, and therefore in elevating the status of the oppressed and untouchables. He denounced untouchability as inhuman and as being against vedic religion. Any Shudra, in his scheme of things could become a dwija (twice-born) provided he practiced cleanliness, character training and improvement in environment.

Q5. Examine the views of Swami Dayanand Saraswati on women, education, and democracy.

Ans. On the question of women, Dayanand was opposed to the evil practices of child marriage and enforced widowhood, which according to him did not have the sanction of Vedas. The pitiable condition of child-widows in Hindu society, which prohibited remarriage, evoked his deepest concern. He therefore, suggested 'nigoga' (a non-permanent co-habitation of widows and widowers) and later, even widow re-marriage.

For the 'prosperity of Aryavarta' (India), Dayanand's world view had a crucial place for education. An education based on moral and religious foundations and meant for all the four classes of men and women, was what Dayanand wanted. The burden of this education was, according to him, to be shouldered by the king/state. He stood for compulsory education. India's awakening he thought, hinged on this factor. He was in favour of an educational system which would emphasise on grammar; philosophy, Vedas, sciences, medicine, music and art.

The political philosophy of Dayanand Saraswati has two central ideas-somewhat contradictory to each other.

The first is the ideas of an 'Enlightened Monarchy' - a concept that he borrowed from Manusmriti - that is, a monarchy thoroughly rooted in obedience to Dharam. The second, somewhat contradictory notion is that elective representation i.e. democracy, though, there really is no contradiction since, in the Vedas, there are references to assembly and the election of the king. Stressing the principle of election, he interprets the king as a president of the assembly. Moreover, politics, for him, was inseparable from morality and he therefore argued strongly for the guidance of political leaders by spiritual leaders. Dayanand extended his democratic elective principle into the functioning and organisational structure of the Arya Samaj. He further visualised a polity which would be the embodiment of decentralisation - a vast commonwealth with the village as the unit.

The following are some of the principles out of the ten important principles of the Arya Samaj (founded in 1857), which moulded a generation of freedom fighter, especially in northern India:

i) The source of pure knowledge is God.

ii) The link between Vedas as guardians of true knowledge and an Arya Samajist is inseparable. He must assimilate its contents and make it popular among the people.

iii) Ethical justifications of actions are a must

iv) The Arya Samaj is devoted to the idea of the emancipation of the world in all its aspects.

v) Rays of knowledge must dispel the darkness of ignorance.

vi) One must leave enough for other. Man's well-being can only be identified with the collective development of his fellowmen.

Q6. Critically examine Vivekananda's views on Freedom.

Ans. Philosophy and Concept of Freedom

Swami Vivekananda was one of the most influential religious thinkers of 19th century India. His writings basically dealt with the freedom of man, its nature, norms, scope, and the idea of equating freedom with equality.

According to Vivekandanda the universe was an illusory expression of the Brahma, the creator. Maya or illusion contained virtues such as knowledge, creativity, and instinctive desires which in fact was the visible image of the Creator. 'Brahma' had immense power to hold the universe together and its influence was felt in each and every object of its creation. The difference between 'Brahma' and his creations was the finitude of virtues in its material forms. The reference here is to mankind at large. What separated man from his creator was the kind of virtues in grained in him. Each person had a different combination of unequal development of virtues. In contract, this relationship was so complete and perfect in 'Brahma' that no difference could be discerned between the triple virtues of knowledge, creativity and instinctive desires and those which lay beyond virtues. Every person with his dominant virtue therefore formed a part of the larger whole; that is, the all-encompassing, all comprehensive totality, in the form of 'Brahma'. Hence, the goal of an individual could only find its true expression in the entire humanity (the Brahman mould). Vivekananda called the attaining of the 'Brahma'ness' by man, the state of 'moksha'.

Vivekananda goes on to add that man was born free but life constrained his natural freedom making him an atomised, isolated 'individual' who was solely interested in the unrestrained pursuit of his desires and aims which would sooner or later bring him into conflict with the equivalent freedom of another, thus cancelling each other out. While the virtues of individuality were essential for the development of his creative potentialities, so also was it necessary to bring out his social nature, his spiritual self. Vivekananda felt that it was possible for both individuality and sociality to go together so that when man's individuality was restrained by his built in sociality it would provoke resistance from the others of his kind.

Since freedom was natural to human beings, limits to freedom would also have to the natural in order to retain its spontaneity. Hence such constraints on freedom will have to come from religion, since it alone could develop in human beings the relationship between individuality and sociality and raise it to a sufficiently higher place of spiritual consciousness. Vivekananda felt that certain circumstances compelled man to act in a way which inhibited the freedom of others as well as went against his won will. This could not amount to a realisation of true freedom. Thus, the purpose of limiting man's freedom should be refinement and not suppression. Religion defied any precise formulation and at times gave prominence to 'raj' relegating 'satwa' to the background for a time.

The pursuance of one's goals through freedom as well as acknowledging similar freedom for the other goes on to prove that man is essentially social, and therefore, would very much prefer living in a community. Vivekananda elucidates his thoughts with some examples. He stresses the evolution of natural communities in India as an outcome of the 'varna' system in which the 'Brahmins' and the 'Kshatriyas' were categorised under the 'raj' (creativity) and the 'Vaishyas' and the 'Shudras' under the 'Tam' category (instinctive desires). Such a categorisation finds similar reference in ancient Greece where Plato talked of three virtues: Reason, Courage, Appetite.

Vivekananda also adds that while social life in India called for emphasis on the role of specification of man as such within the society, comprehensiveness or totality was stressed by its western counterparts. Therefore with the decline of the pre-political age in India, the importance of 'man' steadily decreased while he held the centre stage in western society for long. This naturally sensitised the western society towards liberal principles such as freedom, equality, liberty etc.

Freedom, in a materially conditioned world no longer remained freedom but became a right. Freedom in his view belonged to the natural man i.e. pre-political man. Once the political order was created it became clear that freedom degenerated into rights. Since men fought for rights, not for true freedom which was a spontaneous and universal process, for instance:

PURE FORM	CORRUPT FORM
1). Varnashrama (free mobility on merit)	Transformed into hereditary, hierarchical caste system(caste status and inter-caste mobility restricted by birth)
2) True Freedom	Degenerated into fight for Rights
3) Social Man	Characterised by fight for power, patronage and supremacy; decline in position of Shudras

Thus, it was precisely due to the overriding concern for rights ('adhikarvad') that India has been reduced to its present state. According to Vivekananda 'adhikarvad' had become synonymous with 'tam' (instinctive desires) since man, even if he belonged to the privileged class could not maintain his privileges as he had been drained spiritually. So, whether a man belonged to the higher strata or the lower made no difference whatsoever as all were interested in the realisation of their material desires. Since the hierarchical caste system had rigidified the role of the individual, Indian civilisation had also become inhuman. Thus, nothing short of a cultural revolution would be India back to its blissful state of affairs. Vivekananda also set out to explain that the British as well as the previous foreign conquerors were able to establish their suzerainity over India because India lay enchained in the tentacles of 'adhikarvad'. Vivekananda said that the establishment of a British political order would not bring back India's freedom since it did not lie in their hands. He, however, urged the people of India, especially the youth, to join the nationalist struggle under the auspices of the INC against the British in the hope that it would wake up the 'sleeping nation from all sides' and perhaps free India from the vice-like grip of 'adhikarvad'. Vivekananda singled out the prevailing caste system in India as the all important cause for the present state of affairs in India. The way out would be to return to one's true religious self, and the first step towards freedom would be the emancipation of the poor by restoring dignity and respect (Ramakrishna Mission/ Mathas). He spoke at length about 'Daridra Narayan' or the 'poor as God' where service to the cause of their upliftment would raise the impoverished to a desired level of prosperity. This would then become the single most important desire of all within the folds of 'satwa', since true concern for others could only be the result of 'Truth' that bound. Vivekananda seems to be a supporter of equality since equality could bring back freedom. He also made a distinction between material and spiritual communism. One of the basic aims of the former was equal distribution of material resources.

What appealed to Vivekananda was its obsession with equality. However, in such a system man was treated as a mere functionary composed of matter itself. The latter one was favoured by Vivekananda. Its setting was pre-political communism where there would be perfect harmony between freedom and equality. Thus a communistic society appeared to be standing at both ends of the spectrum of human civilisation. Society begins as a body of individuals equal to one another, then passes through instability, disequilibrium and turmoil and finally ends up as a community of equals. However, freedom formed the core of the former while in the latter one it was absent.

Q7. Discuss Vivekananda's theory of nationalism and politics.

Ans. Concept of Nationalism and Politics: Vivekananda elabourated and developed a theory of nationalism that was based on religion. According to him, like music, each nation had "a main note, a central theme" compared to which everything else was secondary. India's theme, he identified as religion and it had to be made the backbone of national life. The future greatness of any nation could be built only on the foundations of its past greatness. Religion had been a creative force of integration and stability and it helped to retrieve and strengthen even political authority when it became weak. He thus advocated the organisation of national life on the basis of a religious ideal. But religion, in his conception was not a set of barbaric customs or a set of dogmas and rituals etc. It was rather, the realisation of certain eternal principles.

On the basis of such a theory of nationalism, Vivekananda developed a conception about the relation of nationalism to politics and power. This conception of Vivekananda's had a lot in common with the western anarchist thought which viewed politics and power anywhere with suspicion. In his conception politics and power in India were linked to western influence. Anyone who knows India, in his opinion, must understand that politics power and even intellect form a secondary consideration here. Religion, therefore, is the one dominant consideration in India "So he showered ridicule on western political institutions like 'parliaments' which he referred to as 'jokes' and party politics, as degenerate 'fanaticism and sectarianism'. Preoccupation with political power was part of a distinctly western 'vanity' and 'material tyranny'.

In line with such a conception of nationalism, politics and power, was Vivekananda's emphasis on individual morality and social change. He believed that a nation is great or good because of the innate greatness, goodness of its people and not because the state so desires and enacts legislations to that effect. Here again religion is much more important since it moulds the individualities and conduct of people—makes them good or great. In his view, the spiritual tradition of Hinduism calls for resistance to the legalised oppression embodied in the crushing tyranny of castes, kings and foreigners.

It is no exaggeration to say, therefore, that Vivekananda's ideas influenced the theory and practice of politics in India in such a decisive manner that hardly any subsequent political trend could break with the anarchist parameters set by him.

Q8. Discuss about the political carrier of Vinayak Damodar Savarkar.

Ans. Vinayak Damodar Savarkar was one of the most dynamic, outspoken and revolutionary leaders of the freedom struggle. Born on May 28, 1883 into a family of 'jagirdars in the village of Bhagpur near Nasik. Vinayak was one of four children. His elder brother Ganesh (Babarao) was to have a strong influence in his life.

Vinayak lost his parents at a very young age. The burden of the family fell on elder brother Babarao's shoulders. Vinayak spent his youth in fighting against the British Raj. As an extremely brilliant, outspoken and confident school boy, he was famous amongst his teachers and friends. In 1898 when Chaphekar brothers were hanged for assassinating the British Officer - Mr. Rand, Savarkar was just 15 years old. But Chaphekar's martyrdom impressed him and he decided to devote all his efforts for India's freedom. His patriotic spirit found an outlet when he formed an organisation called the 'Mitra Mela'. He encouraged the young, patriotic members of the Mela to strive for "absolute political independence for India" by whatever means necessary. The Mitra Mela also played an important role in Nasik during the plague by serving the victims.

After matriculation in 1901, Savarkar took admission in Fergusson College of Poona and very soon dominated campus life. He, along with a group of students began dressing alike and using swadeshi goods only. He renamed the "Mitra Mela" as "Abhinav Bharat" and declared "India must be independent". In 1905, Savarkar and his friends expressed their resentment on the partition of Bengal by lighting a huge bonfire of foreign goods.

His instigating patriotic speeches and activities incensed the British Government. As a result the British Government withdrew his B.A. degree. In June 1906 he left for London to become Barrister. However, once in London, he united and inflamed the Indian students in England against British. He believed and advocated the use of arms to free India from the British and created a network of Indians in England, equipped with weapons.

The British government arrested Savarkar in London on 13 March 1910 on some fabricated charges and he was sent to India for trial. However as the ship in which he was being taken neared Marseilles in France, Savarkar escaped and swam to the port. According to the plan his friends were to be there beforehand, but they reached late and he was caught by the French Police.

Savarkar was declared guilty and was sentenced to 50 years of 'Kala Paani' in Andaman on 24 December 1910. Life for the prisoners was very harsh and the conditions inhuman. Since 4 July 1911, he was in Andaman Jail in solitude.

Savarkar withdrew within himself, quietly and mechanically doing the tasks presented to him. He was successful in getting permission to start a jail library. With great effort and patience he taught the illiterate convicts to read and write. In 1920, Vithalbhai Patel demanded the release of the Savarkar brothers in the Central Legislative Assembly. Tilak and Gandhi also appealed for the release of Savarkar. On May 2, 1921, Savarkar was brought back to India.

Savarkar remained imprisoned in Ratnagiri Jail and then in Yeravada Jail until January 6, 1924 when he was freed under the condition that he would not leave Ratnagiri district and abstain from political activity for the next five years. On his release, Savarkar founded the Ratnagiri Hindu Sabha on January 23, 1924 that aimed to preserve India's ancient culture and work for social welfare.

Later Savarkar joined Tilak's Swaraj Party and founded the Hindu Mahasabha as a separate political party. He was elected President of the Mahasabha and toiled for building Hindu Nationalism and later joined the Quit India movement.

Savarkar was not only a fervent freedom fighter but he was also a good orator, prolific writer, a poet, a historian, a philosopher, and a social worker. His contribution to Marathi literature is immense.

Savarkar breathed his last at the age of 83. He passed away on February 26, 1966.

Q9. Discuss the political ideas of V. D. Savarkar. [June 08, Q 8]

Ans. V.D. Savarkar's political philosophy revolved around the nationhood of India. The geographical expression of Indian nationalism was equated with its cultural aspect. He intensely argued that contrary to the notion that Hinduism is system of religion followed by a larger number of Hindus, it is the 'Hindutva' or the Hindu factor residing in the minds and the conscience of Indian people that lay at the crux of India's nationhood. This 'Hindutva' thus encompassed the variety of religions indigenous to this land as also its people residing within the geographic proximity of the country. Emphasising his point Savarkar said; "...that millions of our Sikhs, Jains; Lingayats, several Samajis and others would deeply resent to be told that they—whose fathers up to the tenth generation had the blood of Hindus in their veins...had suddenly ceased to be Hindus...Hindu dharma of all shades and schools, lives and grows and has its being in the atmosphere of Hindu culture, and the dharma of Hindu being so completely identified with the land of the Hindus, this land to him is not only 'Pitribhu' (fatherland) but 'Punyabhu' (holyland also)..."

He then went on to assert that since Hindus were born and bred in Hindustan their devotion and sacrifices for the country became limitless. Thus, it would not be wrong if we equate nationalism with the cultural aspects of the Hindu community. Hindus being a majority would shape the nation. The minorities, namely the Christians, Muslims and Sikhs along with the Jains, in order to foster the growth of 'Hindutva', should co-operate freely with the majority and immerse themselves in the social, economic, and political life to the nation. While specifying the clear identity of the Hindu nation, Savarkar warned that those who have converted themselves for petty gains and advantages have no place in this sacred place. On another count he rejected the claims of Muslims and Christians as being equal partners to the cause of the nation. Political power could, then, only be shared with those whose emotional chords sentiments lay in this country and who considered this country as their holy land (Jains, Sikhs, Lingayats, Samajists, etc.). Hindus would be willing to accept the assistance provided by the minorities in the process of building a unified India so long as proportional representation and equitability was stressed even at the level of civic and political life and matter of public appointment. But he would not accept a demand for equality; preferential treatment and sharing of power as equals, though equal rights and representation and fair competition on the basis of merit should be there.

Seeing the exigencies of the political situation brewing in the country at that time, the accommodative politics of the Congress and the dominance of Pan-Islamism Savarkar delineated certain steps:

i) He extolled at length on the virtue and wisdom of Shivaji in keeping the Mughal rulers in check, to influence the Hindu community to galvanise itself against such intrusions by capturing the leadership in the leadership struggle.

ii) The process of 'Shuddhikaran' or purification to bring back ex-Hindus into the Hindu fold. He felt that it would isolate the hardliners among the non-Hindus. Such an action taken by the majority Hindu community would mean damage to India's composite national culture which also had Islamic contributions. But in the wake of increasing Muslim militancy, he saw no alternative way out.

Savarkar's position on many a matter of principle is very well laid out in the following quotation:

"A Hindu patriot worth the name cannot but be an Indian patriot as well. To the Hindus Hindustan being their fatherland and holyland, the love they bear to Hindustan is boundless. What is called nationalism can be defined as in fact the national communalism of the majority community... Thus, in Hindustan it is the Hindus, professing Hindu religion and being in overwhelming majority that constitutes the national community and create and formulate the nationalism of the nation. It is so in every country of the world... The minorities, while maintaining their separate religions and civilisations, co-operate with the majority communities and merge themselves in the common life and administration of these countries."

Q10. Briefly discuss the political thoughts of Sir Syed Ahmed Khan.

Ans. The political thought of Sir Syed Ahmed Khan can be divided into two phases: First phase spanned up to 1887, and the second phase started after 1887. During the first phase Sir Syed Ahmed Khan stood for Hindu-Muslim unity. Expressing the need for Hindu-Muslim unity he said that for "centuries we have been living on the same soil, eating the same fruit on the same land breathing the air of the same country." In 1873, he declared that religion should not be an obstacle for nationalism. He advocated separation between religious and political matters. According to him the religious and spiritual matters were not linked with mundane affairs. As a member of the Viceroy's legislative council he strove for the welfare of both Hindus and Muslims. In 1884, he made it clear that "by the word qaum, I mean both Hindus and Muslims. What we see is that all of us, whether Hindus or Muslims, lie on one soil, are governed by the one and the same ruler, have the same sources of benefit and equally share the hardships of a famine". He was not a religious bigot or Hindu baiter. He worked closely with the Hindus in the scientific society and the Aligarh British India Association. He sought donations from the Hindu Rajas and Zamindars for MAO College. Hindus were well represented in the management and the teaching community. In the initial years of the college, the Hindu students outnumbered the Muslims. Cow slaughter was banned in the college. Along with Surendra Nath Banerjee he demanded restoration of age for civil services examination from 18 to 21 years. He revived the British Association at Aligarh for his purpose.

But surprisingly during the second phase Sir Syed Ahmed Khan changed his views (in December 1887). Until then he had a background which was almost similar to that of the Congress. But during this phase imperialist thought found expression in his writings. They were based on the "emancipatory", "democratic" and "progressive" characterisation of the British rule. Unlike before he opposed the application of principles of equality. Democracy believes in the rule of the majority. In his opinion such a system would lead to the domination of the more educated and more numerous Hindus over the less educated and less numerous Muslims. He opined that the congress demand for a representative form of government would hurt the Muslims most.

He said that so long as the religious, castiest and racial differences exist in India, the western model of democracy could not be established. He felt that if the western model of democracy was adopted in India, "the large community would totally override the interests of the smaller community." This argument was carried forward by the communalists who believed in the two-nation theory. According to this theory Hindus and Muslims were two separate nations which has separate economic, political and social interests and different cultural and historical background, and who cannot from a single nation and Sir Syed Ahmed Khan was averse to the process of elections. In 1888 he said that the system of election would, put the legislation into the hands of "Bengalis or Hindus of Bengali 'type', a condition of utmost degradation" and the Muslims would become slaves of Hindus. On similar grounds, he rejected the applicability of the Self-government in India, which in his opinion would result in the "maltreatment" of Muslims. He even opposed the freedom of speech and the press. He openly supported the Lyttous attack on the freedom of press.

Sir Syed Ahmed Khan was even opposed to political agitations. He argued that they would tantamount to sedition and being anti-government or at least it would arouse the suspicion of disloyalty in the official mind. He exhorted Muslims to shun politics and remain non-political and non-agitational or politically passive and "complete a breach" between the Muslims and the Bengali-dominated Congress. He sought to establish Anglo-Muslim alliance to arouse the Muslim feelings against the Congress. He changed his views because of the influence of British officials on him. He required the help of the government for the college founded by him. The British officials took advantage of Sir Syed Ahmed Khan's desparation. They influenced his views to the extent that he became a man of ideas which were totally different from those he had cherished earlier. The MAO college principal, Theodore Beck, influenced him the most. Beck set out to counter the "evil" influence of Congress by counter posing Sir Syed Ahmed Khan against it. He worked hard to create a 'strong conservative school of thought" and "complete a breach" between the Muslims and the Bengali dominated Congress.

Sir Syed Ahmed Khan relented under the influence of Beck. Its turned against Congress. The growth of Indian revivalism and its links with the Congress intensifies his anti-congress feelings. Sir Syed Ahmed Khan had limited influence on the North-Indian Muslims. He catalysed social and educational reforms among sections of Muslims. His influence was not all pervasive. His sustained campaign against the Congress prevented the movement from going beyond Aligarh and its neighbouring districts. A large number of Muslims remained uninfluenced by him.

Q11. Discuss Mohammad Iqbal's views on nationalism and Islamic democracy.

Ans. Nationalism

In Iqbal's opinion 'nationalism provides a psychological and political justification for the nation-state. The capitalist system was responsible for its emergence. It is based on the consideration of territory. Nationalism merely attaches an individual to a territory. Patriotism, according to Iqbal is different from nationalism. Patriotism is “a perfectly natural virtue and has a place in the moral life of a man”. But nationalism according to Iqbal, is a political concept and is not in consonance with the spirit of Islam. He believed that if nationalism was accepted in its ideal form, Islam would no more remain a living factor. Nationalism “comes into conflict with Islam when it begins to play the role of the political concept demanding that Islam should recede to the background of a more private opinion and cease to be a living factor in the national life.” Iqbal, however, was not opposed to the concept of nationalism which had potentialities of uniting people of a particular country for the achievement of freedom. Such a concept of nationalism, according to Iqbal, was not inconsistent with the spirit of Islam. But religion could be a more uniting factor of people than nationalism.

He believed that the Westerners wanted to use nationalism “to shatter the religious unity of Islam to pieces”. lqbal was not opposed to the national movement but viewed nationalism as a disturbing element in politics. Iqbal felt that the modern-world had become a danger aiming at ‘de-islamisation’ of the Muslims. Nationalism was one such danger. Iqbal was afraid of the possible growth of nationalism in India. He started with the assumption that India was not a nation. Muslims and nationalism are not identical according to him because they were a minority. In the countries where Muslims are a majority, Islam has accommodated nationalism. Muslims in India constitute a cultural entity. He believed that Muslims were “bound together not by racial, linguistic, or geographical ties, but their communal brotherhood”.

He concluded that India was not a single nation. The idea of nationalism would be an obliteration of diversity, which would be most undesirable according to Iqbal. But it does not mean that Iqbal was not in favour of a United India. He felt that fusion of the communities was not possible in India. Instead, mutual ‘harmony and cooperation of different communities should be sought. To him the talk of one nation was “futile”. Iqbal’s insistence on the maintenance of distinct communities by recognising them as separate entities gave rise to Muslim Nationalism. This has made him the father of the Idea of Pakistan.

According to Moin Shakir the feeling that the Muslim League carried Iqbal’s concept of Muslim Nationalism to its logical end is not valid. He never thought of partitioning India. Instead he suggested the idea of a separate Muslim state in the North in his presidential address to the Muslim League in 1928. He demanded only “a state within a state”, and not a separate state. Moin Shakir says “Thus, Iqbal’s scheme seems to have no relation to the league demand for partition. But the league leadership exploited Iqbal’s name to give strength and sanctity to the demand for Pakistan”. Even Jinnah’s and other Muslim leaders’ attempts to rally the anti-Hindu forces in the parties under the guise of the two-nation theory was more profoundly inspired by Rahmat Ali than Iqbal.

Iqbal had great respect for non-Muslim Communities. He was opposed to the narrow and sectarian nationalism inside and outside India as the basis of polity. He had great passion for India's freedom.

Islamic democracy

He condemned the western concept of democracy and urged an acceptance of Islamic democracy. Islamic democracy did not "grow out of the extension of economic opportunity". It is based on the assumption that every human being is a centre of latent power, which can be developed by cultivating a certain type of character. In Islamic democracy emphasis is more on moral considerations. Iqbal's democracy does not belong to the people but to unique individuals. He was convinced that Islamic democracy would not degenerate into autocracy. The basis of Islamic democracy is shifted "from economic exploitation to better spiritual purification and better economic adjustment". Iqbal thought that a government based on the concept of one God would be more suitable than democracy of the western type. The cardinal principles of Islamic democracy would be: the principle of Unity of God, obedience to law, tolerance and universalism. Iqbal appreciated the adoption of democratic institutions in the western countries, but desired that they be in conformity with the basic principles of Islam. In the context of India also, Iqbal felt that western democracy was not suitable. He felt that if democracy was applied to India, the "communal oligarchy in the garb of democracy" would prevail in India. He, therefore, pleaded for the modification of the democratic institutions. He felt that a monarch guided by a religious and ethical code, may establish a government which may aim at the realisation of spiritual ideals through a human organisation.

Q12. Discuss M.A. Jinnah on nationalism, liberalism and two-nation theory.

Ans. Jinnah was initially influenced by British liberalism. He was associated with the leading Indian liberals i.e. Dadabhai Naroroji, G.K. Gokhale, S.N. Banerjee and R.C. Das. His early liberalism was a product of his English education and the influence of Indian liberals. He had uncompromising faith in the concept of nationalism, democracy, secularism and the unity of the country. The core of his liberalism consisted of liberty - civil, fiscal, personal, social, economic, political and international; moral worth and spiritual equality of each individual, dignity of human personality, impartial judiciary, cheap legal procedure and accessible courts, abolition of class privileges and abolition of power of money. His liberalism, to sum up, stood for : freedom, constitutionalism, absence of any type of fanaticism in social and political life, co-operation with the British government, constitutional form of agitation for the right cause, rule of law and the unity of country. He did not support the extra-constitutional method in an agitation. He felt that even the non-co-operation movement was a non-liberal movement.

He acknowledged the positive contribution of the British rule. He believed that developments such as the growth of feelings of patriotism and nationalism were the result of attitudes and polices of the British government. He expressed belief in the democratic institutions of local self-government. According to him government should not be above public criticism. A civilised government is known for the respect it has for public opinion. Undemocratic functioning of the government leads to revolution. But he did not grant people the right to revolt. He stood for the establishment of democracy. But he felt that it should not be given to them as a gift but as a right. Jinnah adheres to liberalism as a spokesman of the liberal middle class. According to him the middle class could not fit in with a movement of the masses. Jinnah felt that with the emergence of Gandhi and Mohammad Ali masses started taking part in national movement. He felt that the involvement of the masses affected the liberal character of the Indian National Congress. Therefore, he left the Indian National Congress, and started contradicting whatever he had said earlier. 1920 was the dividing year in the political understanding of Jinnah.

His approach to politics during the liberal phase was secular. He emphasised that the people should forget religious differences. Religion should be separated from politics. He said the co-operation of all the communities was necessary for the cause of the motherland. Only if the Indians forgot their religious differences, would they be deserving "real political franchise, freedom and self-government". He did not agree with the Aligarh movement (or Sir Syed Ahamed Khan) that if the British left India, Hindu Raj would be established. He disagreed with Gandhi on the issue of mixing religion with politics. He did not even support the Khilafat movement because it blended religion with politics.

Nationalism

According to Jinnah the emergence of nationalism in India was the result of colonial policies—integration of India into a political and social unit and spread of English education. Initially he believed in the one-nation theory. He emphasised the unity between the Hindus and the Muslims. India had a single nationality. This nationalism was a liberal and secular nationalism. He did not locate patriotism in religion. He did not consider pan-Islamism as a sound ideology for the Muslims of India. In the initial phase of his career, Jinnah strived for Hindu-Muslim harmony. He labeled the "supposed rivalry" between the Hindus and Muslims as nothing more than an attempt to divert the attention from the problems and to defer reforms. Jinnah was also impressed by Gopal Krishna Gokhale when he met him in Bombay in 1904. He was so impressed by Gokhale that he stated his ambition of becoming the "Muslim Gokhle".

According to Sarojini Naidu Jinnah emerged as the "ambassador of Hindu-

Muslim unity" at this meeting. He rejected the separate electorate proposed by the Morley-Minto reforms of 1909. But paradoxically, he became the Calcutta Council's Muslim member from Bombay. Though not the formal member of the Muslim League, Jinnah supported the resolution of the Muslim League that strove to attain a "system of self-government suitable to India" to be brought about "through constitutional means, a steady reform of the existing system of administration, by promoting national unity and fostering public spirit among the people of India, and by co-operating with other communities for the said purposes".

But after Jinnah was appointed as the permanent president of the Muslim League, his views on Hindu-Muslim unity underwent significant changes. He supported the resolution of the Muslim League which resolved to work for Swaraj, "full religious liberty" and "separate electorates".

On the eve of the Simon Commission, Jinnah rejected the Nehru report which was opposed to the system of "separate electorates". He described the Nehru report as nothing more than a statement of the "Hindu position". He had sensed even before 1923 that the Hindu Mahasabha was influencing the Congress. Jinnah made three amendments on March 27, 1927 in a conference chaired by him (in relation to the Nehru report.) i) Those were separate electorates should remain, ii) there should be reservation for Muslims to the extent one third of the seats in the central legislature and iii) residuary powers should be vested in the provinces. This proposal was rejected by the Congress in 1928. Agha Khan the founder president of the Muslim League, who presided over the All Parties Muslim Conference in 1929, wrote about Jinnah that "For him (Jinnah) there was no future in Congress or in any camp- allegedly on all India basis - which was in fact Hindu dominated. We had at last won him over to our view". At this conference Jinnah declared that the Simon Commission Report was "dead". But he spelt out what was later to become his strategy for the promotion of Pakistan.

Two-Nation Theory

Jinnah's passion for Hindu-Muslim unity was replaced by his belief in the two- nation theory after he had rejected the Nehru and the Simon Commission reports. For him Hindus and Muslims no more constituted a unity. Instead, they now came to represent two separate nations. He emphasised that Muslims were a separate "party", and he spoke the "language of a bargainer". As a chairman of the federal subcommittee he said "no constitution would work unless it gave a sense of security to the Muslims and other minorities." He began to emphasise that since Muslims are a nation, they must preserve their culture and separate identity. He said that Hindu extremism could be dangerous to Muslim existence. He ruled out the possibility of harmony between Hindus and Muslims. He called Congress a Hindu party which wanted to establish

"Hindu Raj". Establishment of democracy would mean complete extinction of Islam, he said.

Almost during the same period the Muslim students in Cambridge University were launching an agitation for the separate state of Pakistan. Rahmat Ali, a student of Cambridge University founded Pakistan National Movement. He was inspired by the poet Iqbal. He wrote a pamphlet -"Now or Never : Are We to live or perish?" He strove for the formation of Pakistan which would supposedly include the following regions-Punjab, N.W. F.P. (Afghanistan), Kashmir, Sindh and Baluchistan. The Muslim League met on March 4, 1934 in New Delhi for establishing unity in the party. This terrorised the pro-British elements. Though Jinnah supported the communal award, which was opposed by the Congress, he abstained from voting on it.

Jinnah continued to ignore Rahmat Ali's call for Pakistan and his angry attack even in 1937. But he changed his position during the election campaign of 1937.

He further emphasised that "historical" and "cultural" differences existed between the Hindus and Muslims. He held that Hinduism and Islam were "two entirely distinct and separate civilisations". They belong to different religions, philosophies, social customs and cherish two distinct bodies of literature. They neither inter-marry nor do they interdine. They belonged to two different societies. Jawaharlal Nehru did not acknowledge the existence of the Muslim League during the election campaign in 1937. Jinnah reacted to this attitude of Nehru and said, "there is a third party (a part from the Congress and the government) in this country and that is the Muslims". He asked the Congress "to leave Muslims alone". Jinnah complained at the All India Muslim League session held in October 1937 that the Congress discriminated against the Muslim League in the Hindu dominated areas. He made building up of a mass party of Muslims one of his priorities during 1938 and 1939. The membership of the Muslim League multiplied manifold between the Lucknow session of 1937 and the Lahore session of 1940. He still strove for an India which was independent, and where the interests of the Muslims would be safeguarded. He denounced Congress for imposing "Bande Matram (Hail to the Mother)". He compared the Muslims of India with "the Negroes of Africa" and "Slaves" in January 1938. In April 1938, he labeled Congress as a "Hindu Party". On March 20, 1940 Jinnah demanded the division of Indian into "autonomous national states". But he did not use the word Pakistan. But after Jinnah finished speaking at Lahore, the historic Pakistan resolution was hammered. Jinnah said that the Hindu leaders of Hindu Mahasabha wanted to treat Muslims "like Jews in Germany". Jinnah considered the "Quit India" demand as an attempt to "force Mussalmans and surrender to Congress terms of dictation."

Jinnah maintained that "Muslims cannot divorce their religion from politics….. Hence, Hindu-Muslim unity or nationalism, signifying homogeneity between them in all non-religious matters, is unimaginable". Therefore, a separate homeland for Muslims was demanded. Jinnah exhorted the Muslims to prepare for the battle for getting Pakistan in Baluchistan in July 1948. In the 1940s he reminded the Muslims of the discrimination they faced in the earlier decades. Jinnah said in his message on the Pakistan Day on March 23, 1944:
"Pakistan is within grasp…. Insha-Allah, we shall win."
Jinnah told a public meeting in Ahmedabad in October 1945 "Pakistan is a question of life and death for us". He campaigned in the 1945elections on the issue.
On June 20, 1947, the members of the Bengal legislative Assembly voted for the partition of their province by a large majority. Sind did it later.
The 'Partition Council' was formed.
The birth of separatist Muslim Nationalism had taken place much before Jinnah started advocating it. But before Jinnah supported it, the character and content of separate Muslim Nationalism had largely been cultural. Jinnah made it a political weapon for the creation of Pakistan - a new state. He successfully gave an ideological and religious tinge to the two-nation theory.
Jinnah's two-nation theory even distorted his earlier concept of liberal democracy. His new concept of democracy was limited to his idea of separate homeland for Muslims. He did not deny the spiritual aspects of democracy in Islam. He opposed the application of the western type of democracy in India. According to him, India was not fit for democracy. He said the majority of the people are "totally ignorant, illiterate, untutored, living in old superstitions of the worst type, thoroughly antagonistic to each other, culturally and socially… It is impossible to work a democratic parliamentary government in India". Majority rule will become tyrannical in India. Muslims will suffer in economic, social, cultural and political aspects of life. He said that the joint-electoral system would lead to the enslavement and virtual extinction of the minority community. This aspect of the Aligarh movement, which was rejected by Jinnah earlier, influenced the later phase of his politics and thought.

Q13. Write in brief about political career of Abul Kalam Azad.

Ans. Maulana Abul Kalam Azad was born on November 11, 1888 in Mecca, Saudi Arabia. A leading figure in India's struggle for freedom, apart from being a noted writer, poet and journalist, he adopted the pen name Azad (Free). In his childhood, he had a traditional Islamic education, alongwith training in subjects like mathematics, philosophy, world history and science by tutors at his home. Through his own efforts, he learnt English, alongwith Western philosophy, history and contemporary politics. He visited countries like

Afghanistan, Iraq, Egypt, Syria and Turkey. He opposed the partition of Bengal in 1905. He established an Urdu weekly newspaper in 1912 named Al-Hilal. It was consequently banned in 1914, following which he started a new journal, the Al-Balagh.

Abul Kalam Azad

He published many works criticising the British rule and advocating self-rule for India. It was as a leader of the Khilafat movement that he became close to Mahatma Gandhi. He became the youngest President of the Indian National Congress in 1923.He always supported the cause of Hindu-Muslim unity and opposed the demand for a separate Muslim state of Pakistan. After India's independence, he served as the first Minister for Education.

He served in the Constituent Assembly formed to draft India's constitution and was elected to the Lok Sabha in 1952 and in 1957. In 1956, he served as president of the UNESCO General Conference in Delhi. His exhaustive book on India's freedom struggle titled India Wins Freedom was published in 1957. This great leader passed away on February 22, 1958

Q14. Examine the thoughts of Abul Kalam Azad on nationalism and democracy.

Or

Comment on Abul Kalam Azad's romantic phase of Ideas.[June 09, Q 9]

Ans. Nationalism

According to Azad Indian nationalism was neither Hindu nor Islamic. This was secular and was a synthesis of Hindu and Muslim cultures. He became an advocate of Islam in liberal and Islamic sense. We no longer remained hostile to the western civilisation. He said that religion and reason were not opposed to each other. There are two aspects of Azad's concept of nationalism. They are first, his attitude towards the British, second, his attitude towards his countrymen. Up to 1905, Azad was not anti-British. He was influenced by Sir Syed Ahmed Khan, though he did not subscribe to the philosophy of Aligarh movement. Afterwards he got disillusioned with the British and became anti-imperialistic. Till the end of the Khilafat movement though Azad emphasised the Hindu-Muslim unity, he was still under the influence of Pan-Islamism. He still wanted a separate party for the Muslims. After he came in contact with Gandhi following the Jalianwalabagh tragedy and the Khilafat movement, he emphasised that the Hindus and Muslims formed a single nationality. He felt that nationalism could be a strong force, if it was liberated from religious orthodoxy and narrow-mindedness. Gandhi said Azad's faith in nationalism was "as robust as his faith in Islam". Azad believed a unity between Hindus and Muslims would bring nationalism in India. He was opposed to the partition of India on religious grounds. Unlike the liberals, he believed that if constitutional means were not successful in achieving their political purpose, violence could be always taken recourse to. Nonviolence for him was a matter of policy, not creed.

Democracy

He supported democracy during the **"romantic" phase** of Al-Hilal. He remained a firm supporter of democracy even after he abandoned "romanticism". He preached two different types of views during the "romantic" and "post-romantic" phases of his ideas. In the first phase, he did not regard democracy as a way of life. He considered only Islam as a true and perfect religion. The Prophet was considered the personification of all values beneficial to mankind. He held that unity and sovereignty of god and establishment of supremacy of righteous order are the real elements of democracy. Unity of God implied the sovereignty of Islam, which aimed at abolishing the sovereignty of man. To him democracy is based on the will of people, characterised by tolerance, equality and liberty. Liberty was an essential prerequisite for the development of individuals in every society. He said the absence of liberty resulted in slavery which was against the tenets of Islam. He, however, said in case of war liberty of a person could be curtailed. He said unrestricted liberty is dangerous. Liberty like Islam demands faith and action. That is why he supported the Indian National Movement. Azad said Islam recognises the value of equality. He said Islam "swept off racial and national distinctions and showed the world at large that all human beings held an equal rank and all possessed equal rights. It proclaimed that excellence did not lie in race, nationality or colour. It was only righteous action that counted and the noblest among man was he who did his work most righteously." Islamic conception of equality is thus not mechanical but spiritual. Sovereignty of the Prophet and the Khalif constituted the perfect conception of equality, and it only could take the shape of the whole nation's free will, unity, suffrage and elections. That is the reason why the sovereign or president of a republic is designated Khalif. Khalif literally means nothing more or less than representation. It gives full rights to women and puts them at par with men. Islam is superior to western ideologies. Western system of equality is not real. Islamic way of life is full of equality—economic and political as well as social.

Chapter 6

Gandhism: Evolution and Character

Q1. What do you understand by Gandhi's Swaraj?

Ans. Definition and Meaning

Gandhi defined swaraj briefly as self-rule and self-restraint, or in the spirit of the Brhadarannyaka Upanishad, as the autonomy of the moral self, referring to who has acquired mastery over the senses. The word "swaraj", Gandhi writes, "is a sacred word, a Vedic word, meaning self-rule and self-restraint, and not freedom from all restrain, which 'independence' often means." Swaraj, so defined, he said, is an 'all-satisfying goal for all time.' The major ingredients or constitutive processes of swaraj are:

(i) decentralised participatory democracy and **(ii)** the spiritualisation of politics and economics or, in other words, the integration of politics and economics with the principles of satya and ahimsa. To quote Gandhi:

Let there be no mistake about my concept of swaraj. It is complete independence of alien control and complete economic independence. So at one end you have political independence, at the other the economic. It has two other ends. One of them is moral and social, the corresponding end is Dharma. i.e. religious in the highest sense of the term. It includes Hinduism, Islam, Christianity, etc., but is superior to them all. You may recognise it by the name of Truth that pervades everything and will survive all destruction and all transformation. Moral and social uplift may be recognised by the term we are used to; i.e. non-violence. Let us call this the square of swaraj, which will be out of shape if any of its angles is untrue. In the language of the congress, we cannot achieve this political and economic freedom without truth and non-violence, in concrete terms without faith in God and hence moral and social elevation.

In his Hind Swaraj, after commending Mazzini's people-centred (rather than king-centred) concept of Italian nationalism, Gandhi clarified that his goal for India was not the mere transfer of the reins of government from British rulers into the hands of the Indian elite but the securing of self-rule by the "millions of India". Real swaraj, he wrote in 1925, "will come not by the acquisition of authority by a few but by the acquisition of the capacity by all to resist authority when it is abused. In other words, swaraj is to be obtained by educating the masses to a sense to their capacity to regulate and control authority."

Swaraj or Participatory Democracy

In place of centralised, representative government, the swaraj of the masses would mean a system of decentralised participatory democracy. "True democracy," Gandhi wrote, "cannot be worked by twenty men sitting at the Centre. It has to be worked from below by the people of every village." In fact, Gandhi likened the swarajist social set-up to an "oceanic circle" of village republic. He writes: In this structure composed of innumerable villages, there will be ever-widening, never-ascending circles. Life will not be a pyramid with the apex sustained by the bottom. But it will be an oceanic circle whose centre will be the individual always ready to perish for the village, the latter ready to perish for the circle of villages, till at last the whole becomes one life composed of individuals, never aggressive in their arrogance but ever humble, sharing the majesty of the oceanic circle of which they are integral units.

Swaraj and Freedom

Gandhi also spoke of swaraj in terms of "freedom for the meanest of our countrymen" and "the welfare of the whole people." In practical terms, this would mean, he said, "truthful relations between Hindus and Mussalmans, bread for the masses and removal of untouchability." "Hind Swaraj", he said in 1931, "is the rule of all the people, is the rule of justice."

Q2. Discuss Gandhi on modern civilisation.

Ans. Gandhi condemned modern civilisation not because it was Western or scientific but because it was materialistic and exploitative. Speaking to the Meccano Club, Calcutta, in August 1925, he said: Do not for one moment consider I condemn all that is Western. For the time being I am dealing with the predominant character of modern civilisation, do not call it Western civilisation and the predominant character of modern civilisation is exploitation to the weaker races of the Earth. The predominant character of modern civilisation is to dethrone God and enthrone Materialism. I have not hesitated to use the word 'Satan'. I have not hesitated to call this system of Government under which we are labouring 'Satanic'.

On Science and Machinery

On several occasions Gandhi clarified that he was not opposed to science of machinery as such. Far from opposing the progress of science, he admired the modern scientific spirit of the West and maintained that the world needs "the marvelous advances in science and organisation that the Western nations have made." One of the basic errors of the Western, post-Enlightenment modernity, he said, was the exploitation of "the weaker races of the earth" and the destruction of the "lower order of creation" in the name of science and humanism. Modern civilisation, Gandhi said, is based on a faulty concept or model of man as materialistic or body-centred, limitless consumer of utilities. Such a view of man places sensual or materialistic wants over spiritual or moral values. It regards the individuals as wholly independent or self-centred atoms with no moral or spiritual bonds or obligation.

Acting as infinite consumers of utilities, modern or rather modernist persons resort to the mechanised or industrial production of articles which are meant, not for immediate use, but for exchange between town and village and between metropolis and colony. In this exchange, the town and metropolis gain at the expense of the village and the colony. "industrialisation on a mass scale", wrote Gandhi, "will necessarily lead to passive or active exploitation of the villagers as the problems of competition and marketing come in." On another occasion, Gandhi wrote, "Europeans pounce upon new territories like crows upon a piece of meat. I am inclined to think that this is due to their mass-production factories." Similarly, in his Hind Swaraj, he wrote:

When I read Mr. Dutt's Economic History of India, I wept; and as I think of it again, my heart sickens. In is machinery that has improverished India. It is difficult to measure the harm that Manchester has done to us. It is due to Manchester that Indian handicraft has disappeared.

Gandhi says that modern civilisation seeks to increase our "bodily comforts" through better houses, better clothes, faster modes of travel and transport, mechanized production, etc. These however have failed to bring happiness to the people. On the contrary, they have brought about newer diseases, dehumanisation of the workers, more efficient and large-scale means of the diseases, dehumanisation of the workers, more efficient and large-scale means of the destruction of life, etc. "Formerly", writer Gandhi, "men were made slaves under physical compulsion. Now they are enslaved by temptation of money and of the luxuries that money can buy. There are now diseases of which people never dream before...This civilisation takes note neither of morality nor of religion...Civilisation seeks to increase bodily comforts, and it fails miserably even in doing so." Divorced from ethics or morality, the modern self or the individual is left to the play of self-interest, greed, competition, exploitation, brute force, violence, etc. Modern man feels no moral or spiritual restraints in conquering or colonizing other peoples. Imperialism and fascism were to Gandhi the mere political expressions of the satanic character of modern civilisation.

On separation of morality and politics

The modern exorcism of morality or spiritually from politics is a central target of Gandhi's attack. The moderns or liberals dichotomize or separate the private sphere from the public or political sphere of the life of the individual. Morality or public sphere is supposed or expected to operate, not according to any moral or spiritual values, but according to the criteria of expedience or pragmatism. In this way, modern political institutions and political representatives or agents are supposed to be morally neutral "procedural" or "methodical" functionaries or instruments.

According to Gandhi, this modern dissociation of politics from morality or spirituality enables the rich and the strong to manipulate the machinery and procedures of politics and government to their further advantage at the expense of the poor ant the weak. The so-called neutrality of the state and the legal fiction of equality before the law, he said, only serve to perpetuate social and economic inequalities. Often these inequalities and social divisions are promoted and even created by politicians, bureaucrats and lawyers. Criticising the modern profession of law, Gandhi pointed out that lawyers manufacture and promote quarrels among the people rather than resolve them. "It is within my knowledge that they (lawyers) are glad when men have disputes. Petty pleaders actually manufacture them." Similarly, says Gandhi, the colonial state, which professes to be neutral as regard social divisions and caste-discriminations, actually upholds and strengthens those divisions and discriminations.

On Parliament

Turning to the central institution of modern representative democracy, viz. the parliament, Gandhi compared it to a sterile woman in so far as it acts only under pressure from outside forces and not on its own accord. He also compared it to a prostitute since it is always "under the control of ministers who change from time to time". Further, he writes:

It is generally acknowledged that the members (of parliament) are hypocritical and selfish. Each thinks of his own little interest. It is fear that is the guiding motive.....Members vote for their party without a thought. Their so-called discipline binds them to it. If any member, by way of exception, gives an independent vote, he is considered a renegade….The Prime Minister is more concerned about his power than about the welfare of Parliament. His energy is concentrated upon securing the success of his party. His care is not always that Parliament should do right…If they are considered honest because they do not take what are generally known as bribes, let them be so considered, but they are open to subtler influences. In order to gain their ends they certainly bribe people with honours. I do not hesitate to say that they have neither real honesty nor a living conscience.

According to Gandhi, the evil effects of the exorcism of morality from modern civilisation is seen clearly in the case of modern medicine, which, instead of removing disease actually promotes it. He writes:

I overeat, I have indigestion. I got to the doctor, he gives me medicine. I am cured. I overeat again, I take his pills again. Had I not taken the pills in the first instance, I would not have overeaten again. The doctor intervened and helped me to indulge myself.

Q3. What do you understand by Purna Swaraj?

Ans. According to Gandhi, under swaraj, the people would "shun the evils of capital" and would strive to attain "a juster distribution of the products of labour." Swaraj, he said, will not be purna swaraj until the poor are enabled to enjoy the necessities and amenities of life" in common with those enjoyed by the princes and the monied men." He defined purna swaraj as that swaraj which is "as much for the prince as for the peasant, as much for the rich land owner as for the landless tiller of the soil, as much for the Hindus as for the Mussalmans ..." Purna swaraj, thus understood, merges into sarvodaya, which is the topic of the next unit of this course. Gandhi also referred to his ideal of Purna Swaraj as Rama Rajya, Khudai Raj, or the Kingdom of God on Earth. He explained its meaning as follows:

... politically translated it is perfect democracy in which inequalities based on possession and non-possession colour, race or creed or sex vanish. In it, land-and state belong to the people, justice is prompt, perfect and cheap and, therefore, there is freedom of worship, speech and press-all this because of the reign of the self-imposed law of moral restraint.

Purna Swaraj: The Economic Dimension

According to Gandhi, besides its moral and political dimensions, Purna Swaraj or Rama-Rajya has also an economic dimension, which means "entire freedom from the British capitalists and capital, as also their Indian counterpart. In other words, the humblest must feel equal to the tallest. This can take place only by capital or the capitalists sharing their skill and capital with the lowliest and the least."

Q4. What do you know about Hind swaraj of Gandhi?

Ans. Gandhi put forward his political ideas in several of his speeches and writings, the most notable of which is the booklet, 'Hind Swaraj', which he wrote in Gujarati on board S.S. Kildonan Castle during his return voyage from London to South African 1909. It was first published in two parts in Indian Opinion, a weekly edited and published by Gandhi and it refers to Indian anarchists living in London. The Indian anarchists stood for using terrorist methods against the foreign rulers of India. Once freed from foreign rule, India, according to the anarchists, was to pursue the same western model of modernity. Gandhi's objective in writing Hind Swaraj was to condemn both the cult of violence and the claims of superiority of modern civilisation.

The three recurrent themes in Hind Swaraj are: colonial imperialism, industrial capitalism, and rationalist materialism.

Colonial imperialism: Gandhi categorically insisted that "the English have not taken India; we have given it to them. They are not in India because of their strength: but because we keep them". He was one of the earliest to realise that colonialism was something to be overcome in our own consciousness first. Unless this 'Intimate Enemy' was exorcised and exiled, unless we addressed this 'Loss and Recovery of Self Under Colonialism', we would always be a people enslaved by one power or another, whether foreign or native. Certainly, Gandhi would not want to exchange an external colonialism for an internal one, a white sahib for a brown one, or compensate the loss of 'Hindustan' with 'Englistan'. British India colonialism was first justified by a supposedly Christianising mission, but very soon this was articulated in terms of a civilising one. In rejecting this modern civilisation, Gandhi is subverting the legitimacy of the colonial enterprise at its core. For there could be no colonialism without a civilising mission since it could hardly be sustained in India by brute force.

Industrial capitalism: Gandhi sees capitalism as the dynamic behind colonial imperialism. Lenin too had said as much, and like Marx, Gandhi's rejection of capitalism is based on a profound repugnance to a system where profit is allowed to degrade labour, where the machines are valued more than humans, where automation is preferred to humanism. It was this that moved Gandhi to his somewhat hyperbolic claim: "Machinery is the chief symbol of modern civilisation; it represents a great sin". However, by 1919 his views on machinery do begin to change right up to 1947, as he gradually comes to concede some positive aspects like time and labour saving, even as he warns against the negative ones of concentrating wealth and displacing workers. He was acutely sensitive to how machinery can dehumanise and technology alienate, and he extends his critique to the professions of medicine and law. The poor hardly benefit from these professional services, though they are often their victims. He backs up his criticism of these professions in Hind Swaraj with a later suggestion for their nationalisation.

Rationalist materialism: Technology is but the expression of science, which in modern civilisation becomes an uncompromising rationalism. For Gandhi this is but a dangerously truncated humanism. His incisive remark is much to the point: "Just as dirt is matter misplaced, reason misplaced is lunacy! I plead not for the suppression of Reason, but for a due recognition of that in us which sanctifies reason itself'. Certainly, Gandhi is right in insisting on the unreasonableness of not setting any limits to reason.

More recently a post-modern world has emphasised the aggressive and destructive march of this 'age of reason'. However, Gandhi would test his faith with his reason, but he would not allow his reason to destroy his faith. What makes such technological rationalism even more destructive in Gandhi's view, is its flawed materialism. That is, the negation of the spiritual, the transcendent, or in other words, the denial of a religious worldview.

For Gandhi truth, was much more than could be grasped by science or reason. For him there was a reality beyond that perceived by the senses. It is this transcendent reality that gave meaning and value to our present one. In this Gandhi is very much in the mainstream of Hindu tradition. Indeed, most religious traditions would be similarly sensitive to such a transcendent world, even when it is not perceived as wholly other-worldly. In a more secular world today we may not be sympathetic to such a worldview. And yet a materialism that is deterministic leaves no scope for human freedom and hope. Gandhi emphasises this reaching out to a beyond, that gives this freedom and hope its dynamism and a reach beyond its grasp.

Q5. Define Satyagraha? What are the principles on which Satyagraha is based?

Ans. Satyagraha is fundamentally a way of life, which guides the modes of political activism undertaken by the followers of its principle (or satyagrahis). On a personal front it involves a life committed to truth, chastity, non-attachment and hard-work. On the political front, satyagraha involves utilisation of non-violent measures to curb the opponent, and ideally to convert him rather than to coerce him into submission. A satyagrahi wants to make the evil-doers see the evil that they are indulging into, and realise their injustice. In an ideal way, it involves transforming them into acceptance of the right, and if that fails to come around, then at least to stop them from obstructing the right. Picketing, non-cooperation, peaceful marches and meetings, along with a peaceful disobedience of the laws of the land were typical modes of resistance adopted by satyagraha.

Reverence to the opposition was one of the unique features of the satyagraha preached by Gandhi. Under no circumstance, should the opposition or the flag of the opposition be insulted in a Satyagraha movement. Resistance on the part of the authorities would be expected, but a true Satyagrahi had to bear all hardships, including physical assault with patience, not ever stooping to anger, and to defend the faith even at the cost of life. Gandhi believed that the Satyagrahis had to be extremely strong in inner strength and moral courage in order to do that, and also realised that could not be achieved unless the Satyagrahis maintained a pure and simple life. He made his own life a veritable example of his teachings, and also turned his ashram at Sabarmati as a haven for individuals who chose to maintain a life based on his teachings. Non-violence of all forms were to be resisted and refrained from. Abuses and swearing were strictly prohibited and all forms of abstinence from sensual pleasures were highly advocated. Hard labour was an integral part of Satyagraha. Everyone was meant to work for his or her food and the clothes. Khadi developed as the very mark of nationalism, and simple life became the order of the day. Absolute secularism and eradication of every shade of untouchability were also distinct characteristics of satyagraha. It was only in such a way, Gandhi believed, that the Indians would be strong enough to tread the paths of a truly non-violent revolution.

Principles for Satyagrahis

Gandhi envisioned satyagraha as not only a tactic to be used in acute political struggle, but as a universal solvent for injustice and harm. He felt that it was equally applicable to large-scale political struggle and to one-on-one interpersonal conflicts and that it should be taught to everyone.

He founded the Sabarmati Ashram to teach satyagraha. He asked satyagrahis to follow the following principles:

i) Nonviolence (ahimsa)

ii) Truth — this includes honesty, but goes beyond it to mean living fully in accord with and in devotion to that which is true

iii) Non-stealing

iv) Chastity (brahmacharya) — this includes sexual chastity, but also the subordination of other sensual desires to the primary devotion to truth

v) Non-possession (not the same as poverty)

vi) Body-labour or bread-labour

vii) Control of the palate

viii) Fearlessness

ix) Equal respect for all religions

x) Economic strategy such as boycotts (Swadeshi)

xi) Freedom from untouchability

On another occasion, he listed seven rules as "essential for every Satyagrahi in India":

a) must have a living faith in God

b) must believe in truth and non-violence and have faith in the inherent goodness of human nature which he expects to evoke by suffering in the satyagraha effort

c) must be leading a chaste life, and be willing to die or lose all his possessions

d) must be a habitual *khadi* wearer and spinner

e) must abstain from alcohol and other intoxicants

f) must willingly carry out all the rules of discipline that are issued

g) must obey the jail rules unless they are specially devised to hurt his self respect

Rules for Satyagraha Campaigns

Gandhi proposed a series of rules for satyagrahis to follow in a resistance campaign:

i) harbour no anger

ii) suffer the anger of the opponent

iii) never retaliate to assaults or punishment; but do not submit, out of fear of punishment or assault, to an order given in anger

iv) voluntarily submit to arrest or confiscation of your own property

v) if you are a trustee of property, defend that property (non-violently) from confiscation with your life

vi) do not curse or swear

vii) do not insult the opponent

viii) neither salute nor insult the flag of your opponent or your opponent's leaders

ix) if anyone attempts to insult or assault your opponent, defend your opponent (non-violently) with your life

x) as a prisoner, behave courteously and obey prison regulations (except any that are contrary to self-respect)

xi) as a prisoner, do not ask for special favourable treatment

xii) as a prisoner, do not fast in an attempt to gain conveniences whose deprivation does not involve any injury to your self-respect

xiii) joyfully obey the orders of the leaders of the civil disobedience action

xiv) do not pick and choose amongst the orders you obey; if you find the action as a whole improper or immoral, sever your connection with the action entirely

xv) do not make your participation conditional on your comrades taking care of your dependents while you are engaging in the campaign or are in prison; do not expect them to provide such support

xvi) do not become a cause of communal quarrels

xvii) do not take sides in such quarrels, but assist only that party which is demonstrably in the right; in the case of inter-religious conflict, give your life to protect (non-violently) those in danger on either side

xviii) avoid occasions that may give rise to communal quarrels

xix) do not take part in processions that would wound the religious sensibilities of any community

Q6. Illustrate the western Influences on M.K. Gandhi. [Dec 08, Q 7]

Ans. Western Influences on Gandhi

Gandhi's critique of modern civilisation was influenced by the writings of some Western romantic thinkers. Edward Carpenter's Civilisation: Its Cause and Cure greatly influenced Gandhi's critical attitude towards modern science and medicine. Similarly, Leo Tolstoy's The Kingdom of God is within You exerted a tremendous influence on Gandhi's views on the repressive character of the modern state and his commitment to non-violent resistance. Gandhi acknowledged that reading Tolstoy made him realise the "infinite possibilities of universal love" and made him a "firm believer in ahimsa". Gandhi and Tolstoy corresponded with each other. In his last letter to Gandhi, Tolstoy, wrote that the former's satyagraha movement in South Africa was a new mode of emancipatory struggle by the oppressed. Gandhi's activity in Transvaal seemed to Tolstoy to be "the most essential work, the most important of all the work now being done in the world." Gandhi was also influenced by Henry David Thoreau's writings. In Thoreau's essay, "On the Duty of Civil Disobedience", Gandhi found confirmation of his views on the coercive features of the state on the individual's obligation to his own conscience."From Thoreau and Ruskin". Gandhi wrote' "I could find out arguments in favour of our fight."

John Ruskins Unto This Last was yet another source of inspiration for Gandhi. 'Buskin's moralistic critique of the so-called science of the political economy of self-interest brought about "an instantaneous and practical transformation" of Gandhi's life. He translate Ruskin's book, entitling; it Sarvodyas. From it, Gandhi learned three lesions, viz. **(i)** that the good of the individual is contained in the good of all **(ii)** that a lawyer's work has the same value as the barber's in as much as all have the same right of earning their livelihood from their work; and **(iii)** that a life of labour, i.e., the life of the tiller or the soil and the handicraftsman is the life worth living.

Q7. Write a note on the followings:-

(i) Gandhi on Hinduism

Or

Discuss Gandhi's theory of Social Change. [Dec 09, Q 4]

(ii) Village Panchayat

Ans. (i) Gandhi on Hinduism- Gandhi accepts the four stages of life which is the underlying principle of any normative order. Everybody despite one's caste position has a right to practice these stages of life. In his scheme, second and third stages are important stages. Second stage, when one gets involved in the social and biological production which helps in continuation of a civilisation. Third stage, when one takes one's actions beyond the family boundary and enters into public domain. It helps everybody to contribute to the betterment of society. Every citizen takes to the public domain, and then politics become everybody's profession. Gandhi was against the professional politicians whose encouragement corrupts public life. If every citizen is concerned about public activities, then the political order does not collapse. Management of individual, community and society become easier. Centralisation of political power in a small group cannot help in creating popular and participatory democracy. Moreover, democratic institutions work efficiently only when technological needs of a society remain under human control. Technological advancement might create an alienated being which creates a psychological basis for doing violence. Technological advancement may be the basis of creating unemployment and in the end result, it creates poverty. Unemployment and poverty are the root causes of economic unit; a person cannot be an active social unit. Technological advancement creates the gap between the poor and the rich, which is against the basic principles of a Sarvodaya society.

Role of Industrialisation

Sarvodaya society has space for industrialisation and technological advancement, but it should not go beyond human control, nor it should destroy the ecological basis of a society. Industrialisation and urbanisation should not disturb the village society which is the soil of India. Industrialisation leads to concentration of economic power which cuts at the roots of democracy. Concentration of economic and political power helps a small minority who can sabotage the institutional basis of a democracy. Gandhi opposes the centralisation of economic power in rural India. Distribution of land is an economic and political programme for Gandhi.

Role of Education

Education remains a major means for achieving a Sarvodaya society. A Sarvodaya social order can be created by giving **'nai talim'.** Gandhi was favouring compulsory primary education. Gandhi was in support of basic education it a critical look of own and a deeper understanding of the problems of a society which is the responsibility of a Pedagogic system. A better society can be created only by locating the defects of a society. Social defects in the social organisation can be noted with the help of education. Practice of untouchability, division of labour on the basis of caste system has no place in a Sarvodaya society. Basic education creates love for manual labour which help a child to question the division of labour on the basis of caste system. Acquiring some skill to make somebody an effective element of a society is possible through education. Creating community awareness which becomes the basis of a Sarvodaya society is done through education. Education plays a vital role in mediating between individual consciousness and community consciousness. Unless community consciousness is created, collective energies can not be channelised in a creative manner.

Theory of Social Change

This leads us to the point that Gandhi has an evolutionary concept of social change. Logic of historical development convinced him that the process of social change is very slow. Stages of history are the connected points in a chain. Slow change in a society does not lead him to pessimism. Gandhi was very optimistic that goodness of an individual would compel him to do something good for the society. Something good can be done by an individual only by knowing the wrong things of a society. Individual, social groups, community play a crucial role in restructuring a society which breeds less tension and violence. Gandhi recognises the concept of class and the role of violence in changing a society. In his thought he was trying to minimise their role. Gandhi like Buddha understands the structural basis of violence in Indian society. Conflict and violence cannot bring a better society. Gandhi's reaching of nonviolence, and Satyagrah has a Buddhist philosophical underpinning. At the same time, he allows the individual to take initiative. Social groups can get activated and collective will can bring social change. As a result a non-violent social order can be created only if there are no structural basis of violence. Gandhi found that in the Indian society, there are multiple bases for violence. Economic, caste, religion all can erupt into violent politics. Gandhi by recognising material and non material basis of violence contributed to the body of human knowledge.

(ii) Village Panchayat

Gandhi's sarvodaya centres around the small republic where the mass of people arrange their affairs without depending on the state. In Gandhi's scheme, village panchayat plays a crucial role in policy making. Village panchayat consists of all the ablest youths from all castes and religions. In a face to face society, people have an informal arrangement for the management of their affairs. Village republics are a part of India's traditions. Many institutions of Indian society must be used for strengthening democracy. Indigenous institutions must have a place in a democratic system. In other words, western democracy can suit India only by adopting to the Indian conditions. As Gandhi says, "In the domain of politics, I should make use of the indigenous institutions and serve them by curing them of their proved defects." Gandhi was conscious of the historical fact that colonisation had destroyed the basic institutions of a village society. Revival of these institutions in a true spirit may strengthen democracy. Moreover, political institutions at the grass roots level may be able to restrict 'the power of state. Gandhi's concept of state is that of a limited state which does not interfere in the day-to-day activities of people. As Indian society consists of a large number of villages, the Village Republic can be a nucleus of a democratic organisation. Otherwise, state as a coercive organisation can destroy the vitality of village society.

Once village panchayat is formed, it is easy to create a sarvodaya economy. Political institutions can be a means for the management of local resources. Rich people can hand over their surplus land to the village panchayats which can distribute it to the needy. Labourial community contributes their labour to the village fund. The individual remains at the centre of political organisation remains small enough to be influence by the individual. But the individual's initiative is necessary for creation of social wealth. But individual contributes his surplus wealth for the welfare of the community. Village Panchayat must look after the economy of the village which will help the prosperity of village people. The main agenda of Gandhian political programme is the social reconstruction issue. The village panchayat can take care of education, health, sanitation. It can help in abolition of untouchability and weaving khadi for their needs. Thus, the village community can turn into a self-sufficient economy. Their needs are taken care of by their collective effort without much dependence on the urban economy. Individual initiative will create a community bond. Gandhi was not opposed to the varna system. Varna system should not be based on pollution and purity. Division of labour which creates a basis for some castes to do intellectual labour and the others manual labour is not proper. Those castes that do manual work have a lower position in the Hindu society. Gandhi does not allow any separation of intellectual and manual labour. Practice of untouchability is an institutional arrangement for creating violence in a society. Combination of hand and head creates an integral personality. Gandhi understood the real dynamics of a caste society. By removing the basis on which the ideology of caste system stands, the reconstruction of a society is possible.

Q8. Discuss the Gandhi's concept of sarvodaya. [June 09, Q 7]

Ans. Sarvodaya is a term meaning 'universal uplift' or 'progress of all'. The term was first coined by Mohandas Gandhi as the title of his 1908 translation of John Ruskin's tract on political economy, *Unto This Last*, and Gandhi came to use the term for the ideal of his own political philosophy. Later Gandhians, like the Indian nonviolence activist Vinoba Bhave, embraced the term as a name for the social movement in post-independence India which strove to ensure that self-determination and equality reached all strata of India society. The main purpose of Sarvodaya is to create moral atmosphere in the society. Truth, non-violence and purity are the foundations of Sarvodaya.

Feature :

(i) Sarvodaya is a strong ideology for prevention of socio-economic ills of the society. **(ii)** It is based on 'Advaita Vedanto' doctrine **(iii)** It stands for creating high moral character in the society. It is only possible by truth, nonviolence, self-sacrifice and purity etc. **(iv)** at aims at adopting self-sacrifice for the sake of others, taking and giving to others. It is the best principle in Sarvodaya. **(v)** It puts importance for the development of villages. For this villages should be given priority in giving aids. Villages form the keystone of Indian Democracy. It is the duty of every individual to look to the welfare of village people. **(vi)** Truth and non-violence are the two main points of sarvodaya. If everybody practices these two principles, the social corruptions and irregularities will be checked. **(vii)** It is one nonpolitical ideology. It is rather a socio-religious creed. It stands for self-limitation of human wants. **(viii)** Sarvodaya stands for national unity and solidarity. It condemns provincialism and regionalism. Gandhiji's Sarvodaya has its roots in the Vedantic concept of spiritual unity of existence and the Gita. The idealism of Sarvodaya is opposed to the concept majoritarism, concept of class racial struggle and the principle of 'greatest good of the greatest numbers.' The ethics of idealism of Gandhi is profounded by his philosophy Sarvodaya. Gandhi considered the state as an organisation of violence and force. Being an apostle of non-violence he was repelled by the coercive character of the State.

Sarvodaya is concerned with Gandhiji's social ideas and ideal of a community. In the words of Gandhiji, It is casteless and classless society. At the very outset it can be noted here that in order to overcome the difficulties of the problems of caste, communal evils, economic inequalities and social divisions, Ganjhiji had propounded the philosophy of Sarvodaya. He desired a classless society and partyless Democracy. Freedom, equality, justice and fraternity form the basic part of Sarvodaya. Thus, the Philosophy of Sarvodaya is hostile to the state. According Gandhiji for 'Swaraj', Sarvodaya is necessary. In Sarvodaya, there is no space of politics of power. It is the base for politics of cooperation. Sarvodaya is the realisation of the happiness and elevation of all. There are two techniques for stabilisation of power of the people.

(i) constant propaganda and publicity

(ii) Decentralisation of power. The aim is to change the heart of the people.

Sarvodaya opposes to the ideas of egoism and wealth. There is no scope for class struggle in Sarvodaya. Social good, rationality and communal harmony are basic principles of Sarvodaya. Sarvodayas accept the universalisation of self-government. Thus, the political philosophy of Sarvodaya is a powerful intellectual attempt to build a plan of political and social reconstruction on the basis of metaphysical idealism.

Q9. What do you know about Bhoodan movement? Discuss the limitation of this movement.

Ans. The leadership of the Bhoodan Movement fell on Vinoba Bhave who was taken by people as a **'Saint'.** He moved from village to village and propagated the gospels of Sarvodaya. The movement started in 1951 when Telengana peasant movement on the land question reached peak. It was a violent struggle launched by poor peasants against the local landlords. Vinoba looked into the problem and came out with a novel solution, viz., the landlords' voluntary gift of land would help in solving the problems of landlessness in India. This would pave the way for a non-violent radical solution born out of love and not out of hatred. In village Pochampali, in Telangana District one Ram Chandra Reddy created history by donating 100 acres of land to Vinoba in response to his appeal.

Limitation of the bhoodan movement

The bhoodan movement was inspired by the Gandhian workers under the leadership of Vinoba Bhave and J.P. They did not strengthen the organisation. In early 1970s when there was conflict between Vinoba and J.P., the Sarva Seva Sangh split vertically. Moreover, that idealism could not sustain for a long period. Also, organisationally it remained an authoritarian structure. There was hardly any democratic discussion within the organisation on the issues affecting the organisation. The bhoodan movement could not inculcate democratic values at the village level. On the contrary, it reinforced the old values of patron-client relations. There were no popular movements from below on the land question. They appealed to the conscience of the landlords for donating land. This created situations when the landlords started demanding back their land. In the end, however, it should be said that the bhoodan movement was a novel experiment started on the Indian soil. It created a new awareness among people. It aimed at creating an egalitarian society. Gandhi's framework of social change brought the issue to the surface. It was realised by one and all that land distribution cannot be tackled by the laws of the state alone.

Chapter 7

Nationalism and Social Revolution-I (Socialism)

Q1. What is evolutionary socialism?

Ans. Evolutionary socialism is one of the types of socialism. It has got different brands — utopian socialism, democratic socialism, parliamentary socialism, revisionism, fabianism, social democracy, welfare socialism and euro-communism. Marxian socialism holds that socialism can be brought about only by a violent revolution. The new society created would be socialist; by abolishing private property, establishing dictatorship of the proletariat and by bringing about the monopoly of the Communist Party. Evolutionary socialism, as the very term suggests, believes in the evolutionary method of establishing socialism. It implies that there is no need of overthrowing the system (State) existing before. Instead, the social forces wishing to bring about socialism should do it by using the organs of the State i.e. legislature. They should help form the policies which are socialistic and should get them implemented. It is against the concepts of dictatorship of the proletariat and single party monopoly. Evolutionary socialism is in fact, a synthesis of the Marxist and liberal views of democracy. Like Marxism it believes in the establishment of a society which is free from exploitation and inequality, and like liberal democracy, it favours multiparty system, periodic elections and free expression of views.

Q2. Give your comments on socialism's basic philosophy.

Ans. Philosophy of socialism developed in the 19th century, although the ideas regarding socialism were propounded even before. For instance, the ideas of philosophers such as Rousseau, Morelly and Babeuf propounded before the French Revolution, formed important features of socialism, as it came about later. Mention can be made of ideas such is the abolition of private property and faith in equality.

Utopian Socialists

After the industrial revolution (1760-1830) the condition of the workers worsened in European countries. The workers suffered from the different crises of capitalism - their diving conditions were miserable, there was massive unemployment, inflation etc. Many humanist and social reformers reacted to this. The trio of Saint Simon (1760-1825), Charles Fourier (1772-1873) and Robert Owen (1771-1858) attacked the capitalist socio-economic order. They supported the establishment of a socialist Society. They emphasised the need for equal distribution of wealth and gave support to the trade union movement. They were mainly utopian socialists. They believed that if the capitalists changed their attitudes the conditions of the workers would be improved within the given capitalist system. They did not, however, analyse the capitalist mode of production. They also failed to give scientific theory for removing the exploitation of the capitalist society.

Influence of Utopian Socialism

Utopian socialism, however, influenced the French and German socialists on the one hand and Marx and Engels on the other. Blanc(1813-1882), a reformer and a scholar gave the economic principle "from each according to his ability, and to each according to his work." He is regarded as the chief precursor of the welfare state. He influenced both the Social Democrats and the revisionists. Proudhan (1809-1865) attacked private property. He associated the economic system with political system. He pleaded for the overthrow of the capitalist system. Pre-Marxian socialism, except Proudhan, based itself upon the humanitarian hope that people will treat each other better if production increased. But they failed to analyse scientifically the functioning of tbe capitalist economic system and the exploitation inherent in it.

German Social Democracy

In the 1860s the phenomenon of German Social Democracy assumed considerable significance. Lassale (1825-1864) was one of the early German Social Democrats. He urged that the working class must have a separate party, which can represent their interests in the legislature. He was a supporter of the producers' coperative. The socialists and the Marxists reached a compromise in Germany and proposed the famous Gotha Programme (1875). This programme was moderate and it supported the evolutionary method of bringing about socialism. Marxists and Karl Marx himself criticised this programme and drafted another programme on Marxist lines known as Erfurt Programme. This programme emphasised the importance of the interrelationship between history and revolutionary programme. In reaction to the Erfurt Programme emerged revisionism. The main advocate of revisionism was Bernstein (1850-1932). He said that the Marxists emphasise only the economic factor but the non-economic factors are equally important. The Marxian theory of value, according to him, is not applicable always. His theory provided substantive foundation to evolutionary socialism.

Bernstein's revisionism influenced British Parliamentary Socialism and Fabianism. To propagate these views the British Labour Party was founded in 1906. It developed the trade union movement. It said that socialism could be established, by the participation of the labour parties in the government. The party believed that the state could introduce pro-working class policies and this would give birth to socialism. It sought to combine the economic principles of socialism with the principle of parliamentary democracy and welfare liberalism. Ramsay MacDonald, Harold Laski and Clement Attlee were the important leaders of the British Labour Party. The British parliamentary democracy believed in planning, reform, gradual change, progressive taxation and faith in the parliamentary methods as against the revolutionary methods of overthrowing capitalism. It did not believe in the theory of class struggle, dictatorship of the proletariat and in the capacity of the state to bring about change.

Euro-communism which developed mainly in France, Italy and Germany also believes in the principles of evolutionary socialism. On June 4, 1884, the Fabian Society was set up in England by some arm chair intellectuals. It aimed at establishing a socialist society in England through democratic, gradual and peaceful means. The society was named after a Roman General Fabius, who adopted a policy of "wait and hit hard at the right moment." C.D.H. Cole and H.J. Laski were among its main advocates. The Fabian Society maintained that socialism and democracy are supplementary and complementary to each other. Socialism can be brought about by the gradual way through democratic means.

Q3. Briefly discuss the formation of the national socialist party.

Or

Trace the genesis of the formation of Communist Party of India.

[Dec 07, Q 10]

Ans. The **Congress Socialist Party** (CSP) was founded in 1934 as a socialist caucus within the Indian National Congress. Its members rejected what they saw as the anti-rational mysticism of Mohandas Gandhi as well as the sectarian attitude of the Communist Party of India towards the Congress Party. Influenced by Fabianism as well as Marxism-Leninism, the CSP included advocates of armed struggle or sabotage (such as Jayprakash Narayan and Basawon Singh (Sinha) as well as those who insisted upon ahimsa or nonviolent resistance (such as Acharya Narendra Deva). The CSP advocated decentralised socialism in which co-operatives, trade unions, independent farmers, and local authorities would hold a substantial share of the economic power. As secularists, they hoped to transcend communal divisions through class solidarity. Some, such as Narendra Deva or Basawon Singh (Sinha), advocated a democratic socialism distinct from both Marxism and reformist social democracy. During the Popular Front period, the communists worked within CSP. Basawon Singh (Sinha) along with Yogendra Shukla was among the founder members of **Congress Socialist Party** from Bihar. JP Narayan and Minoo Masani were released from jail in April 1934. Narayan convened a meeting in Patna on May 17, 1934, which founded the Bihar Congress Socialist Party. Narayan became general secretary of the party and Acharya Narendra Deva became president. The Patna meeting gave a call for a socialist conference which would be held in connection to the Congress Annual Conference. At this conference, held in Bombay October 22-October 23, 1934, they formed a new All India party, the **Congress Socialist Party**. Narayan became general secretary of the party, and Masani joint secretary. The conference venue was decorated by Congress flags and a portrait of Karl Marx. In the new party the greeting 'comrade' was used. Masani mobilised the party in Bombay, whereas Kamaladevi Chattopadhyaya and Puroshottam Trikamdas organised the party in other parts of Maharashtra. Ganga Sharan Singh (Sinha) was among the prominent leaders of the Indian National Congress Party as among the founders of the **Congress Socialist Party**. The constitution of the CSP defined that the members of CSP were the members of the Provisional Congress Socialist Parties and that they were all required to be members of the Indian National Congress. Members of communal organisations or political organisations whose goals were incompatible with the ones of CSP, were barred from CSP membership. The Bombay conference raised the slogan of mobilising the masses for a Constituent Assembly.

In 1936 the Communists joined CSP, as part of the Popular Front strategy of the Comintern. In some states, like Kerala and Orissa, communists came to dominate CSP. In fact communists dominated the entire Congress in Kerala through its hold of CSP at one point.

In 1936, the CSP began fraternal relations with the Lanka Sama Samaja Party of Ceylon. In 1937 the CSP sent Kamaladevi Chattopadhyaya on a speaking tour of the island.

The CSP had adopted Marxism in 1936 and their third conference in Faizpur they had formulated a thesis that directed the party to work to transform the Indian National Congress into an anti-imperialist front.

During the summer of 1938 a meeting took place between the Marxist sector of the Anushilan movement and the CSP. Present in the meeting were Jayaprakash Narayan (leader of CSP), Jogesh Chandra Chatterji, Tribid Kumar Chaudhuri and Keshav Prasad Sharma. The Anushilan marxists then held talks with Acharya Narendra Deva, a former Anushilan militant. The Anushilan marxists decided to join CSP, but keeping a separate identity within the party. With them came the Anushilan Samiti, not only the Marxist sector. The non-Marxists (who constituted about a half of the membership of the Samiti), although not ideologically attracted to the CSP, felt loyalty towards the Marxist sector. Moreover, around 25% of the membership of the Hindustan Socialist Republican Association joined the CSP. This group was led by Jogesh Chandra Chatterji. The Anushilan marxists were however soon to be disappointed by developments inside the CSP. The party, at that the time Anushilan marxists had joined it, was not a homogeneous entity. There was the Marxist trend led by J.P. Narayan and Narendra Deva, the Fabian socialist trend led by Minoo Masani and Asoka Mehta and a Gandhian socialist trend led by Ram Manohar Lohia and Achyut Patwardan. To the Anushilan marxists differences emerged between the ideological stands of the party and its politics in practice. These differences surfaced at the 1939 annual session of the Indian National Congress at Tripuri. At Tripuri, in the eyes of the Abnushlian marxists, the CSP had failed to consistently defend Subhas Chandra Bose. Jogesh Chandra Chatterji renounced his CSP membership in protest against the action by the party leadership.

Soon after the Tripuri session, Bose resigned as Congress president and formed the Forward Bloc. The Forward Bloc was intended to function as a unifying force for all leftwing elements. The Forward Bloc held its first conference on June 22-23 1939, and at the same time a Left Consolidation Committee consisting of the Forward Bloc, CPI, CSP, the Kisan Sabha, League of Radical Congressmen, Labour Party and the Anushilan marxists. At this moment, in October 1939, J.P. Narayan tried to stretch out an olive branch to the Anushilan marxists. He proposed the formation of a 'War Council' consisting of himself, Pratul Ganguly, Jogesh Chandra Chatterjee and Acharya Narendra Deva. But few days later, at a session of the All India Congress Committee, J.P. Narayan and the other CSP leaders pledged not to start any other movements parallel to those initiated by Gandhi. The Left Consolidation Committee soon fell into pieces, as the CPI, the CSP and the Royists deserted it. The Anushlian marxists left the CSP soon thereafter, forming the Revolutionary Socialist Party.

Narayan organised the CSP relief work in Kutch in 1939.

On the occasion of the 1940 Ramgarh Congress Conference CPI released a declaration called *Proletarian Path*, which sought to utilise the weakened state of the British Empire in the time of war and gave a call for general strike, no-tax, no-rent policies and mobilising for an armed revolution uprising. The National Executive of the CSP assembled at Ramgarh took a decision that all communists were expelled from CSP.

Members of the CSP were particularly active in the Quit India movement of August 1942. Although a socialist, Jawaharlal Nehru did not join the CSP, which created some rancour among CSP members who saw Nehru as unwilling to put his socialist slogans into action. After independence, the CSP broke away from Congress, under the influence of JP Narayan and Basawon Singh (Sinha), to form the Socialist Party of India. Basawon Singh (Sinha) went on to become the first leader of opposition in the state of Bihar (and assembly as well) and Acharya Narendra Deva became the first leader of opposition in U.P. state and assembly.

Q4. Write a note on the followings:-
(i) Jawaharlal Nehru and Socialism
Or
Comment on Jawaharlal Nehru's views on socialism. [Dec 08, Q 9]
(ii) Subhash Chandra Bose and Socialism
Or
Examine Subhash Chandra Bose's concept of socialism. [Dec 08, Q 10]
(iii) Jaya Prakash Narayan on Socialism
(iv) Ram Manohar Lohia and Socialism

Ans. (i) Jawaharlal Nehru and Socialism : The relevance of Jawaharlal Nehru remains undiminished today. In fact, his ideas and approach to political, economic and social issues are more relevant now than even in his life-time. It is necessary to state this basic truth and assess the continuing validity and vitality of his approach, because some who unabashedly use his name seek to project him as a pragmatist rather than as the firmly committed socialist that he was.

It is the fashion these days to say that socialism is a vague term, that it is a slogan, that there is no precise definition of what it means. This is essentially the argument of the believers in the status quo, of those who are afraid of radical change that will either hurt their own interests or destroy their pet theories.

It is no doubt true the despite his massive personal popularity and the power at his disposal in the government and in the party, Jawaharlal Nehru could not put into practice many of the ideas he spelt out regarding the radical changes, social and economic, that our society required. But this must be seen in the background of the dilemma he faced as an honest politician committed to socialism on the one hand and to democracy on the other. Rightly, he saw no contradiction between the two, for, who can deny that true democracy is the only viable basis for genuine socialism and that without advance towards the goal of socialism democracy will be bereft of meaning? Nehru would not discard the democratic processes or bypass the democratic institutions in order to put his ideas into practice. In our context, with a long history of feudalism, caste hierarchy, religious divergence, multiplicity of languages and customs, in fact of stratification of society in a variety of ways, it has not been easy to correlate tradition and change, to work out a viable compromise between the best of cherished values and the urgency of eliminating social and economic inequalities. Jawaharlal Nehru realised that revolution in our situation had to be by consent and could not be by imposition. He admired the Soviet achievements and accepted the ultimate ideals of Marxism, but he did not make a secret of his reservations about applying the same methods in the case of our country.

In an underdeveloped nation with many layers of development within itself, both vertical and horizontal, and with a variety of vested interests wielding tremendous influence and extremely articulate, the difficulties involved in bringing about radical changes by consent were obvious enough. Yet the alternatives to the democratic system are so risky and unpredictable that he would not lightly discard his faith, even if this meant a visible, often frustrating, slowing down of the process of change.

Nehru's acceptance of political democracy was not unqualified. "I am perfectly prepared to accept political democracy," he said, "only in the hope that this will lead to social democracy." He was clear in his mind that political democracy "is only the way to the goal and is not the final objective". He saw clearly that if profound economic changes did not take place fast enough, the political structure would be rendered unstable.

If political or social institutions stand in the way of such change, they have to be removed.

Socialism, whose essence is the removal of poverty and establishment of equal opportunities if not of equality in the strictest sense, has necessarily to suit the conditions of each country, and Nehru's constant effort was to bring about changes without destroying the fabric of Indian society, even if certain parts of that fabric were to be replaced.

Nehru saw the socialist society as some kind of a cooperative society, in which each individual would give of his best and would find full scope for his own development. The very first step had to be the ending of the profit motive of the acquisitive society to which we are accustomed. The dilemma he faced was the result of his desire to avoid a violent upheaval that could have disastrous consequences for future generations of our people and to take the maximum number of people along with him on the new path. This was no easy task, for the vested interests in the acquisitive society which he wanted to end were entrenched in the party and in the administrative apparatus which had necessarily to be his major instruments. Also, it was these interests which were active during the freedom struggle, and even more in the years of freedom, and they were able to create the illusion of democratic functioning without active participation by the masses of our population who were to gain by the changes Nehru envisaged.

Once Nehru said that two contradictory and conflicting processes could not go on side by side that unfortunately is what has been happening. The Directive Principles contain a broad outline of the kind of socialist society envisaged, but the many amendments to other chapters of the Constitution that have been necessited have brought out the dichotomy in thinking that characterised the Constitution-making body. On another plane, the formulation of the concept of "mixed economy" represented on the one hand the "half-way house" Nehru thought of and on the other the ability of the vested interests to keep "two contradictory and conflicting processes" going on side by side, a situation Nehru did not desire. It is no coincidence that the "mixed economy" in operation has resulted in a strengthening of the monopoly and big business houses, and a consequent tightening of their hold on the administrative apparatus. If corruption has increased and the public sector has not been enlarged and strengthened to the extent it should have been, this is because of acceptance of the "mixed economy" as something of a "half-way house".

I think it is possible to establish socialism by democratic means provided, of course, the full democratic process is available.

There has been mass awakening as never before in our history, and despite massive illiteracy our people have demonstrated their capacity to reject what is against their interests. But the real problem is that the democratic process is not yet fully developed, and the people have only limited choice. The limitations imposed by our circumstances, both historical and man-made, have helped both the urban and rural vested interests to twist the democratic process to suit their own ends which are diametrically opposed to the interests of the masses.

In thinking of a form of socialism suited to our national needs and national genius, Nehru envisaged a limited place for the private sector, but he was quite clear about the framework.

In all that counts, in a material sense, nationalisation of the instruments of production and distribution seems to be inevitable. The question is whether there can be a step-by-step approach in this matter. Our experience with the takeover of the wholesale trade in foodgrains shows that partial measures in dealing with production and distribution of essential commodities can defeat the very objective. The fate of the land reform measures has shown that an administrative machinery that is not geared to the task can work havoc. The continuing importance and influence of the big business houses must be seem as the direct result of the failure to involve the people at the grassroots level more and more in the processes of planning, production and distribution.

It is possible to find fault with Jawaharlal Nehru for not having made the maximum use of his popularity to force the pace of change, but to do so is to overlook the historical forces that had shaped him and the historical circumstances in which he had to function, apart from his own commitment to the democratic processes as well as to the instruments at his disposal. It is debatable how much more he could have achieved in his life-time, but it is indisputable that he laid firm foundations for the kind of society we want to build in this country. It is for us and for future generations to build on these foundations.

Nehru was conscious that the Indian Revolution would be long and arduous, for he said: "Leaders and individuals may come and go; they may get tired and slacken off; they may compromise and betray; but the exploited and suffering masses must carry on the struggle, for their drill sergeant is hunger." If the social and economic burdens of the masses "continue and are actually added to, the fight must not only continue but grow more intense". The masses would ultimately assert themselves, and of this he had not the least doubt. It was his hope that the political parties and the administrative apparatus would help the masses to assert themselves and secure their rights. He was quite clear in his mind that a leadership that failed to take the masses nearer the goal of socialism would be thrown aside, and the mass upsurge in 1969 following the elimination of the Syndicate from the Congress would appear to bear this out, even if only in a very limited sense.

Nehru said: We have to plan at both ends. We have to stop the cumulative forces that make the rich richer and we have to start the cumulative forces which enable the poor to get over the barrier of poverty.

The planning process unfortunately has not gone on the way he had intended it to, and this is where the two main instruments on which he had to depend come in.

Nehru wanted the services to "cease to think of themselves as some select coterie apart from the rest of the people", and he rejected people with the "coat and necktie" mentality. In other words, he wanted a new type of administrator to emerge, who could identify himself with the common people without effort and who would not become either a tool in the hands of vested interests or a self-seeker without a conscience. Unfortunately this kind of change has not come about; on the other hand, the expanded administrative structure has careerists and self-seekers in many key positions. This has to change.

As for the other instrument, the Congress, it may now be in better shape than in Nehru's time, but what he said about Congressmen remains relevant. Congressmen should make the organisation strong and effective. Use of money for boosting individuals in the organisations is extremely undesirable. Bogus members should be weeded out. Those in the organisation for whom the Congress is not an instrument for serving the country, who serve themselves and exploit it for their own ends...should be turned out.

He wanted the party to be a mass party, constantly in touch with the people and reflecting their aspirations, constantly struggling to end social and economic injustice. Some changes have taken place in the party in recent times, but it is still far from being the kind of instrument for change that Jawaharlal Nehru wanted it to be. It is to be hoped that the new forces at work within the Congress and the mass consciousness that has developed in the country will make it so.

Our aim and our problems were succinctly summed up when Jawaharlal Nehru said:

Socialism is the inevitable outcome of democracy. Political democracy has no meaning if it does not embrace economic democracy. And economic democracy is nothing but socialism. Monopoly is the enemy of socialism. To that extent it has grown during the last few years, we have drifted away from the goal of socialism.

(ii) Subhash Chandra Bose and Socialism- Subhash Chandra Bose was a believer in socialism. He asserted that he wanted a 'Socialist Republic of India'. However, his concept of socialism was different from that of the others and he called it Indian socialism. Addressing ***Bharatiya Naujawan Sabha*** in 1931, he said, "If we undertake a comparative analysis of different social and political ideals that have inspired human endeavor and activity throughout the ages, we shall arrive at certain common principles that should form the basis of our collective life. These are justice, equality, freedom, discipline and love." In order to be just and impartial, he advocated treating all men as equal. He asserted that bondage of any kind, economic or political, robs men of their freedom and gives rise to inequalities of various kind. Therefore in order to ensure equality it is necessary to get rid of bondage of every kind. However, he also warned that freedom did not mean indiscipline or license or absence of law. It rather means the substitution of law and discipline, which is very necessary for the struggle for freedom the basis of life.

Besides these fundamental principles, Bose asserted that love is the highest principle. Without a feeling of love for humanity neither one could be just to all, or treat men as equal, nor feel called upon to sacrifice, and without that the right sort of socialism could not emerge. Thus, for Bose the cardinal principles of socialism are justice, equality, freedom, discipline and love. He advised his countrymen and women not to ignore the history and traditions of the country while adopting the social and political institutions of the other countries. He asserted that these were all kinds of active nation building programmes and socio-political ideologies in the Western world, such as Socialism, State Socialism, Guild Socialism, Syndicalism, Philosophical, Anarchism, Bolshevism, Fascism, Parliamentary Democracy, Aristocracy, Absolute Monarchy, Dictatorship etc. He accepted some wisdom in each of them. However, he warned that in a progressive world like ours it would not be proper to accept any one of them as the last word for an ideal or the final solution of all the social and political - problems. Because he reasoned that the results of the transplantation of an entire idea or institution in one country from another may not necessarily be agreeable or fruitful. A national institution is the natural result of the history of the people concerned - their thoughts and ideals and the activities of their day to day life. This should be borne in mind. According to Bose social and political institutions cannot be built by ignoring history and the traditions of the people of the country, besides their present condition or prevailing atmosphere of life. For the above reason, he could not agree with the communists in India also. He felt that the Bolshevik Socialism of Soviet Union did not suit India. There should be assimilation of only those socialistic principles which could suit on Indian requirements. He explained that the Bolshevik theory had been passing through an experimental stage and the communists were departing from Lenin and other Bolsheviks. This departure had been caused by the peculiar conditions and circumstances prevailing in Russia, which compelled a modification of the original theory. He also warned against the unsuitability of Marxian ideas and said that Marxian ideas were coming from the West like 'boisterous breakers' and some people in India we unnecessarily excited and stirred up with these. Most of them, Bose said, who believed that adoption of Marxism in its pure and complete form would make India a land of joy and plenty and pointed their fingers towards Russia, in fact were wrong because the Bolshevism adopted and practiced in Russia was not the same as classical Marxian socialism. The other reason for rejection of communism was the methodology and tactics communists generally employed to achieve their ends. These methods and tactics, he thought, did not suit India and that is why communism could not make much headway in this country.

Indian socialism would therefore be different, he asserted. He said that at that stage it was difficult to chalk out the details of a socialist state (of his dreams). He could only give an outline, the main features and principles of the socialist State. He said, "We want political freedom whereby it meant the Constitution of an independent Indian state, free from the control of British imperialism. It should be quite clear to everybody that independence means severance from the British Empire, and on this point there should be no vagueness or mental reservation. Secondly we want complete economic emancipation. Bose elabourated his view of economic emancipation and held that every human being must have the right to work, and the right to a living wage. There shall be no drones in the society and no unearned income. There must be equal opportunities for all, and there should be a fair, just and equitable distribution of wealth. For this purpose, it may be necessary for the state to take over the control of the means of production and distribution of wealth. Besides economic equality Bose also felt that the third essential feature of real socialism is complete social equality. Social equality means that there shall be no caste or depressed classes. Every man will have the same rights, the same status in society. Bose was not only a believer of eradication of caste hierarchy, but also a supporter of women's equality in social status or in law. Woman will be an equal partner of man was Bose's firm faith. Nevertheless, the ideal of socialism could not be achieved without social change. Bose had a specific view about social change.

(iii)Jaya Prakash Narayan on Socialism- Jaya Prakash Narayan (1902-1979) was the main force behind the formation of the Congress Socialist Party in 1934. He began his political career as a participant in the non-cooperation movement. He was influenced by Marxism as a student in the USA, when he came in contact with the East European intellectuals. He was also influenced by M.N. Roy. But he did not support Russian Socialism. He favored a popular Front with the Communist in the thirties. But he denounced this in 1940, and became a critic of the Soviet Union. He opposed the Cabinet Mission Plan in 1946. As a member of the Congress Socialist Party, he thought in terms of a mass revolution. He said that if the British government did not accept the constitution prepared by the Constituent Assembly, there would be a mass revolution in India. After Gandhi's death there was transformation in Jaya Prakash Narayan's personality. He became skeptical of any structural and institutional change in India. He committed himself to the inner metamorphosis suggested by Gandhi. He resigned from the national executive of the Praja Socialist Party and ceased to be a member of any political party.

Socialism and Socio-economic Construction

Jaya Prakash Narayan regarded socialism as a complete theory of socio-economic construction. He did not agree with the theory that men are biologically unequal. He said that the inequality in society exists due to the disproportionate control of the means of production. He advocated reduction in revenue, limitation of expenditure and the nationalisation of industries. In the Ramgarh session of the Congress in 1940 he advocated collective ownership and control of large-scale production, and nationalisation of the heavy industries, heavy transport, shipping and mining. He made Gandhism the base of his socialism. He said that grass-root level democracy should be introduced in India. The village should be made a self-governing and self-sufficient unit. He favored the distribution of land to the tiller, co-operative farming, and cancellation of agriculture debt.

(iv) Ram Manohar Lohia and Socialism- Rammanohar Lohia became the most prominent socialist leader in the post-independence period. He was active in bringing about the Asian Socialist Conference of 1953. He stood for combining the principles of socialism with those of Gandhism. He laid emphasis on adapting socialism to the specifics of the Indian society. In 1952, he pleaded for greater incorporation of Gandhian ideas in socialist thought. He advocated decentralisation of the economy based on the revival of the cottage industries. He preferred small machines to big machines in the economy of the country. He was opposed to any kind of co-operation with the Congress. He laid foundation of anti-Congressism in India. He was equally opposed to the communists: He supported the principle of "equidistance" vis-a-vis the Congress and the Communists. He broke from the Praja Socialist Party in 1955 on the issue of supporting the Congress. Lohia, in fact, gave a theory of mobilisation of the backward classes. He said that the socialists could capture power by mobilising the backward classes. He held caste to be one of the most powerful exploiting institutions in India. The backward classes, according to him, should form the government to introduce the policies based on the principles of socialism. He accepted the Marxian principle of dialectical materialism, but believed that consciousness played a more determining role than the economy. He believed that in history there was constant clash between the well-organised castes and the loosely organised classes. Caste represented conservative forces in the society, according to him.

Q5. Briefly discuss Nehru's scientific outlook.

Ans. Nehru believed that the methods and approach of science have revolutionised human life more than anything else in the long course of history, and have opened doors and avenues of further and even more radical changes, leading up to the very portals of what has long been considered the unknown. Nehru said: "It is the scientific approach, the adventures and yet critical temper of science, the search for truth and new knowledge, the refusal to accept anything without testing and trial, the capacity to change previous conclusions in the face of new evidence, the reliance on observed facts and not on pre-conceived theory, the discipline of the mind, all that is necessary not merely for the application of science but for life itself and the solution of its many problems."

One of the reasons Nehru advanced for India's extensive use of science and technology was that. it would bring economic power and independence to the country. His intention to promote a scientific outlook in the country and the extensive use of science and technology for the promotion of economic development was also in the direction of settling in motion a social revolution. These steps weakened the irrational traditions of India which was based on status and gradually replaced it by the bourgeois outlook which was based on contract. Another advantage of the extensive use of science and technology was that it would make India an independent and self-reliant economic, political and military power.

Nehru wrote to Gandhi in 1945: "I do not think it is possible for India to be really independent unless she is a technically advanced country. I am not thinking for the moment in terms of just scientific growth. In the present context of the world we cannot even advance culturally without a strong background of scientific research in every department. There is today a tremendous acquisitive tendency both in individuals and groups and nations, which lead to conflicts and wars."

According to Nehru, India should resist the foreign pressures by herself developing her science and technology. Among many other factors, this was one of the reasons for India's refusal to sign the nuclear non-proliferation treaty. Primarily, India wanted to develop nuclear energy for peaceful purposes. And she also did not want to give up the option to make any weapons for self-defence. This takes us to India's independent foreign policy independent foreign policy.

Q6. What are the techniques of national and social revolution according to Bose?

Ans. In a broadcast over Azad Hind Radio Subhash Bose chalked out his methodology of national struggle. He said that the campaign that was going on in India was non-violent guerrilla warfare. He asserted that the object of this guerrilla warfare would be twofold, one to destroy war production in India and the other to paralyse the 'British administration and all people of India should participate in the struggle.

He chalked out a detail programme for the people. He suggested that payment of the taxes be stopped which directly or indirectly brought revenue to the government. The workers in all industries should either launch a stay in strike or try to hamper production by conducting a go-slow campaign inside the factories. They should also carry out sabotage to impede production. The students should organise secret guerrilla bands for carrying on sabotage in different parts of the country. They should also invent new ways of annoying the British authorities, for example, burning stamps etc. in post offices, destroying British monuments etc. The women, especially girl students should do underground work of all kinds, especially as secret messengers or provide shelter for the men who fight. The government officials who are prepared to help the campaign should not resign their posts but those in government offices And in war industries should give all available information to fighters outside and should try to hamper production by working inefficiently. The servants who are working in the houses of Britishers, should be organised for the purpose of giving trouble to the masters, for example, by demanding higher salaries, cooking and serving bad food and drinks etc. The Indians should give up all business with foreign banks, firms, insurance companies etc. For the general public he suggested the following activities:

a) Boycott of British goods, industry, burning of British stalls and government stores;

b) Total boycott of Britishers in India, and those Indians who are pro-British;

c) Hold demonstrations in spite of official prohibition;

d) Publishing of secret bulletins and setting up of a secret radio station;

e) Marching to the houses of British government officials and demanding their departure from India;

f) Organising of processions for entering and occupying government offices, secretarial buildings, law courts etc. with a view to hampering administration.
g) Arranging to punish police officers and prison officials who oppress and persecute people.
h) Begin erecting barricades in the streets where there is a likelihood of attack from the police and military.
i) Setting fire to government offices and factories which a.re working for war purposes.
j) Interrupting postal, telegraph, telephone and communication as frequently as possible.
k) Interrupting railways, bus and tram services, whenever there is a possibility of hampering the transport of soldiers or of war material.
l) Destroying police stations, railway stations and jails in isolated places.

Q7. Do you think that Subhash advocated fascism ?

Ans. Bose has been called a believer in Fascism. This assumption arose from the fact that he wanted to associate India's freedom struggle with Second World War politics and sought the help of Fascist Italy and Nazi Germany. He also showed his admiration for Mussolini. In a chapter 'A Glimpse of the Future' in his book 'The Indian Struggle' he wrote "In spite of the antithesis between communism and fascism, there are certain traits common to both. Both communism and fascism believe in the supremacy of the state over the individual. Both denounce parliamentary democracy. Both believe in Party rule. Both believe in the dictatorship of the party and in the ruthless suppression of all dissenting minorities. Both believe in a planned industrial reorganisation of the country. These common traits will form the basis of the new synthesis. The synthesis is called 'Samyavada." Bose asserted 'that it will be India's task to work out this synthesis. Besides the advocacy of this synthesis, in 1941 in Kabul, Bose had said that dissensions in the country would disappear only when an iron dictator rules in India for twenty years. He asserted that at least after the end of British rule in India there must be a dictatorship. And it is for India's good that she should be ruled by a dictator to begin with. None but a dictator can wipe out such dissensions. He believed India needed a Kamal Pasha to cure its many ailments.

Nevertheless, Bose had advocated dictatorship as a panacea for India's problems.

However, he could not be branded as a fascist. He never sanctioned the extreme tenets of fascism which sanctioned imperialistic expansion and believed in racialism.

He was a votary of the rights of the exploited masses. Thus, although he took armed help from the fascist powers of Europe and Asia, and organised national army for India's liberation, yet he did not preach the ideology of fascism. The Forward Bloc, the party he belonged to summarised its dominant guiding principles on January 1, 1941.

i) Complete national independence and uncompromising anti-imperialist struggle for attaining it.

ii) A thoroughly modern socialist state.

iii) Scientific large-scale production for the economic regeneration of the country.

iv) Social ownership and control of both production and distribution.

v) Freedom for the individual in the matter of religious worship.

vi) Equal rights for every individual.

vii) Linguistic and cultural autonomy for all sections of the Indian community.

viii) Application of the principle of equality and social justice in building up a New Order in Free India.

Q8. What is the basic philosophy of Jai prakash Narayan and Narender Dev?

Ans. Both JP and Narendra Dev wanted to work within the national congress and create political platform for socialists and other left wingers. They realised that the congress was a platform which needed a new orientation. There was no point in creating another political party. According to them the Congress party offered enough space for accommodating different ideological groups. It was also the class character of the Indian national movement that helped in maintaining such a complex ideological framework. Acharya Narendra Dev said "for a subject, colonial state political independence is the first step on the road to socialism. In a middle class revolutionary movement, for the success of the national movement, to base itself on the support of the people together with middle class. The economic well-being of the common people must, however, find a central place in the programme of the movement. The Congress Socialist Party must not divorce the national movement from the revolutionary aspirations of workers, peasants and the middle class." This was the famous speech given by Acharya Narendra Dev at the CSP's first conference at Patna in 1934, Both JP and Narendra Dev recognised the importance of the congress party as the leader of the anti-imperialist struggle. Secondly, they recognised the importance of class politics in the congress. Thirdly, the fact that the ideology of socialism was going to play a significant role in the national movement. Fourthly, the CSP was going to function as a pressure group in the congress. It would be neither a political party nor an alternative to the congress. JP made it all this very clear in his speech which is given below.

"Our work within the congress is governed by the policy of developing into a true anti-imperialist body. It is not our purpose, as sometimes it has been misunderstood to be, to convert the whole Congress into a fulfledged socialist party. All we seek to do is to change the content and policy of that 0rganisation so that it comes truly to represent the masses, having the object of emancipating them both from the foreign power and the native system of exploitation." Furthermore, JP understood the class context of congress leadership and the conservative orientation of the leadership who were scared of the slogan of socialism. As JP stated, "The congress at present is dominated by upper its objectives any programmed aimed at the economic emancipation of the masses."

Q9. Discuss the views of Acharya Narender Dev on socialism.

Ans. The Socialist Party brought out a socialist programme which clearly indicates their viewpoint. First, for nationalisation big capital was necessary, but not abolition of private property. Secondly, their main emphasis was on the abolition of the Zamindaries in rural India. Land reforms should be implemented which would bring land to the tiller. In other words, they pleaded for the growth of the peasant proprietor and small industrial capital.

Narendra Dev was much more clear in the concept of democratic socialism. Democracy cannot survive without socialism and vice versa. Human Freedom is the basis of acquiring a socialistic pattern of society.

Socialism and Democracy

He said socialism for which we stand is democratic because: **(i)** It is opposed to hierarchical conception of society; **(ii)** It is opposed to the control of social power, political or economic by a single person or a privileged class in any form of despotism, dictatorship, feudalism or capitalism; **(iii)** It is opposed to imperialism and foreign domination in all forms and recognises the entire right of democratic freedom; **(iv)** It favours democratisation of social relations and behaviours; **(v)** It establishes the control of the working people over social, economic and political powers; **(vi)** It provides for self govt. in all social, political and economic affairs; **(vii)** It evolves order on the basis of liberty, i.e. free participation of all concerns; **(viii)** It provides for democratic decentralisation of power and responsibility; **(ix)** It assures social equality and justice by attaching priority to the needs as claims for full physical, mental as moral development of all; **(x)** It provides social happiness, of which individual happiness is a constituent; **(xi)** It regards the people as a source of authority and recognises their right to revolt in case a single person or a minority group or class attempts to seize or retain control over government, institutions or social power and **(xii)** if favours a democratic organisation for peace and international relations.

Opposition to the Third International

Narendra Dev stoutly opposed the policy of the Third International which split and weakened the anti-imperialist forces and sought to discredit Indian nationalism and its leaders. He said that nationalism was a potent social forces and it was not meant to create a head-on-clash between nations or class struggles.

Socialism not a borrowed ideology

Socialism was not a borrowed ideology for Narendra Dev. He never abused Gandhi's constructive programme. He only felt that it must be supplemented by a class organisation for the abolition of vested property rights. He was prepared to accept Satyagraha as an instrument of class conflict in India. But he felt that it would be unrealistic to believe that feudal landlords who levied unlawful exactions upon their tenants and capitalists who cared more for profits than for protection could become dependable trustees of national resources.

The failure of the civil disobedience movement could not be explained in terms of the moral inadequacy of the Satyagrahis. The freedom movement was only an expression of the educated middle class. If it had to gain strength, it must evoke new response from the people working in fields and factories. Political freedom must be translated in terms of long delayed relief of economic and social leaderships.

Student of Eastern and Western Thought

Narendra Dev was a keen student of both, eastern and western thought. His study of ancient Indian culture was deep and wide. He could easily claim to be a scholar of Buddhist Philosophy. While he had a great regard for the cultural heritage of India, he was also conscious that "many old ideas had become effete and obsolete by the afflux of time would have to be discarded." In his opinion, "the task before us is the presentation of careful and scientific analysis of our culture, the preservation of its vital elements and their synthesis with modern thought." In his thinking, he has kept enough space for understanding Indian religious traditions: viz., what is the source and essence of Bharatiya Dharma? It will be better to quote him: " People of different races and culture migrated to India from time immemorial and made it their home. They were absorbed in the Indian community and the religion of land, its customs and ideas. Different communities following different ways of life have lived together in amity and religious feuds and conflicts are rare in Indian history. The Indian spirit had tried through the ages to seek unity in diversity. It was the catholic spirit of Hindu religion that made this miracle possible. Hinduism is not a creedal religion. It does not forcible impose its way of life upon others. It does not believe that the only true way of life is the one which is professed by it….. Truth manifests itself in many ways and therefore, no individual religion has the monopoly of truth. Hinduism is perhaps the only religion which believes that followers of other religions can also attain salvation.

It does not attach much importance to external forms and penetrates the inner spirit of man. It is also because of this comprehensive charity that Hinduism does not believe in proselytisation. Hindu Saints have, therefore, initiated their Muslim or Christian followers into spiritual sadhna without demanding of them renunciation of their faith and practice. "Indian religious traditions have integrated the best elements from all religions Hindu Saints, Muslim Fakirs and Sufis, who preached oneness of the Supreme being and bhakti (devolution) as a means of reaching him, did not recognise caste, community as external forms of worship. They were a continuation of the Sharman culture which disregarded external norms and emphasised good deeds."

Cultural Marxist

Narendra Dev was basically a cultural Marxist. He was deeply influenced by the Indian cultural traditions, specifically Buddha. He was much influenced by the gospel of love as Ahimsa preached by Buddha. He spent more than a decade working on his book on Buddhist philosophy - 'Buddha Dharma Darshan' a treatise of considerable historical value. Interestingly, he had a profound understanding of Indian religious traditions. But at the same time, he was not in favour of religion and politics being comprise the collective consciousness of people. Marxists must bring certain democratic elements of religions to make the human being an ethical being.

Opposition to combining Religion and Politics

He was dead opposed to mixing up religion with politics, as mentioned already. Once he contested a by-election where the congress party put up a religions man to defeat him. Narendra Dev felt very sad and castigated the political opportunism of the Congress which according to him had mixed religion with politics. Political opportunism was opposed by him always. After independence, he left both the congress and the socialist parties. Once the socialist party split, he remained till death with the PSP (Praja Socialist Party).

Q10. Discuss the concept of total revolution of J.P. Narayan.

[June 08, Q 13(c)]

Ans. JP's total revolution is basically an extension of his concept of Sarvodaya, where he was for village Swaraj. Indian society is basically a village society. Villages should be the nucleus of public administration. All the elders of the village must sit together and settle their problems. This is possible only if the village economy has an egalitarian character. Unequal distribution of wealth is not going to create democracy. For democracy at village level here, rural economy needs an egalitarian character. Rich landowners should voluntarily give up their land to the poor. Non-violent social order creates space for real radical democracy. Violence breeds hatred and conflict. The structural basis of violence should be abolished. That is why he was for the concept of party less democracy. Parties monopolise political power which creates tensions. Political violence negated the basis of any democratic political order. He was in agreement with the cause of the Naxalites but the means that they adopt, he was opposing.

Q11. Briefly discuss about the political life of Ram Manohar Lohia.

Ans. Ram Manohar Lohia was born on March 23, 1910 in a village named Akbarpur in the District of Faizabad. Ram's father, Hira Lal, was a nationalist by spirit and a teacher by profession. His mother, Chanda, died when Ram was very young. Ram was introduced to the Indian freedom struggle at an early age by his father through the various protest assemblies Hari Lal took his son to. Ram made his first contribution to the freedom struggle by organising a small hartal on the death of Lokmanya Tilak.

Hari Lal, an ardent follower of Gandhiji, took his son along on a meeting with the Mahatama. This meeting deeply influenced Lohia and sustained him during trying circumstances and helped seed his thoughts, actions and love for swaraj. Ram was so impressed by Gandhiji's spiritual power and radiant self-control that he pledged to follow the Mahatma's footsteps. He proved his allegiance to Gandhiji, and more importantly to the movement as a whole, by joining a satyagraha march at the age of ten!

While in school reading the prescribed history book, Lohia noted that the British author of the textbook referred to the great Maharashtrian king Chatrapati Maharaj Shivaji as a "bandit leader" (lutera sardar). Lohia researched the facts and proved that the label "bandit leader" was an unjust description of the Maharaj. Lohia launched a campaign to have the description striken from the textbook. Lohia organised a student protest in 1918 to protest the all-white Simon Commission which was to consider the possibility of granting India dominion status without requiring consultation of the Indian people.

Lohia met Jawaharlal Nehru in 1921. Over the years they developed a close friendship Lohia, however, never hesitated to censure Nehru on his political beliefs and openly expressed disagreement with Nehru on many key issues.

Lohia attended the Banaras Hindu University to complete his intermediate course work after standing first in his school's metric examinations. In 1929, Lohia completed his B.A. from Calcutta University. He decided to attend Berlin University, Germany over all prestigious educational institutes in Britain to convey his dim view of British philosophy. He soon learned German and received financial assistance based on his outstanding academic performance.

While in Europe, Lohia attended the League of Nations assembly in Geneva. India was represented by the Maharaja of Bikaner, a well known puppet of the

British Raj. Lohia took exception to this and launched a protest there and there from the visitors' gallery. He fired several letters to editors of newspapers and magazines to clarify the reasons for his protest. The whole incident made Lohia a recognised figure in India overnight. Lohia helped organise the Association of European Indians and became secretary of the club. The main focus of the organisation was to preserve and expand Indian nationalism outside of India.

Lohia wrote his PhD thesis paper on the topic of "Salt Satyagraha," focusing on Gandhiji's socio-economic theory.

When Lohia returned to India in 1933, a comical situation arouses. Ram had no money to reach his hometown from the airport. He quickly wrote a nationalistic article for "The Hindu," the most popular and widely read newspaper and got money to pay for the fare home.

Lohia joined the Indian National Congress as soon as he returned home. Lohia was attracted to socialism and helped lay the foundation of Congress Socialist Party, founded 1934, by writing many impressive articles on the feasibility of a socialist India. Lohia formed a new branch in the Indian National Congress—the All India Congress Committee (a foreign affairs department). Nehru appointed Lohia as the first secretary of the committee. During the two years that he served he helped define what would be India's foreign policy.

In the onset of the Second World War Lohia saw an opportunity to collapse the British Raj in India. He made a series of caustic speeches urging Indians to boycott all government institutions. He was arrested on May 24, 1939, but released by authorities the very next day in fear of a youth uprising.

Soon after his release, Lohia wrote an article called "Satyagraha Now" in Gandhiji's newspaper, Harijan on June 1, 1940. Within six days of the publication of the article, he was arrested and sentenced to two years of jail. During his sentencing the Magistrate said, "He (Lohia) is a top-class scholar, civilised gentleman, has liberal ideology and high moral character." In a meeting of Congress Committee Gandhiji said, "I cannot sit quiet as long as Dr. Ram Manohar Lohia is in prison. I do not yet know a person braver and simpler than him. He never propagated violence. Whatever he has done has increased his esteem and his honor." Lohia was mentally tortured and interrogated by his jailers. On December of 1941, all the arrested Congress leaders, including Lohia, were released in a desperate attempt by the government to stabilise India internally.

He rigorously wrote articles to spread the message of toppling the British imperialist governments from countries in Asia and Africa. He also came up with a hypothetical blueprint for new Indian cities that could self-administer themselves so well that there would not be need for the police or army.

Gandhiji and the Indian National Congress launched the Quit India movement in the 1942. Prominent leaders, including Gandhiji, Nehru, Azad and Patel, were jailed. The "secondary cadre" stepped-up to the challenge to continue the struggle and to keep the flame for swaraj burning within the people's hearts. Leaders who were still free carried out their operations from underground. Lohia printed and distributed many posters, pamphlets and bulletins on the theme of "Do or Die," on his secret printing-press. Lohia along with freedom fighter Usha Mehta, broadcast messages in Bombay for three whole months before detection from a secret radio station called "Congress Radio" as a measure to give the disarrayed Indian population a sense of hope and spirit in absence of their leaders.

Lohia went to Calcutta to revive the movement there. He changed his name to hide from the police who were closing in on him. Lohia fled to Nepal's dense jungles to evade the British. There he met he Nepalese people and Koirala brothers (courageous freedom fighters in Nepal), who remained Lohia's allies rest of their lives Lohia was captured in May of 1944, in Bombay. Lohia was taken to a prison in Lahore, notoriously known throughout India for its tormenting environment. In the prison he underwent extreme torture. His health was destroyed but his courage remained. Even though he was not as fit his courage and willpower strengthened through the ordeal. Under Gandhiji's pressure the Government released Lohia and his comrade Jayaprakash Narayan. A huge crowd waited to give the 2 a heroes welcome. Lohia decided to visit his friend in Goa to relax. Lohia was alarmed to learn that the Portuguese government had censured the peoples freedom of speech and assembly. He decided to deliver a speech to oppose the policy but was arrested even before he could reach the meeting location. The Portuguese government relented and allowed the people the right to assemble. The Goan people weaved Lohia's tale of unselfish work for Goa in their folk songs. As India tryst with freedom neared Hindu-Muslim strife increased. Lohia strongly opposed partitioning India in his speeches and writings. He appealed to communities in riot torn regions to stay united, ignore the violence surrounding them and stick to Gandhiji's ideals of non-violence. Lohia comforted the Mahatama as nation that once wielded the power of non-violence took refuge in killing their own brothers and sisters. Lohia remained beside Gandhiji as son would remain beside a father.

Dr. Lohia was the first to introduce the unification of some 650 Indian princely states together to form larger states, an idea later adopted by Sardar Patel, first Home Minister of India. Lohia favored Hindi as the official language of India, arguing, "The use of English is a hindrance to original thinking, progenitor of inferiority feelings and a gap between the educated and uneducated public. Come, let us unite to restore Hindi to its original glory."

He was one of the greatest thinkers the Indian Parliament would ever see. He realised that the prevailing poverty would create an India with a weak foundation. As an economically crippled India tried to find ways to get rid herself of its abject poverty, Lohia decided to make the mass public realise the importance of economic robustness for the nation's future.

He encouraged public involvement in post-freedom reconstruction. He pressed people to construct canals, wells and roads voluntarily in their neighborhood. He volunteered himself to build a dam on river Paniyari which is standing till this day and is called "Lohia Sagar Dam." Lohia said, "satyagraha without constructive work is like a sentence without a verb." He felt that public work would bring unity and a sense of awareness in the community. He also was instrumental in having 60 percent of the seats in the legislature reserved for minorities, lower classes, and women.

As a democracy, the Indian Parliament was obliged to listen to citizens' complaints. Lohia helped create a day called "Janavani Day" on which people from around the nation would come and present their grievances to Members of Parliament. The tradition continues even today.

Lohia wanted to abolish private schools and establish upgraded municipal (government) schools which would give equal academic opportunity to students of all casts. This he hoped would help eradicate the divisions created by the caste system.

At the Socialist Party's Annual Convention, Lohia set up a plan to decentralise the government's power so that the general public would have more power in Indian politics. He also formed Hind Kisan Panchayat to resolve farmers' everyday problems.

Lohia was a socialist and wanted to unite all the socialists in the world to form a potent platform. He was the General Secretary of Praja Socialist Party. He established the World Development Council and eventually the World Government to maintain peace in the world.

During his last few years, besides politics, he spent hours talking to thousands of young-adults on topics ranging from Indian literature, politics and art.

Lohia died on October 12, 1967 in New Delhi. He left behind no property or bank balance but prudent contemplations.

Q12. State the main principles of Lohia's theory of history.

Ans. A critique of Marx's theory of history is the starting point of Lohia's own theory of history as stated in his book *Wheel of History*. His main criticism against Marx's theory was that it projects a reading of European history as the history of mankind. As an alternative to it, he developed his own version of philosophy of history. According to his theory there are two main principles which explain the movement of history. The first principle relates to the struggle among various societies for supremacy in terms of power and prosperity. According to Lohia, in this respect history moves like a cycle, i.e., no society can stay at the top forever. Throughout history the centre of power and prosperity has shifted from one region of the world to another. The second principle is about the internal social organisation of any society. In every society there is a constant shift between two kinds of social divisions: one permits social mobility, the other does not. The one that allows people to move to higher or lower positions is 'class'. The other which freezed individuals in the social position they were born in is 'caste'. So every society oscillates between class and a caste. You would have noticed that for Lohia the meaning of both these words differs from their common usage.

The central idea of Lohia's theory of history is that both the principles described above are related to each other: the external and the internal changes take place together. A society which is at the centre of the world tends to have class division; a society which has lost the external struggle develops caste system. Can you see what connects the two principles?

It is not simply a matter of chance. The connecting link, according to Lohia, is the search for technological efficiency by every society. When a society succeeds in attaining increasing levels of efficiency, this success has both internal and external consequences. Externally, that society rises in power in relation to other societies. Internally, it can accommodate social struggle for mobility. However, such maximisation takes place only in one or two dimensions, and at the cost of all other dimensions. Therefore after some time this process reaches a dead-end. Then the society starts declining. Internally it has to adopt the rigid division of castes because there are lesser goods for distribution. In its relationship with other societies, it is no longer the centre of power. The centre shifts to some other nation. That is how the wheel of history moves.

Will the wheel of history go on turning endlessly? Fortunately not, Lohia would say. There is also a third principle that operates in history. Unlike the first two, it works for human unity or what Lohia called 'approximation of mankind'. Throughout history several forces have brought humanity closer in various spheres of life: technologies of production, language ideas, religions, etc. This principle works both among different nations and within nations. Till now such approximation has taken place as a result of external forces, independent of human will. However, according to Lohia, today we have reached the stage of 'wilful approximation of human race', a stage where human beings can come together through conscious efforts. This should be the next step in human progress. Only such a step would enable us to stop the march of the wheel of history.

Q13. According to Lohia what were the common features of communism and capitalism?

Ans. Ram Manohar Lohia was highly influenced by Mahatma Gandhi's ideas which instigated the feeling of Swaraj (freedom) into him. 'Salt Satyagraha' was his subject in the PhD thesis paper. Though he had a good affinity with Jawaharlal Nehru but dissented with him on many political issues.

His first contribution as a nationalist leader was organising a 'hartal' on Bal Gangadhar Tilak's death. In 1928, he joined protests against the Simon Commission.

Lohia on capitalism and communism

Faces Lohia analysis two of modern civilisation: capitalism and communism. For the last three to four hundred years Europe (including America) has been at the centre of the world. The distinguishing features of the modern European civilisation are: continuous application of revolutionary technology to the sphere of production, striving for rising standards of living and an attempt to have greater social equality. In his essay 'Economics after Marx', Lohia makes an attempt to understand the historical origins of this system by questioning the Marxist theory regarding the origins of capitalism. His main criticism of the Marxist theory was that it explains the rise of capitalism only actually right from its beginning capitalism has depended upon external resources. These external resources came from colonies. Marx was right in saying that capitalism is based on the exploitation of the worker by the capitalist. But he did not notice that both of them participate in a more fundamental exploitation of the colonies. In this sense capitalism and colonialism were born together. This was the main point of Lohia's theory of 'twin origin of capitalism and colonialisms'.

From this Lohia concluded that non-European societies like India cannot develop capitalism. *Can you see the reason why?* The reasoning is very simple. If capitalism can arise only with the help of colonialism, and if countries like India cannot now have any colonies, it follows that India cannot also imitate the capitalist development of Europe. Lohia did not question the possibility of capitalism only in the non-European world.

He doubted the future of this system even in Europe and America. He reasoned that the shrinking of colonies after the Second World War had posed a serious challenge to the survival of the capitalist system.

What is the alternative to capitalism? Is communism the answer? In Lohia's view communism only appears to be so; in reality it is no different from capitalism. Both of these are just two faces of the modern civilisation. Both depend on heavy capitalisation, centralised economic mechanism and large-scale technology. Communism merely changes the ownership pattern while retaining the technology. Therefore both capitalism and communism are equally irrelevant for non-Western countries like India.

Neither communism nor capitalism can escape the crisis of modern civilisation. This crisis has arisen, according to Lohia, because its technology has now reached a dead-end. This civilisation cannot create a revolutionary technology any more. As a result it cannot spread any further in geographical terms. Gradually it will lose its pre-eminence in the world. The crisis of the modern civilisation can also be seen in the moral and spiritual decline in these societies. The individual has been reduced to a cog in the machine. In the light of all this it naturally seemed to Lohia that the stage was now set for another turning of the wheel of history.

Chapter 8

Nationalism and Social Revolution II (Communists)

Q1. Examine the features of Marxist political thought during pre-independence period in India. [June 06, Q 1]

Or

Write a note on Marxist thought on colonial India. [Dec 08, Q 11]

Ans. The general features of Marxist political thought during pre-independence period in India may be summarised as follows:-

a) Indian Marxists tried to reconcile nationalism with internationalism. As communists they all subscribed to proletarian internationalism. As such they blindly followed the dictates of the Comintern. But they were also great nationalist. They most emphatically pointed out the contradiction between British imperialism and Indian nationalism. They also strongly emphasised that nothing short of complete independence could be the goal of the national movement. In fact, they had a distinct role in forcing the Indian National Congress to adopt the Independence Resolution.

b) Class approach to politics was first introduced in India by the Marxist thinkers. M.N. Roy and others firmly believed that the general principles of historical materialism and the theory of class struggle could well be applied in explaining Indian social development as in the West.

c) Indian communists had a definite understanding of the stage of social development in India. They argued that capitalism had substantially grown in India immediately after the First World War. But with the help of the 'decolonisation' theory they further argued that the Indian capitalist class had aligned itself with imperialism and so had forsaken any moral right to lead the anti-imperialist national liberation movement. This theory was first formulated by M.N. Roy in 1921 in his book *'India in Transition'*. But its more prominent spokesman was Saumendranath Tagore who in 1928 put forward the thesis that to the degree the hindrance in the way of the capitalist development of India has been removed by British imperialism, the bourgeoisie is sliding more and more towards co-operation and one group after the other is capitulating to imperialism. According to this view Indian bourgeoisie was to be regarded as a counter-revolutionary force, in the same camp as imperialism (politically), because they too, like the imperialists, sought to industrialise the country. It may be pointed out that because of this crude lumping together of imperialism and the national bourgeoisie, the CPI, took an ultraleftist stand in the 1930s and 1940s and failed to grasp the depth of the contradiction between imperialism and the Indian bourgeoisie.

d) Despite shortcomings, however, the Marxists quite correctly emphasised the need for forming a revolutionary alliance between the working class and the peasantry, particularly the poor and landless peasants. According to them, it was only this alliance which could provide the true democratic essence to the nationalist movement.

Q2. Discuss the features of Marxist political thought during post-independence period in India.

Ans. After Indian gained her independence in 1947 the whole situation changed radically. Britain or for that matter any imperialist power could no longer be identified as the principal enemy. Hence, the question of the Indian state came to the forefront. As a corollary to it also came the question of the stage of revolution. Unfortunately, even after forty years of independence the traditional communist parties have not been able to develop a dialectical and comprehensive Marxist analysis of the Indian state. The Marxist intellectuals are also not unanimous on this point. Without going into the debate we shall give in brief outlines the major arguments of different parties and intellectuals on this question.

a) The Communist Party of India (CPI) has characterised the Indian state as a national bourgeoisie state. According to the CPI the class of national bourgeoisie does not include the monopolists who tend to compromise with feudalism and imperialism. Rather because of their participation in the anti-imperialist struggle, a large section of the national bourgeoisie has become progressive in their outlook and practice. As a mark of this progressive character the CPI points out the development of a large and strong public sector, the enactment of anti-monopoly MRTP Act, the nationalisation of banks, initiation of land reforms in the countryside and the consistent allegiance to the non-aligned foreign policy. It is because of these factors that the monopolists cannot exercise decisive influence over the policies of the Indian state. The party considers the national bourgeoisie as its ally in this revolution which, according to it, may be accomplished by peaceful means through the non-capitalist path of development.

b) According to the CPI (M) the Indian state is 'an organ of the rule of the bourgeoisie and landlords, led by the big bourgeoisie, who are increasingly collabourating with foreign finance capital in pursuit of the capitalist path of development'. Being reactionary and compromising in character the ruling class in India, the party believes, has failed to accomplish the tasks of democratic revolution. These tasks imply elimination of the feudal, semi-feudal and imperialist elements in India. In order to do this we need a Peoples Democratic Revolution, the essence of which is an agrarian revolution directed against feudalism, imperialism and big bourgeoisie. The revolution is to be led by the working class with poor and landless peasants as its closest allies. However the rich peasants and national bourgeoisie can also be allies in the revolutionary front.

c) The CPI(ML) describes India as a semi-feudal and semi-colonial state which is yet to attain independence. Hence, it considers the destruction of feudalism, distribution of land to the landless and tenants, and achievement of real freedom of the country as the primary object of the present stage of revolution. Now is the stage of New Democratic Revolution, the essence of which is the agrarian revolution. This revolution should bring an end to the class rule of the feudal lords, imperialists and comprador bourgeoisie.

d) Marxist scholars like K.N. Raj, Hamze Alavi, and Pranab Bardhan have liberated themselves from the clutches of economism and instrumentalism and have presented the thesis of the relative autonomy of the Indian state. According to them, certain developments in the post-war world have created conditions which enable the Indian state to enjoy relative autonomy. These developments are: **(1)** numerical dominance of the lower middle classes at the time to independence, **(2)** extensive involvements of the state in economic activities, **(3)** availability of credit from socialist counties, **(4)** inheritance of overdeveloped state from the imperialist power at the time of independence. **(5)** inability of the dominant classes and their parties to use the state as their instrument, **(6)** direct ownership and control of the state in the economic sphere, and **(7)** enormous prestige and sufficiently unified sense of ideological purpose of the state elite. As a result of these factors, the scholars argue the state enjoys relative autonomy which enables it to shape the class alignments, provide material basis for the new classes and undertake the regulating role in the economy.

Q3. How did left wing emerged in India?

Ans. The individuals who ultimately came to constitute left wing in India came from various backgrounds. To begin with, they were nationalists who under the inspiration of the October Revolution were seeking new paths for achieving national independence.

Four Ideological Currents

The majority of them belonged to the following four ideological currents: 1) Indian national revolutionaries operating from abroad in the period of the First World War (mainly from Germany, USA, Turkey and Afghanistan). The outstanding names amongst them were of M.N. Roy and Abani Mukerji. 2)

National revolutionaries from the Pan-islamic Khilafat movement, who went abroad in the war period (1924-26) and those from the great Hijrat movement of the post-war period. Among them are Mohammad Ali Sepassi, Rahmat Ali Khan, Ferozuddin Mansoor Abdul Majid and Shaukat Usmani; 3) National revolutionaries of the Ghadar party organised among the Sikh and emigrant labour in the USA, Rattan Singh and Santokh Singh were two important names. For a long time they were directly in touch with the Communist International and 4) The most important trend was of the national revolutionaries in India itself. They came from the left wing of the National Congress, the terrorist organisations and parities, the Khilafat movement and the Akali movement. After Gandhi withdrew from the non-cooperation movement in 1922 they turned to the ideology of socialism and the class organisation of workers and peasants under impact of the Russian Revolution. Later on many of them became the founders of the early communist groups in different parts of the country, e.g. Dange in Bombay, Singaravelu in Madras, Musaffer Ahmad in Calcutta and the Inqilab Group in Lahore.

In the earlier phase, these groups were sought to be co-ordinated by the communist centre organised abroad on the basis of the Communist Party of India formed at Tashkent on October 17, 1920 by M.N. Roy and others soon after the Second Congress of the Communist International. The Tashkent centre under the leadership of Roy did a lot of ideological and propaganda work as reflected in their documents and published material. It helped the ideological transformation of the radical nationalist groups to make them into truly communist groups.

First Marxist Debate Regarding India's Political Situation

The first Marxist debate regarding the political situation in India took place at the Second Congress of the Third International which opened in Petrograd on 19 July 1920 and then met in Moscow from 23 July to 7 August.

Roy and Lenin Debate

There were serious difference between Lenin and M.N. Roy as far as the political situation in India was concerned. But they also agreed on certain basic points: Nationalism is a bourgeoisie ideology: the proletarian movement must be kept independent and separate from the bourgeoisie movement. Roy and Lenin differed with each other as far as the mutual relationships of the two movements were concerned. Lenin argued that the two movements should co-operate and collabourate with each other while M.N. Roy opposed these ideas and put forward the argument that the Communist International should assist exclusively the institution and the development of the Communist Party in India. Lenin was not sure whether the conditions for building a Communist Party in Indian were ripe or not. But Roy insisted that a Communist Party in India could be built in the very near future.

For Lenin and the Bolsheviks the world revolution was round the corner and he wanted all the anti-imperialist movements to support the marching armies of the revolution. For the time being Roy agreed with Lenin and accepted the tactic of supporting the national liberation movements. This was the period of non-cooperation in India.

Roy and Gandhi

For a short while Roy was very much impressed by Gandhi and saw his non-violent path as the only path available to the Indian revolutionaries under conditions of colonialism. But Roy was disillusioned when Gandhi withdrew the mass movement. Now he returned to his original argument. He had always believed that only a violent uprising could overthrow the British rule in India. Moreover, this violent insurrection could be organised only by a well organised Communist party. Since Gandhi was opposed to violence he was also opposed to the revolution in India.

Q4. Find out the main assumptions of M.N. Roy's framework for understanding Indian society and polity.

Ans. There were a number of theoretical assumptions inherent in Roy's framework which were not applicable as far as India was concerned. Broadly speaking, Roy's framework was based on the following assumptions:

i) Nationalism was the ideology of the bourgeoisie. (In actuality India being a colonial society nationalism was the ideology of all the classes.)

ii) From the very beginning the national movement would be led either by the working class and its party or by the bourgeoisie and its political party: (In actuality the national movement was led by the nationalist intelligentsia with different ideological learnings.)

iii) Indian National Congress was the party of the Indian bourgeoisie more specifically the party of the capitalist class. Gandhi's leadership was the leadership of the capitalist class. (In actuality the I.N.C. was a party of the Indian people as a whole and its ideology and programme were constantly changing. Its ranks were open to all patriots—conservatives, liberals, communists.)

iv) The British rule could be overthrown only through an armed insurrection and not through non-violent peaceful mass movements as was being claimed by Gandhi. A violent insurrection could be organised only by a disciplined and illegal party of the working class. Therefore, there was an ardent need to build a communist party in India and win over the Indians who were under the influence of the I.N.C.

After 1928 this framework was inherited the CPI and continued to influence it till 1947.

Q5. Why did the Indian communists form the WPPs?

Or

Examine the genesis of the formation of the communist party of India.

Ans. Between the period 1920-25, M.N. Roy was constantly in touch with the Indian communists and helped them to imbibe what he thought to be the basic principles of Marxism. In his communications he consistently underlined the need to form a communist party which he knew, could exist only underground. The colonial government was keeping a very strict vigil to stop the entry of Bolshevik literature and Bolshevik trained agitators in India. The government strongly put down all attempts to organise political activities informed by Marxian schemes.

Thus, the main issues in front of Marxists were: Now the communist party could not be formed legally. The government was determined not to allow the communist groups to function openly. How to evolve a plan of action under such conditions? How the Indian masses should be approached? It was then that the idea of forming a legal, open mass party- the Workers' and Peasants' Party (WPP) was mooted for the first time. An open broad based movement could be built only within the legal framework.

WPP as Conceived by Roy

For M.N. Roy WPP was to be a legal party - "a political party of the masses based on the principle of class interest and with a programme advocating mass action for carrying forward the struggle for national liberation." However, legal mass party was to contain al illegal communist nucleus and was to be under the control and direction of the communist party.

Roy believed that without the communist control this organisation would not ensure a leading role for the working class in the national movement. Around 1922, Roy proposed the formation of this two-in-one arrangement - Workers' and Peasants' Party. But he still called this legal mass party the "conscious vanguard of the working class" which was first supposed to carry out the national revolution by overthrowing the British rule and then establish the "dictatorship of the proletariat."

Nationalist and the Question of Revolution

As pointed out above, many individuals inspired by the Russian revolution came to form the left wing of the Congress. They were young Congressmen who were attracted to workers and peasants movements and socialism though without committing themselves to any fixed scheme of Indian revolution and theoretical formulations of the Third International. The Third International and the leaders of the October Revolution were strongly opposed to imperialism. It was natural that this should attract the attention of all nationalists in the colonial countries. They were sympathetic to the revolution but this did not mean that they were willing to accept Bolshevik ideas and their language. For them Russia was a source of inspiration, necessarily the source of relevant ideas and practices.

M. N. Roy, on the other hand, had already accepted Marxism and Russian experience as a model for emulation.

Genesis of the Formation of the Communist Party of India

Therefore he made the idea of violent revolution and the communist party as the touch stone for distinguishing true communists from pseudo-socialists. Those who questioned the programme of violent revolution and the formation of an underground Communist party could not call themselves as genuine communist. Meanwhile, Roy was attempting to form the CPI but it was not getting formed. Through its conspiracy cases the government had terrorised the nationalists. The formation of the WPP was being proposed by him to tide over this problem. This was the first time that a gap appeared between the given theory and Indian social-political reality.

As pointed out earlier, most of the radical groups had sprung up from within the INC. Their professed objective was to radicalise the Congress movement by extending its mass base to working class and poor peasants. For this purpose they were thinking of forming own organisations.

In Bombay, S.A. Dange, in his journal 'Socialist' (September 1922), suggested the formation of a party called the 'Indian Socialist Labour Party of the INC "The idea was to introduce in the existing Congress" an element of strong opposition to vested interests'. The ultimate goal of the party was to be socialism (yet not defined in terms of a strict scheme) while the immediate objective was to disseminate widely a knowledge of socialist principles to organise the workers in trade unions and to work for legislative reforms.

A similar party within the INC was proposed by M. Singaravelu in Madras. Hemanta Kumar Sarkar. Qazi Nazrul Islam and Muzaffer Ahmad formed Peasants' and Workers' Party in Bengal. WPPs were also formed in Bombay (K.N. Jolekar, R.S. Nimbalkar), Punjab (Abdul Majidi & Sohan Singh Josh) and United Provinces (P.C. Joshi). These parties declared that "Gandhian methods". Including non-cooperation, passive resistance, constructive programme, and civil disobedience were equally good for workers' and peasants' struggles.

Meanwhile, in 1925, one Satyabhakta Suddenly called a conference in Kanpur (December 27) to form a legal Communist Party of Indian. To a large number of communists this sudden move on the party of Satyabhakta came as a surprise as they were busy forming WPPs. But they decided to attend the conference and capture it from the hands of Satyabhakta. Therefore, technically speaking, the Communist Party was formed in 1925 in Kanpur but the actual work of organisation was continued through the WPPs. In actually, the CPI began to be formed only after 1928 when the WPPs were disbanded on the orders of the Third International.

Q6. Write a short note on the formation of congress socialist party.

Ans. In 1933, in Nasik jail, a number of young socialists such as Jayaprakash Narayan, Achyut Patwardhan , M.R. Masani, N.G. Gore, Ashok Mehta, S.M. Joshi and M.L. Dantwala floated the idea of forming an all India socialist organisation within the Congress organisation. Their aim was to influence the policies of the Congress towards socialist ideology. The formation of this party was welcomed by Nehru and Bose.

The Socialists put forward the programme of abolition of zamindari, state ownership of land, nationalisation of industries and banks and fixation of minimum wages for the working masses. The first All-India Socialists Conference was held at Patna on 17th May, 1934, under the presidentship of Acharya Narendra Dev. The conference appealed to the Congress to adopt a programme so as to ensure economic freedom for the starving millions. Very soon CSP units were organised in various parts of the country and Jayaprakash Naryan emerged as its popular spokesman.

The right wing within the Congress was critical of the socialist programme and denounced their propaganda as "loose talk". The first annual session of the CSP (21-22 October, 1934) in Bombay was attended by 150 delegates from 13 provinces. Ram Manohar Lohia, P. Ramamurti and E.M.S. Namboodiripad were also Congress socialist leaders at that time.

The socialists were of the view that all left-wingers should unite together in the Congress in order to influence the decisions of the Congress. But they did not ask them to dissolve their separate organisations. The CSP leadership invited the communists and the Royists to join their ranks as individual members. This was their conception of a united front between the left groups. Once again, through the CSP the communists entered the Congress organisational structure. Many of them became the members of the AICC. Some of the socialist were included into the Working Committee by the Congress president, Nehru.

On two important issues, the socialists carried on a massive campaign inside the Congress. They were opposed to the Congress decision of participating in the elections of 1936. But after some time they agreed to the idea that Congress should participate in the elections. However, now they argued that the Congress should not form ministries as this will make them a part of the colonial government administration. Majority of the Congressmen disagreed with them and were for the formation of ministries. Consequently the Congress formed ministries in seven provinces. But the voting made it quite clear that socialists were a growing force.

The Communists and Royists also existed outside the Congress even when they were a part of the CSP and INC. Both of the groups tried to convert the socialists to their side. They began to compete with each other to increase their respective organisational strength. This created mutual quarrels between them. As a result of these dissensions, the United Front collapsed towards the end of 1940.

Q7. Discuss the Indian left's response on Second World War.

Ans. On 15th September 1939, the Congress Working Committee met to discuss the question of India's role in the War. It adopted a resolution which categorically declared that India could not associate herself with a war which claimed to be anti-fascist and for the defence of democracy when the same democratic freedom was denied to her. The resolution demanded that the British government must declare in unequivocal terms their war aims vis-à-vis India. The Indian communists did not distinguish between Hitler's fascism and western democracies. For them it was an imperialist and they demanded of the Congress leaders that they immediately start the mass civil disobedience. At the beginning of the war the communist policy was to continue the tactic of united front with the Congress. The communist leaders were hopeful that after the preliminary round when the Congress leaders could be arrested, the responsibility of conducting the struggle shall fall into their hands. Moreover, the mass movement was supposed to develop towards mass insurrection.

At Ramgarh session of the Congress in March 1940 the Congress adopted a resolution pledging support for the allies in return for national independence. The Congress leadership was being supported by the Congress Socialists, while the communists were getting impatient with the wait and watch policy of the INC.

Bose accused Gandhi of compromising with the British. "I wholly endorse" said Gandhi, "Mr. Subhas Chandra Bose's charge that I am eager to have a compromise with Britain if it can be had with honour." Soon the communists started emphasising the policy of "exposure of Gandhism" and "sharpest opposition to Gandhian leadership." M.N. Roy's group was the only group at this stage which was giving full support to the British war efforts.

With the aim of persuing the "proletarian path" of armed insurrection, the communists began to organise political general strikes in the major industries. Apart from denouncing Gandhi and Nehru, the communist party also attacked Bose and CSP leadership. The communist policy of single handedly leading the national movement was fully endorsed by the ideologues of the Third International.

By following this policy the communists once again separated themselves from the national movement. The government decided to attack the communists. Till February 1941 about 480 leading communist activists were arrested in various parts of the country and the party was completely paralysed.

The government had succeeded in giving the communist party a serious blow. Large numbers of them were detained in the Deoli detention camp.

In June 1941, Hitler attacked the Soviet Union. All the communist parties in Western democracies began to support the war efforts of their respective governments. What should be the policy of the CPI in this changed situation? The interests of the Soviet Union and Britain coincided with each other. However, India was still a colonial country.

The communists who were outside and functioning under the leadership of P.C. Joshi were of the view that earlier policy of mass opposition to imperialism should be continued and further strengthened as the situation for India remained essentially the same. The other camp, the majority of whom were in jail, emphasised the point that the communists policy must address itself to the supreme aim of Russian victory even if it meant jettisoning the national aim of India's freedom.

With the new situation, they argued the "imperialist war" has changed its character and it has become a "People's War". Ultimately it was this late policy which became the policy of the CPI. Of course, there were individual communists who disagreed with this policy. Consequently, the communists now began to support the war efforts of the colonial government. To the extent possible, they prevented strikes in the factories in order to keep the production running.

As far as the Kisan Front was concerned the new slogan was: "Grow more food". The policy of sharpening the anti-feudal contradiction was also suspended.

From 9 August, 1942, onwards the government began to arrest the Congress leaders and thus succeeded in aborting the Quit India Movement as planned by Gandhi. Meanwhile P.C. Joshi, the General Secretary of the communists party, met the Governor and other authorities and requested them to release the detained communist leaders. A large section of the communists were released from various jails.

It was in 1942 that CPI once again became a legal party openly working for its policies. Now the political field was open to the party as the main political party, i.e., the INC was declared an illegal body. During the years 1942-43, CPI gained strength in numerical terms while it lost its prestige in the eyes of national minded public. In 1943 the Party held its first congress openly and legally. Around this time the membership of the party rose to 5000.

In 1945, after the war was over, the political opponents of the CPI denounced its People's War policy as anti-nationalist.

The communists resigned their membership of the INC. However, this was not the only issue on which the party was swimming against the national mainstream. The other important issue was the party's support to the Pakistan movement.

The party declared that the demand for Pakistan was not a communalist separatist demand but a justified demand for national self-determination. The party carried on a campaign to convince the Indian masses and the Congress leadership to recognise, the demand for Pakistan as a democratic demand. This further alienated them from nationalist public opinion in India.

It is well-known how after R.P. Dutt's advice in March 1946, the CPI started suddenly opposing the demand for Pakistan. In December 1945, the Central Committee of the CPI declared that the new strategy of the party was to work as the builder of a new United National Front in the form of a Congress-League-Communist joint front.

The mass upsurge which followed the arrests of the Congress leaders took a violent turn at many places. The Congress socialists played a very important role in the upsurge of 1942. However, like the Civil Disobedience, the movement of 1942 was also suppressed by the British authorities. But the movement expressed the determination and irresistible urge of the Indian people to be free. After the war was over the British rulers realised that it was no longer possible to keep India subservient.

Q8. Discuss M. N. Roy's concept of radical humanism.[Dec 06, Q 11(iv)]

Or

Write a short note on M.N.Roy's Partyless democracy.[June 08, Q 13(b)]

Ans. M.N. Roy criticised the economic interpretation of history given by Marx. He argued that by viewing the individual as only a part of the collectivity, Marxism rejected the autonomy of the individual. According to Roy, the existence of social organisation presupposes the prior existence of the individual. He further contended that neither socialism nor communism but freedom should be the ideal of a civilised society. Describing Radical Humanism in this context he said, "We place man in the centre of scheme of things: others would sacrifice him on the altar of the collective ego."

He now viewed the Marxist model of revolution as an outdated one. Revolution through insurrection was impossible owing to the military power of modern states. He put forward the idea of a revolution by consent, guided by a philosophy with universal appeal.

In the last years of his life 1947-57, Roy became an exponent of Radical Humanism. Like Western philosophers, Turgot and Condorcet, he felt that the progress of science had liberated man's creative energies. He explained the need to coin a new word because the existing philosophies were inadequate to deal with the problems of Indian society. He argued that his political philosophy makes room for the individual and moral values; and he judged the merit of any social order by the freedom it gives to its individual members.

Also politics around him had become opportunistic and the way could be cleared only by introducing the human element in public affairs. He believed that the right to participate in politics had been reduced to mere voting in elections. This must be re-examined in order to establish complete democracy.

Humanist Model of Politics

Roy's theory of a new model of politics aims at the rejection of spiritualism, nationalism, communism and stands for the acceptance of materialism. According to M.N. Roy the latter is the only possible philosophy since it represents the knowledge of nature as it really exists.

The basic elements of New Humanism are three: rationality, morality and freedom. Roy argued that human beings are subject to their environment but the rational nature of man compels him to offer better explanations of the events of nature. As rational creature man is involved in a struggle for material existence. This struggle takes two forms - at the savage plane it signifies the satisfaction of his mundane wants and at the higher plane, it signifies his struggle for freedom. Freedom is a process and not a complete idea. In the quest for freedom, argues Roy, man as a rational being is driven to bring nature his control And freedom "signifies the progressive disappearance of all restrictions on the unfolding of the potentialities of individuals as human beings. Freedom of the individual is one of the central themes of Roy's scientific politics. He challenges al ideologies which deny the sovereignty of man. As an alternative to the existing ideologies, Roy desired to set up a new social order based on the sovereignty of the individual.

Partyless Democracy

Given his experience of party politics, Roy attacked the goal of power as the only incentive for political action. He argued that "politics is as old as organised social life... it should therefore be realised that politics and parties are not invariably related to each other, nor have they always been together." Hence, there was a possibility of political activity without the existence of political parties. The party system is an inadequate medium to represent the people in the eyes of Roy. It denies the individuals any significant opportunity for effective political action. The right to vote does not ensure political participation. Moreover party rule signifies the rule of a minority of citizens who claim to represent the aspirations of the people. Representative government largely represents only the party which controls it and membership of even the largest size is but a small fraction of the people. Finally Roy Claims that party system leads to dishonesty and corruption in public life since such a system works for the leaders and not for the people.

Roy formulated the nation of organised democracy and participant citizenship to overcome the grave defects of parliamentary democracy. Concomitant to this political framework is the need to introduce a new economic order. According to Roy, a decentralised order in which functions of the state are performed by free and voluntary associations of enlightened people will provide a partial solution to the problem. The state will become an advisory and administrative machinery to co-ordinate and supervise policies framed by the people. The people will participate in local committees which will make them conscious of their sovereign rights.

The economic activity of the new social order has three characteristics:

a) Co-operative economy

b) Centralised planning

c) Science and Technology

Since Roy was critical of capitalism and its doctrine of laissez faire and of state socialism, he advanced the view of an economy based on widespread decentralisation and a practice of co-operation. Economic activity should be conducted at the district, regional and national level by multipurpose co-operative societies. Similarly, planning should be initiated at the grassroots level. Science and technology should be used to reconcile the problem of economic development with the human urge for freedom.

From the above discussion we find that M.N. Roy started his career with a commitment to Marxism but became disillusioned with it over the years. What remained with him however was the conviction that revolutions are 'heralded by iconoclastic ideas'. A revolution must be preceded according to him by a philosophical revolution. Thesis 20 in the Principles of Radical Democracy states that a reorganisation of society must be conducive to common progress and prosperity without encroaching upon the freedom of the individual. Thus, revolutions have no relations with violence or the struggle for power amongst individuals but are meant to change the outlook of the people by bringing about a philosophical regeneration.

Q9. Write a note on the followings:-

(i) Indian Marxist and instrumental approach to the state[Dec 06, Q 10]

(ii) Indian Marxist and Congress

(iii) Indian Marxist and Historical materialism

Ans. (i) Indian Marxist and instrumental approach to the state

Indian communists have an instrumental approach to the question of the state. That state is an instrument of the ruling classes and it works in safeguarding and furthering their interests. Otherwise each Communist Party has a political theory of Indian state. Understanding of ruling class helps in characterising Indian state. There are three Communist Parties: CPI, CPI (M) and CPI (ML). We have to understand each party's viewpoint on the character of Indian State. The position of the CPI is as follows: "The State in Indian is the organ of the class rule of the national bourgeoisie as a whole, in which the big bourgeoisie holds powerful influence. This class rule has links with the landlords. These factors give rise to the reactionary pulls in the State Power." This statement has two parts. First, the big bourgeoisie holds the state power which is the national bourgeoisie. At the same time they have not snapped their relations with the landlords in rural India. This helps in the rise of reactionary forces in Indian politics. They recognise the progressive character of the national bourgeoisie. The ruling Congress Party is the party of this class, that is why it can function as the instrument of social progress. Basically, the congress party can fight feudal interests in rural India.

The position of CPI(M) is as follows: "The present Indian state is the organ of the class rule of the bourgeoisie and the landlords led by big bourgeoisie are increasingly collabourating with foreign finance capital in the pursuit of capitalist path of development. This class character essentially determines the role and functions of State in the life of the country."

For CPI(M), the ruling class is composed of the capitalists and landlords. They both share power in Indian state. Moreover, Indian capitalists are collabourating with foreign capitalist. State is an instrument of capitalists and landlords. The Congress Party is a party of these classes. It has a very little capacity to play a progressive role in Indian politics. There is no question of social, economic and political progress unless this state is undermined and destroyed and replaced by a state of People's Democracy.

CPI(ML) is not a homogeneous political grouping. There are many groups working in the platform. Dominant viewpoint in the party is as follows. "India under Congress rule is only nominally independent, in fact it is nothing more than a semi-colonial and semi-feudal country. The Congress Party Administration represents the interests of the Indian feudal princes, big landlords, are bureaucrat-comprador capitalist." In other words, Indian ruling class has a comprador character. They are subordinated to the American and Russian imperialism. Capitalists are very friendly with the landlords. Indian state is an instrument of these classes which do not work in the interests of Indian people. It is a reactionary state. Indian state and the Congress Party cannot become instruments of social change.

Both CPI and CPI(M) give certain autonomy to the Indian state. Within the present class configuration, state can play a decisive role in the development of a society. Both recognise the importance of planning. That planning in Indian economy supplements the strength of Indian capitalist class. Indian capitalist class because of its belated growth does not have sufficient capital and technology for taking an independent path. State sector or public sector can provide them a helping hand in their development. Public Sector in Indian economy has gone for capital intensive industries. That helps the Indian capitalist class not to be so much dependent on foreign capital. It gives them certain manoeuvring capacity in the international economy.

(ii) Indian Marxist and Congress

As the Congress Party under the leadership of Nehru took a forthright and independent stand on the role of planning and foreign policy, it created confusion in the minds of the communist parties. CPI believes that Congress under the leadership of Nehru represented the interests of the national bourgeoisie. The line continued till the Indira Gandhi period. The Congress Party pursued the policy of non-alignment. It gave priority to public sector in Indian economy. Here the perception of CPI(M) differs slightly from CPI. That non-aligned policy is the result of the character of Indian capitalist class which is reasonably developed class in all the third world countries. They pursued the policy of planning to keep Indian autonomous of international capital. There is a possibility that Indian capitalist class goes deeper into economic crisis. It will depend more and more on foreign capital like World bank and IMF.

CPI and CPI(M) agree that the Congress Party is a secular party but every often compromises with communal forces. Domination of single personalities like Nehru, Indira Gandhi in Congress politics makes the party more authoritarian. Congress Party under the leadership of Indira Gandhi has never faced any organisational election. That is why CPI(M) characterises the Congress Party as an authoritarian party, although CPI does not agree with this characterisation.

Both CPI and CPI(M) do not have any political theory of communalism and caste system. Most of the leaders during the national movement acquired certain understanding out of their experience. On both these issues, their understanding does not differ from liberal traditions. India is a multi-community society. Inter-communal harmony is a must for practicing class politics. With radicalisation of mass politics, communal politics will retreat.

(iii)Indian Marxist and Historical materialism [June 06, Q 11(v)]

Communists in India have always been busy in trying to look for answers to problems in a Marxist framework. They have had very little time to do philosophical thinking. Their concern has been basically in the application of historical materialism to Indian situations. Most Indian Marxists have a dialogue with Marx's own writings on Indian society. In constructing Indian history, Marx has made two important points. First, Indian society before the British rule was a stagnant society. Village community and caste society created a social framework for making Indian economy a unchanging economy. Secondly, British rule was blessing in disguise which helped in destroying this aspect of Indian society and created circumstances for regeneration. Marx's own statement is given below. "The historic pages of their rule in India report hardly anything beyond that destruction. The work of regeneration hardly transpires through a heap of ruins. Nevertheless it has began."

The British rule cannot stop the changes introduced by it. Changes would bring national unity. Moreover, introduction of freedom of press and English education have brought about a radical change in Indian society. An educated class with new ideas would be playing an important role in the political transformation of a society.

Marxists have a historical scheme for understanding any history. There are certain stages in history like primitive communism, slavery, feudalism and capitalism. Historical development of each society experiences these stages. Some of the prominent communists themselves applied the historical scheme in a mechanical manner. S.A. Dange, in his book, *India: From Primitive Communism to Slavery* accepted the stage of slavery in Indian history. But most of the Indian communists reject this point and try to understand Indian history in a creative manner. All of them agree to a point that Indian history does not have stage of slavery. Primitive tribal society gets transformed into a caste society without experiencing the stage of slavery. Indian feudalism integrated caste system into it. It has similarities with European feudalism because it does not have serfdom which is an integral part of European feudalism.

Q10. Discuss the views of Nehru and Subhash Chandra Bose on the problem of social transformation of India.

Ans. Nehru's understanding of the problem of social transformation of India was primarily guided by his secular and scientific outlook, which aimed at the modernisation of Indian society. In this venture Nehru had before him two major alternatives. One, the model of free market economy in the West, based on unrestricted capitalism; the other was the model of planned economy as pursued in the USSR. Nehru had reservations against both of these approaches. He could not accept the first one, since this would eventually lead to gross inequality and exploitation, in violations of the basic norms of humanism. As regards the Marxian model of socialism which was being practiced in Soviet Russia, Nehru was deeply impressed by its achievements and he quite openly proclaimed that socialism was the only option for India, if a society free from the clutches of exploitation, injustice and inequality was to be built. His socialist sympathy was most strongly evident in his Presidential address at the Lucknow Session of the AICC in 1936. He could at the same time never reconcile himself to the methods. Thus, he could not accept the idea of the cult of one centralised party, restrictions on rights and freedoms of individuals and above all, Soviet socialism's emphasis on class struggle and the forcible overthrow of an exploitative social order. Nehru's socialism was broadly based on limited public control of private enterprise, planned economy etc. on the one hand, and pluralism freedom of the individual etc. on the other. In developing this perspective, he was deeply influenced by the Fabian idea of democratic socialism in a nationalist framework. While this nationalism was sharply different from the idea of Hindu revivalism with which Nehru never compromised, he emphasised that India's road to socialism would have its foundations based on traditional Indian ideals like co-operation, peaceful development, humanism and accommodation of all religious beliefs, i.e. secularism.

It becomes quite strongly evident that Nehru was projecting a vision which was bound to unleash tensions and difficulties, since it was an attempt to reconcile things which were contradictory. While Nehru's goals was to seek a society based on justice and free from exploitation, he attempted to do it in a framework of thought where rights and freedoms of individuals placed in unequal circumstances would not be restricted. This was a kind of humanism which was unworkable in practice, since the privileged and the underprivileged were advised to work in a spirit of cooperation. Effectively speaking, Nehru's nationalistic vision blurred his perspective of socialism and dissipated the possibility of any real social revolution, since his radical outlook contradicted his path of compromise.

Subhas Chandra Bose

Subhas Chandra Bose's idea of social transformation of India was guided primarily by a spirit of intense nationalism and the considerations of practical politics. While he quite strongly emphasised that political freedom was meaningless without social and economic emancipation of the masses and that in free India it was not the vested interests (i.e., the landlords, money-lenders and capitalists) but the interests of the peasants and workers which would be protected, the ideological framework which he envisaged for realising these goals contradicted his objectives. He distanced himself from the capitalist path of free-market economy and came certainly closer to the radical ideology of socialism. But his spiritual background, particularly the influence of Vivekananda, his militant nationalism and above all, his primary consideration being practical politics, led Bose to reject the Marxist model of socialism with emphasis on class struggle and materialism. Thus, while he was certainly attracted towards socialism's crusade against injustice and exploitation and its advocacy of the cause of equality, he could not endorse the political strategy of Marxism for realisation of these objectives.

His ideological vision became particularly clouded because, guided primarily by militant nationalist sentiments he aimed at realising his goal by adopting a path which would give him quick, immediate and effective results. This inclination towards pragmatism being a major feature of Bose's political outlook, he looked towards fascism with its emphasis on centralised state control and militarism. He felt that the quickest road to social transformation was possible by combining the ideological goal of Marxism, socialism with emphasis on equality and the fascist methods of discipline, militant nationalism and rigid state control. In this regard, the views of Bose sharply differed from those of Nehru, who was uncompromisingly opposed to fascism for its inhuman character.

Bose, however, could not convincingly explain as to how this odd mixture was really possible in practice, since fascism was basically a defence of the vested interests of capitalism, while Marxian socialism was uncompromisingly opposed to capitalism. The result was that Subhas Chandra Bose's nationalist ideological vision did not enable him to develop any real and effective understanding of the problem of social revolution in India.

Q11. What were the alternatives proposed by the communists to understand the problem of social revolution? Discuss the problems of these alternatives.

Ans. The alternative strategy of social revolution proposed by the communists was primarily a product of their critique of the nationalist brand of socialism. While they also were genuine patriots and stood for secularism, opposition to Hindu revivalism and obscurantist practices like untouchability, their basic argument was that the objectives of socialism, i.e. equality, justice and freedom from exploitation could not be realised without a radical restructuring of society. In their vision, this was impossible by adopting the nationalist solution which emphasised primarily the idea of accomplishment of national freedom under the leadership of middle-class oriented parties and groups as represented by Nehru, Subhas, Bose and Congress Socialists. The Communists also could not agree with their perspective of social transformation which mainly justified the values of harmony and co-operation among the contending groups and classes in a society where discrimination between the privileged and underprivileged was extremely acute. In other words, their main objection against nationalism was that it was virtually a defence of the vested interests and real social transformation was impossible by adopting the framework of nationalism.

Motivated by this idea the communists, who professed their adherence to Marxism, developed an alternative approach towards the understanding of the question of social revolution. They followed what is generally known as the class approach and therein lay their fundamental difference with the nationalist approach. They argued that if the ordinary man was to be the real beneficiary of social transformation, then it would have to be the alliance of the working class and peasantry which would be the guiding force of revolution. This, they argued, could not be done by adopting the methods of co-operation and preaching harmony of contending groups and classes in society; to achieve this objective, the communists thus preached the idea of violent, forcible overthrow of the propertied classes which include the nationalists, i.e. the middle classes also. In proclaiming this goal, they were largely inspired by the experience of the Russian Revolution.

This approach, however, despite its strongly radical thrust, proved unworkable for a number of reasons. One, despite the criticism of the nationalists, it could not be appreciated by the communists that nationalist sentiments and appeals were too strongly embedded in the minds of the masses, which could not be just brushed aside. Rather, this virulent attack on nationalism and the castigation of the nationalist leaders like Gandhi, Nehru and Subhas Bose as agents of capitalists quite often isolated the communists from the mainstream of the freedom struggle. Two, the model of the Russian Resolution was virtually unworkable in India, because the material conditions were fundamentally different. Three, the communists overestimated the potential and organisational strength of the working class was somewhat mechanical and to a large extent unreal, with the consequence that their vision of social revolution eventually remained unreal and unworkable.

Question Papers

EPS-3 : MODERN INDIAN POLITICAL THOUGHT
June, 2006

Note:
***(i) Section I** – Answer **any two** out of four questions.*
***(ii) Section II** – Answer **any four** out of six questions.*
***(iii) Section III** – Answer **any four** parts of Q. No. 11.*

SECTION I

Answer any two of the following question in about 500 words each. Each question carries 20 marks.

Q1. Write an essay on Socialism in early 20th century India.

Ans. The post non-cooperation period witnessed a rapid growth of socialist ideas and emergence of numerous Socialist and Communist groups. There were two factors responsible for the development of radical politics in the twenties. The increasing restlessness among Indian youth and the toiling masses who were being drawn into the national movement was coming to the fore. It was Gandhi's signal contribution that he made the Congress led movement a full-fledged mass movement. Yet his insistence on non-violence in the face of brutal repression by the colonial government as witnessed in the Jalianwala Bagh massacre, or his withdrawal of the non-cooperation movement in the wake of the Chauri-Chaura episode when a mob of peasants burned down a police-station manned entirely by the British led to large-scale disillusionment. Increasingly, it was being felt that nonviolent methods will not do. Search for alternative forms thus became imperative. This search was decisively influenced by another factor: the victory of the Russian Revolution and the establishment of a socialist state. The first socialist weekly, *The Socialist,* was started by S.A. Dange in 1923 in Bombay. In Bengal a group of determined organisers led by Muzaffar Ahmed started the foundations of the Communist Party. Earlier M.N. Roy, a revolutionary nationalist, who had left India in search of arms, reached USA and became converted to socialism. Thereafter, in 1921, he along with a band of Mohajirs formed in Tashkent, the Communist Party of India which was affiliated to the communist International. The Mohajirs were those who left the country on hijrat i.e. self-imposed exile—a concept of Islamic faith. In 1924, a number of people, including Dange and Muzaffar Ahmed, were arrested under the Kanpur conspiracy case. Workers and Peasant Parties were formed in Bombay, Bengal and Punjab. They supported the economic and political demands of the workers and peasants and organised them on class lines. They articulated and propagated the programme of national independence and stood for direct action by the workers and peasants. Trade unions were organised and a number of strikes took place. Side by side, the development of revolutionary terrorism into socialism took place. Bhagat Singh and his Hindustan Socialist Republican Association typified such developments.

Revolutionary Socialism

In 1926, a political forum by the name of Naujawan Bharat Sabha was created with the idea of educating young people in social matters, popularizing swadeshi and developing a sense of brotherhood. Apart from this it sought to cultivate a secular outlook, even atheism among the youth. This organisation was a fore-runner of the Bindustan Republic Association, which aimed at overthrowing the British rule by insurrection. It had an elabourate organisation to carry on its clandestine activities. The Sabha propagated the ideal of equality, removal of poverty and equitable redistribution of wealth. This Hindustan Republican Association (HRA) subsequently changed its name to Hindustan Socialist Republic Association (HSRA). When the British Government, in its bid to suppress the working class movement, sought to introduce the Public Safety Bill and the Trade Disputes Bill, the HSRA decided to protest by bombing the Assembly when the bills were placed-the action was carried out by Bhagat Singh and Batukeswar Dutta, while many such activities carried on by the HSRA seem, on the face of it, to be conventional terrorist activities and the Naujawan Bharat Sabha functioned with a much broader perspective. Bhagat Singh clarified in his trial that revolution to him was not the cult of the bomb and pistol but a total change of society culminating in the overthrow of bath Indian and foreign capitalism and the establishment of the dictatorship of the proletariat. The assembly bombs were meant to be purely demonstrative to make the authorities see reason. In a sense the activities of the HSRA exemplified the transition from terrorism to radical socialist politics, as it did for finding the appropriate methods of political agitation.

Now Refer to Chapter-1, Q.No.-9(a) & (b)

Q2. Evaluate Gokhale as a liberal thinker.

Refer to Chapter-2, Q.No.-13

Q3. Discuss Tilak's political ideas.

Refer to Chapter-3, Q.No.-5

Q4. Discuss Dr. Ambedkar's views on democracy.

Refer to Chapter-4, Q.No.-14

SECTION II

Answer any four of the following questions in about 250-300 words each. Each question carries 10 marks.

Q5. Write a note on revivalist nationalist politics in early 20th century India.
Refer to Chapter-7

Q6. Discuss the political ideas of Swami Dayanand Saraswati.
Refer to Chapter-5, Q.No.-4

Q7. Mention the salient features of Gandhi's Constructive Programme.
Refer to Chapter-6

Q8. Write a short note on the Socialists in the post-Independence period.
Refer to Chapter-8, Q.No.-4 & Q.No.-5

Q9. Discuss Marxist political thought in pre-Independence India.
Refer to Chapter-8, Q.No.-1

Q10. Comment on M.N. Roy's critique of Marxism.
Refer to Chapter-8, Q.No.-5

SECTION III

Q11. Write short notes on any four of the following in about 50 words each. Each part carries 5 marks.
(i) Equality before law.
Refer to Chapter-4, Q.No.-14

(ii) Ranade on methods of social reforms.
Refer to Chapter-2, Q.No.-9

(iii) Distinct characteristics of militant nationalism.
Refer to Chapter-3, Q.No.-1

(iv) Nehru on social transformation.
Refer to Chapter-7, Q.No.-5 & 6

(v) Indian Marxists and Historical Materialism.
Refer to Chapter-8, Q.No.-9

(vi) JP's concept of Total Revolution.
Refer to Chapter-7, Q.No.-13

EPS-3 : MODERN INDIAN POLITICAL THOUGHT
December, 2006

Note:
(i) Section I *– Answer* ***any two*** *out of four questions.*
(ii) Section II *– Answer* ***any four*** *out of six questions.*
(iii) Section III *– Answer* ***any four*** *parts of Q. No. 11.*

SECTION I

Answer any two of the following question in about 500 words each. Each question carries 20 marks.

Q1. Discuss the British colonial intervention in the Indian polity.
Refer to Chapter-1, Q.No.-2(2)

Q2. Describe the broad contours of the social reform ideology in 19th and early 20th century India.
Refer to Chapter-2, Q.No.-1

Q3. Critically examine Bhagat Singh's ideas on Atheism and Social Revolution.
Refer to Chapter-3, Q.No.-12

Q4. Write an essay on Tribal Movements in colonial India.
Refer to Chapter-4, Q.No.-3

SECTION II

Answer any four of the following questions in about 250-300 words each. Each question carries 10 marks.

Q5. Enumerate the main trends of the Muslim political thinking in early 20th century India.
Refer to Chapter-5, Q.No.-10 & 14

Q6. Discuss the political ideas of V.D. Savarkar.
Refer to Chapter-5, Q.No.-8

Q7. Examine Mohammad Iqbal's views on Nationalism.
Refer to Chapter-5, Q.No.-11

Q8. Give an account of Gandhi's critique of modern civilisation.
Refer to June-2003, Q.No.-7

Q9. Examine Lohia's view on Capitalism and Communism.
Refer to Chapter-7, Q.No.-16

Q10. Comment on the Indian Marxists' view on the nature of state.
Refer toChapter-8, Q.No.-9(i)

SECTION III

Q11. Write short notes on any four of the following in about 50 words each. Each part carries 5 marks.
(i) Religious Revivalism
Refer to Chapter-1, Q.No.-4

(ii) Raja Rammohan Roy
Refer to Chapter-2, Q.No.-6

(iii) Sri Aurobindo's views on the nature of British rule
Refer to Chapter-3, Q.No.-7

(iv) Abul Kalam Azad's view on nationalism
Refer to Chapter-5, Q.No.-14

(v) Self-respect Movement
Refer to Chapter-4, Q.No.-12

(vi) M.N. Roy's concept of partyless democracy
Refer to Chapter-8, Q.No.-8

EPS-3 : MODERN INDIAN POLITICAL THOUGHT
June, 2007

Note:
(i) Section I *– Answer* ***any two*** *out of four questions.*
(ii) Section II *– Answer* ***any four*** *out of six questions.*
(iii) Section III *– Answer* ***any four*** *parts of Q. No. 11.*

SECTION I

Answer any two of the following question in about 500 words each. Each question carries 20 marks.

Q1. Discuss the British colonial intervention in social and cultural spheres in India.
Refer to Chapter-1, Q.No.-2

Q2. Describe the circumstances leading to the social reform movement in Colonial India.
Refer to Chapter-2, Q.No.-1

Q3. Trace the influence of militant nationalism on the Indian National Congress.
Refer to Chapter-3, Q.No.-1 & 2

Q4. Write an essay on Tribal Movements in British India.
Refer to Chapter-4, Q.No.-3

SECTION II

Answer any four of the following questions in about 250-300 words each. Each question carries 10 marks.

Q5. Identify the main trends of Muslim political thinking in early 20th century India.
Refer to Dec-2006, Q.No.-5

Q6. Describe Abul Kalam Azad's views on democracy.
Refer to Chapter-5, Q.No.-14

Q7. Discuss Gandhi's views on science and machinery.
Refer to Chapter-6

Q8. Write a note on Nehru's scientific outlook.
Refer to Chapter-7, Q.No.-6

Q9. Examine Subhash Chandra Bose's conception of Socialism.
Refer to Dec-2005, Q.No.-4

Q10. Describe M.N. Roy's concept of partyless democracy.
Refer to Chapter-8, Q.No.-8

SECTION III

Q11. Writes short notes on any four of the following in about 50 words each. Each parts carries 5 marks.
(i) Religious revivalism in colonial India.
Refer to Chapter-1, Q.No.-4

(ii) Methods of social reform.
Refer to June-2006, Q.No.-7

(iii) Sri Aurobindo's views on nature of British rule.
Refer to Chapter-3, Q.No.-7

(iv) Jyotiba Phule's views on gender equality.
Refer to Chapter-4, Q.No.-6

(v) Swami Vivekananda's concept of nationalism.
Refer to Chapter-5, Q.No.-7

(vi) Gandhi's view on education.
Refer to Dec-2003, Q.No.-11(iv)

EPS-3 : MODERN INDIAN POLITICAL THOUGHT
December, 2007

Note:
(i) Section I – *Answer* **any two** *out of four questions.*
(ii) Section II – *Answer* **any four** *out of six questions.*
(iii) Section III – *Answer* **any four** *parts of Q. No. 11.*

SECTION I

Answer any two of the following question in about 500 words each. Each question carries 20 marks.

Q1. Discuss different stands of Liberalism in British India.
Refer to Chapter-1, Q.No.-6

Q2. Examine Rammohan Roy's reinterpretation of Hinduism.
Refer to Chapter-2, Q.No.-6

Q3. Discuss G.K. Gokhale's views on economic and social issues.
Refer to Chapter-2, Q.No.-12 & 13

Q4. Examine B.R. Ambedkar's views on caste system.
Refer to Chapter-4, Q.No.-17

SECTION II

Answer any four of the following questions in about 250-300 words each. Each question carries 10 marks.

Q5. Discuss Swami Vivekananda's concept of freedom.
Refer to Chapter-5, Q.No.-6

Q6. Write a note on Sir Syed Ahmed Khan's views on education.
Refer to Chapter-5, Q.No.-10

Q7. Discuss Gandhi's concept of Swaraj.
Refer to Chapter-6, Q.No.-1

Q8. Examine the role of village panchayat in Gandhi's scheme.
Refer to Chapter-6, Q.No.-7(2)

Q9. Comment on whether Subhash Chandra Bose was an admirer of Fascism.
Refer to Chapter-7, Q.No.-9

Q10. Trace the genesis of the formation of Communist Party of India.
Refer to Chapter-7, Q.No.-3

SECTION III

Q11. Write short notes on any two of the following in about 50 words each. Each part carries 5 mark.
(i) Army in British India.
Refer to Chapter-1, Q.No.-2

(ii) Rammohan Roy on Sati
Refer to Chapter-2, Q.No.-6

(iii) Partition of Bengal
Refer to Chapter-3

(iv) Impact of Birsa Munda's Movement
Refer to Chapter-4, Q.No.-21(1)

(v) M. Iqbal on Islamic Democracy
Refer to Chapter-5, Q.No.-11

(vi) Bhagat Singh as a revolutionary
Refer to Chapter-3, Q.No.-10

EPS-3 : MODERN INDIAN POLITICAL THOUGHT
June, 2008

Note:
(i) Section I *– Answer* ***any two*** *out of four questions.*
(ii) Section II *– Answer* ***any four*** *out of six questions.*
(iii) Section III *– Answer* ***any four*** *parts of Q. No. 11.*

SECTION I

Answer any two of the following question in about 500 words each. Each question carries 20 marks.

Q1. Discuss the British (colonial) intervention in social and cultural fields in 19th century India.
Refer to Chapter-1, Q.No.-2

Q2. Trace the emergence of Nationalism in early British India.
Refer to Chapter-1, Q.No.-7

Q3. Critically examine Gopal Krishna Gokhale's political thought.
Refer to Chapter-2, Q.No.-12

Q4. Assess B.G. Tilak as a political leader.
Refer to Chapter-3, Q.No.-5

SECTION II

Answer any four of the following questions in about 250-300 words each. Each question carries 10 marks.

Q5. Write a note on anti-caste movements inspired by liberal philosophy in colonial India.

Ans. Anti-Caste Movements under the Influence of Liberal Philosophy: The third major way in which the caste structure was affected was through powerful anti-caste and social reform movements under the Arya Samaj in Northern India, Raja Ram Mohan Roy in Bengal, Jyotiba Phule in Maharashtra, Sri Narayan Guru in Kerala, Ramaswami Naicker in Madras and so on. The major themes taken up by these movements were reform in regard to the position of women, equality for oppressed castes, general reform in religion and rituals. So, for instance, social reformers had exerted enough pressure for the enactment of the Special Marriage Act in 1872, that made inter-caste marriage possible.

Questions of widow remarriage, Sati, women's education etc. were important issues of struggle waged by the social reformers, particularly in Bengal.

The mobility of a few low castes had in Srinivas' words, a 'demonstration effect' on all others in the region. The latter felt that they were no longer condemned to a life of poverty and oppression. Provided they made the effort, they could also rise up the ladder. Perhaps this feeling significantly contributed to lending a strength to the movement of lower and backward castes. What has come to be known as the 'Backward Classes Movement' acquired a widespread character and was particularly strong in Southern parts of India. These movements, passed through two stages: in the first, the lower castes tried to acquire the symbols and rituals of high status, while in the second aspirations moved towards acquisition of political power, education and share in the new economic opportunities.

The emergence of caste sabhas or associations gave organisational impetus to the movement of backward castes. Initial activity of these sabhas were directed at trying to reform caste customs and undertake welfare activities of the benefit of their caste brethren, in the form of building hostels, houses on a co-operative basis, setting up colleges and hospitals and provide scholarships.

An overview of the most important anti-caste movements mentioned above suggests that, despite widely differing approaches and methods they had a common stand, in that they were motivated by similar issues which became the total point of reform. While the social reformers of Bengal explicitly challenged the very basis of caste oppression by advocating nationalism, the Arya Samaj and/or the Ramakrishna Mission sought to modify the caste system by efforts in the direction of removal of untouchability. Phule and Naicker organised the 'lower castes' to lead an assault on the upper caste domination in all spheres of social life. However, it has been pointed out that such movements which organised the lower castes against upper caste domination, in due course got transformed into a movement of caste solidarity themselves.

Q6. Discuss Jyotiba Phulel's critique of Varna and the caste system.

Refer to Chapter-4, Q.No.-6

Q7. What were the main trends of Muslim political thinking in early 20th century India?

Refer to Chapter-5, Q.No.-10 & Q.No.-14

Q8. Discuss the political ideas of V.D. Savarkar.

Refer to Chapter-5, Q.No.-9

Q9. Examine M.K. Gandhi's critique of modern civilisation.
Refer to Chapter-6, Q.No.-2

Q10. Briefly describe M.K. Gandhi's concepts of Satyagraha.
Refer to Chapter-6, Q.No.-5

Q11. Trace the growth of socialist ideas in early 20th century India.
Refer to June-2006, Q.No.-1

Q12. Enumerate the main assumptions of M.N. Roy's analytic framework.
Refer to Chapter-8, Q.No.-4

SECTION III

Q13. Write short notes on any of the following in about 100 words each. Each part carries 6 marks.

(a) Formation of the congress socialist party.
Refer to Dec-2007, Q.No.-10

(b) M.N. Roy's partyless Democracy.
Refer to Chapter-8, Q.No.-8

(c) JP's concept of Total Revolution.
Refer to Chapter-7, Q.No.-10

(d) Subhash Chandra Bose's views on History.
Refer to Chapter-7, Q.No.-7 & Q.No.-8

EPS-3 : MODERN INDIAN POLITICAL THOUGHT
December, 2008

Note:
(i) ***Section I*** *– Answer* ***any two*** *out of four questions.*
(ii) ***Section II*** *– Answer* ***any four*** *out of eight questions.*
(iii) ***Section III*** *– Answer* ***any two*** *parts of Q. no. 13.*

SECTION I

Answer any two of the following questions in about 500 words each. Each question carries 20 marks.

Q1. Discuss the British (colonial) intervention in the Indian economy.
Refer to Chapter-1, Q.No.-2 (3)

Q2. Write an essay on political liberalism in 19th century India.
Refer to Chapter-2, Q.No.-4

Q3. Discuss militant nationalism in Colonial India.
Refer to Chapter-3, Q.No.-1 & Q.No.-2

Q4. Write a note on E.V. Ramaswamy Naicker's self-respect movement.
Refer to Chapter-4, Q.No.-12

SECTION II

Answer any four of the following questions in about 250 words each. Each question carries 12 marks.

Q5. Discuss the political ideas of Swami Dayanand Saraswati.
Refer to Chapter-5, Q.No.-4

Q6. What were Mohammad Iqbal's views on nationalism?
Refer to Chapter-5, Q.No.-4

Q7. Illustrate the Western influences on M.K. Gandhi.
Refer to Chapter-6, Q.No.-6

Q8. Discuss the role of Village Panchayat in M.K. Gandhi's scheme.
Refer to Dec-2007, Q.No.-8

Q9. Comment on Jawaharlal Nehru's views on socialism.
Refer to Chapter-7, Q.No.-4 (1)

Q10. Examine Subhash Chandra Bose's concept of socialism.
Refer to Chapter-7, Q.No.-4 (2)

Q11. Write a note on Marxist thought in Colonial India.
Refer to Chapter-8, Q.No.-1

Q12. Trace the goals genesis of the formation of the Communist Party of India.
Refer to Dec-2007, Q.No.-10

SECTION III

Q13. Write short notes on any two of the following in about 100 words each. Each part carries 6 marks.
(i) Police system in British India
Refer to Chapter-1, Q.No.-2

(ii) Social reform versus Political reform
Refer to Chapter-2

(iii) Sri Aurobindo's theory of nationalism
Refer Chapter-3, Q.No.-8

(iv) B.R. Ambedkar on conversion
Ans. Throughout his life Ambedkar made efforts to reform the philosophical basis of Hinduism. But he was convinced that Hinduism will not modify its disposition towards the untouchables. So, he searched for an alternative to Hinduism. After careful consideration, he adopted Buddhism and asked his followers to do the same. His conversion to Buddhism meant reassertion of his faith in a religion based on humanism. Ambedkar argued that Buddhism was the least of injustice and exploitation was the goal of Buddhism. By adopting Buddhism, the untouchables would be able to carve out a new identity for themselves. Since Hinduism gave them nothing but sufferings, by renouncing Hinduism, the untouchables would be renouncing the stigma of untouchability and bondage attached to them. To live a new material life, a new spiritual basis consistent with the liberal spirit was essential. Buddhism would provide this basis.

Therefore, at the social level, education; at the material level new means of livelihood; at the political level, political organisation and at the spiritual level, self-assertion and conversion constituted Ambedkar's overall programme of the removal of untouchability.

EPS-3 : MODERN INDIAN POLITICAL THOUGHT
June, 2009

Note :
*(i) **Section I** – Answer **any two** out of four questions.*
*(ii) **Section II** – Answer **any four** out of eight questions.*
*(iii) **Section III** – Answer **any two** out of four questions.*

SECTION I

Answer any two of the following questions in about 500 words each. Each question carries 20 marks.

Q1. Describe the different strands of Liberalism that emerged during the colonial period in India.
Refer to Dec-2007, Q.No.-1

Q2. Explain Rammohan Roy's views on Caste, Women's rights and Sati.
Refer to Chapter-2, Q.No.-6

Q3. Evaluate the nature of Tribal movements during the colonial period.
Refer to Chapter-4, Q.No.-3

Q4. Assess Gandhi's revised views on modern Civilisation and Swaraj.
Ans. Within about a decade after the publication of Hind Swaraj, Gandhi softened his moral condemnation of some of the institutions and values of the modern Western civilisation. Broadly speaking, his position changed, over the years, from an outright indictment of modernity to a limited appreciation of the emancipatory relevance of some of its values and institutions, especially, parliamentary democracy, constitutional government, the scientific spirit and technological inventions.

SECTION II

Answer any four of the following questions in about 250 words each. Each question carries 12 marks.

Q5. Write a note on Aurobindo's positive programme of Political Action.
Refer to Chapter-3, Q.No.-8

Q6. Describe Dr. B.R. Ambedkar's views on Social and Economic Democracy.
Refer to Chapter-4, Q.No.-14

Q7. Discuss Gandhi's concept of Sarvodya.
Refer to Chapter-6, Q.No.-8

Q8. Examine Iqbal's views on Nationalism.
Refer to Dec-2008, Q.No.-7

Q9. Comment on Abul Kalam Azad's romantic phase of Ideas.
Refer to Chapter-5, Q.No.-14

Q10. What technique was suggested by Subhas Chandra Bose for national revolution?

Ans. In a broadcast over Azad Hind Radio Subhash Bose chalked out his methodology of national struggle. He said that the campaign that was going on in India was non-violent guerrilla warfare. He asserted that the object of this guerrilla warfare would be twofold, one to destroy war production in India and the other to paralyse the British administration and all people of India should participate in the struggle. He chalked out a detail programme for the people. He suggested that payment of the taxes be stopped which directly or indirectly brought revenue to the government. The workers in all industries should either launch a stay in strike or try to hamper production by conducting a go-slow campaign inside the factories. They should also carry out sabotage to impede production. The students should organise secret guerrilla bands for carrying on sabotage in different parts of the country. They should also invent new ways of annoying the British authorities, for example, burning stamps etc. in post offices, destroying British monuments etc. The women, especially girl students should do underground work of all kinds, especially as secret messengers or provide shelter for the men who fight. The government officials who are prepared to help the campaign should not resign their posts but give all available information to fighters outside and should try to hamper production by working inefficiently. The servants who are working in the houses of Britishers, should be organised for the purpose of giving trouble to the masters, for example, by demanding higher salaries, cooking and serving bad food and drinks etc. The Indians should give up all business with foreign banks, firms, insurance companies etc. For the general public he suggested the following activities:

a) Boycott of British goods, industry, burning of British stalls and government stores;

b) Total boycott of Britishers in India, and those Indians who are pro-British;

c) Hold demonstrations in spite of official prohibition;

d) Publishing of secret bulletins and setting up of a secret radio station;

e) Marching to the houses of British government officials and demanding their departure from India;

f) Organising of processions for entering and occupying government offices,

secretarial buildings, law courts etc. with a view to hampering administration.
g) Arranging to punish police officers and prison officials who oppress and persecute people.
h) Begin erecting barricades in the streets where there is a likelihood of attack from the police and military.
i) Setting fire to government offices and factories which are working for war purposes.
j) Interrupting postal, telegraph, telephone and communication as frequently as possible.
k) Interrupting railways, bus and tram services, whenever there is a possibility of hampering the transport of soldiers or of war material.
l) Destroying police stations, railway stations and jails in isolated places.

Q11. Write a note on Nehru's scientific outlook.
Refer to Chapter-7, Q.No.-6

Q12. Examine M.N. Roy's views on Partyless Democracy.
Refer to June-2008, Q.No.-13(b)

SECTION III

Answer any two of the following questions in about 100 words each. Each questions carries 6 marks.

Q13. Write a brief note on Ranade's criticism of Hindu Religious practices.
Refer to Chapter-2, Q.No.08

Q14. Describe Santhal Revolt of 1855.
Refer to Chapter-7, Q.No.-21(2)

Q15. Write a note on Narendra Dev as a Cultural Marxist.
Ans. Narendra Dev was basically a cultural Marxist. He was deeply influenced by the Indian cultural traditions, specifically Buddha. He was much influenced by the gospel of love as Ahimsa preached by Buddha. He spent more than a decade working on his book on Buddhist philosophy—'Buddha Dharma Darshana' a treatise of considerable traditions. But at the same time, he was not in favour of religion and politics being combined. For him religious traditions are a millennia old phenomena which comprise the collective consciousness of people. Marxists must bring certain democratic elements of religions to make the human being an ethical being.

Q16. Describe briefly the Indian Marxist's views on nationality.
Refer to Chapter-8, Q.No.-1, Q.No.-2 & Q.No.-5

EPS-03: MODERN INDIAN POLITICAL THOUGHT
December-2009

Note:
(i) ***Section I-*** *Answer* ***any two*** *out of four questions.*
(ii) ***Section II-*** *Answer* ***any four*** *out of eight questions.*
(iii) ***Section III-*** *Answer* ***any two*** *out of four questions.*

SECTION I

Answer any tow of the following questions in about 500 words each. Each question carries 500 words each. Each question carries 20 marks.

Q1. Examine the cause of the third stage of British Colonialism.
Refer to Chapter-1, Q.No.-1

Q2. Analyse Bhagat Singh's views on Atheism.
Refer to Chapter-3, Q.No.-12

Q3. Describe political ideas of Savarkar.
Refer to June-2008, Q.No.-8

Q4. Discuss Gandhi's theory of social change.
Refer to Chapter-6, Q.No.-7 (i)

SECTION II

Answer any four of the following in about 250 words each. Each question carries 12 marks.

Q5. In what way was Prarthana Samaj different from Brahmo Samaj?
Refer to Chapter-3

Q6. Comment Boycott as a means for anti-colonial struggle.
Refer to Chapter-6

Q7. Describe E.V. Ramaswami Naicker's view on Varnashram Dharma.
Refer to Chapter-4, Q.No.-11

Q8. Briefly describe the principles on which Arya Samaj was founded.
Refer to June-2006, Q.No.-6

Q9. Explain the basic principles of Satyagraha.
Refer to June-2008, Q.No.-10

Q10. How did Gandhi define Swaraj?
Refer to Dec-2007, Q.No.-7

Q11. Examine Nehru's view on socialism.
Refer to Dec-2008, Q.No.-9

Q12. How did the Indian Marxists view the colonial role?
Refer to Dec-2008, Q.No.-11

SECTION III

Write short notes on any two of the following in about 100 words each. Each question carries 6 marks.

Q13. Aurobindo's views on nature of the British rule.
Refer to Chapter-3, Q.No.-7, P-74

Q14. Ambedkar's understanding of conversion.
Refer to Dec-2008, Q.No.-13 (iv)

Q15. Meaning of socialism according to Subhas Bose.
Refer to Dec-2008, Q.No.-10

Q16. Congress Socialist Party (CSP).
Refer to June-2008, Q.No.-13

EPS-03: MODERN INDIAN POLITICAL THOUGHT
June-2010

Note:
(i) ***Section I***- *Answer **any two** out of four questions.*
(ii) ***Section II***- *Answer **any four** out of eight questions.*
(iii) ***Section III***- *Answer **any two** out of four questions.*

SECTION I

Answer any two of the following questions. Each question carries 20 marks:

Q1. Discuss the evolution of nationalist idea in colonial India.
Refer to Chapter-1, Q.No.-7

Q2. Analyze the philosophical foundations of Shri Aurobindo's political thought.
Ans. Aurobindo's writings reflect diverse influences. Of these, the Indian tradition of idealism in philosophy seems to have impressed him the most. The great European philosophers from Homer to Goethe influenced him the maximum during his formative period and the study of Geeta, Upanishads and Vedanta had a deep impact on him political thinking. As Romain Rolland said, Sri Aurobindo was "the highest synthesis of the genius of Asia and the genius of Europe". He tried to integrate the materialist trend in western philosophy with the idealist tradition in Indian philosophy. Vedantic philosophy as propounded by Ramakrishna and Vivekanand also influenced Aurobindo's thinking. He was also inspired by the remarkable vitality and diversity of the Indian intellectual tradition. He believed that the writings of the Vedantic sages and the Buddha reflect the genius of the Indian mind. However, at a later stage, according to dynamism and vitality. As against this, western philosophy managed to retain its dynamism and continued to grow. Aurobindo wanted to combine the best elements of the Indian and western philosophical tradition. He explained the origin, nature and destiny of this world in his theory of evolution. According to his theory of creation, matter passes through various stages development; from the plant and animal stages to that of the mind and the supermind. In his view, matter is spirit in a hidden form, growing progressively towards the revelation of the spirit which is the supreme, unconditioned and absolute reality. In this process of evolution, in the transformation from the mind to the supermind, the technique of 'yoga' helps human beings to hasten the process. Sri Aurobindo developed his own technique called 'Integral Yoga' or 'Purna Yoga' which

incorporates the techniques of four yoga i.e. Karma yoga, Bhakti yoga, Jnana yoga and Raja yoga—as well as the Tantrik philosophy. Through this integral Yoga, a Yogi can rise to the supremental level, which will being him joy (Anands). The attainment of Anands helps in self-realization and assists in the service of humanity. According to him, since 'matter' is not different from 'spirit' gradual evolution of matter will convert it into pure spirit. Despite the obstacles in the way which may slow down the process, the advancement of humanity in the direction of spiritual perfection will continue. In this process, a few developed souls will work as pathfinders and will struggle hard to find the path for others. Aurobindo believed that India's tradition of spiritual thought and practice was very advanced and the whole of humanity could benefit from this in its spiritual journey. He wanted India to take the lead and for this reason, thought that India ought to be free, to play her true role in the spiritual regeneration of the world.

Q3. Was Jinnah a liberal? Discuss his Two Nation Theory.
Refer to Chapter-5, Q.No.-12

Q4. Write an essay on Gandhi's revised views on modern civilization and Swaraj.

Ans. It must indeed be admitted that even at the time of writing Hind Swaraj Gandhi was deeply appreciative of and committed to the civil liberties guaranteed by modern liberalism. As early as 1903, he had fought for the extension of the rights and liberties of liberalism to the Indians in Sought Africa. Ever since then, he remained proud of his "reformist liberalism". Yet, until the 1920s, he remained very critical of constitutional government and parliamentary democracy, which he contrasted with his ideal of swarajist democracy. He had even said that he was not interested in constitution-making as he did not see it as means to his ideal swaraj. Soon however, under the influence of Jawaharlal Nehru, Chittaranjan Das, etc. he revised his views and re-drew his ideal. He now came to regard parliamentary democracy and constitutional government as important means to his ideal swaraj. Accordingly, he spoke of the Constituent Assembly as constitutive of "constructive satyagraha." Regarding parliamentary democracy, law courts, etc., he wrote in his 1921 Foreword to Hind Swaraj. I must warn the reader against thinking that I am aiming at the swaraj described therein. I know that India is not ripe for it. It may seem an impertinence to say so. But such is the conviction. I am working for the self-rule pictured therein. But today my corporate activity is undoubtedly devoted to the attainment of parliamentary swaraj in accordance with the wishes of the people of India. I am not aiming at destroying railways or hospitals, though I would certainly welcome their natural destruction. Neither railways nor hospitals are a test of a high and pure civilization. At best they are a necessary evil. Neither adds one inch to the

moral structure of a nation. Nor am I aiming at a permanent destruction of law courts, much as I regard it as a consummation devoutly to be wished for. Still less I am trying to destroy all machinery and mills. It requires a higher simplicity and renunciation than the people are prepared for. Reiterating these revisions, Gandhi wrote in 1942: It must be remembered that it is not the Indian Home Rule depicted in that book that I am placing before India. I am placing before the nation parliamentary, i.e., democratic swaraj. I do not suggest a destruction of all machines, but I am making the spinning-wheel the master machine. The Indian Home Rule depicts an ideal state. The fact that I cannot come up to the ideal condition of things laid down therein is to be attributed to my weakness. What I have said about hospitals is also true. And yet I suppose I shall resort to the few medicines I hold lawful so long as I retain the least attachment for my body.
Now refer to Chapter-6, Q.No.-1

SECTION II

Answer any four of the following questions. Each question caries 12 marks.

Q5. Write a note on Raja Rammohan Roy as a social reformer.
Refer to Chapter-2, Q.No.-6

Q6. Discuss Phule's views on the caste system.
Refer to Chapter-4, Q.No.-6

Q7. Analyze the assumptions of the Moderates about the British rule.
Ans. Extremism as an ideology was different from the ideology of the moderates. The basis of each of these ideologies was different.
The liberal (Moderates) cherished the illusion that British rule was for the good of India. Their assumptions were:
(i) The British had an extreme sense of justice and fair play.
(ii) They had come to deliver Indians from the bondage of stagnation, backwardness and irrational tradition.
(iii) British Raj was a part of the divine plan for India's progress, and
(iv) That the continuation of British Raj was beneficial to India and hence they desired its continuance.
The conclusions that logically flowed from these assumptions were:
(i) Appealing to British conscience was sufficient to get one's demands granted. Pressure politics was uncalled for. Constitutional methods should be strictly followed.
(ii) Politics is a secular matter. Mixing of religion with politics is undesirable and uncalled for.

(iii) We should win and preserve British sympathy for our cause. It is in our own interest. For this, purity of both the ends and the means is necessary. Wrong ends and wrong means, it was feared, would lead to British hostility and damage our cause. Sp they insisted that the British should be true to their promises and fulfil them. The British had proclaimed that the good of India was at their heart. In this respect, the moderates were only demanding what citizens of British Empire could rightly demand. They would not use the argument of the Natural Right to freedom and independence. In contrast to the above, we propose to study in brief, the ideology of extremism *I* in two parts: (A) Assumptions and (B) Logical conclusions. Tilak contributed to the development of this ideology in a big way.

(A) The Assumptions: Characterization of British Raj

Unlike the liberals, the extremists had no illusion either about the generous or philanthropic nature of British Raj or the British sense of justice and fairplay. To them, the British were as good or as bad as people anywhere. It was meaningless to ascribe superior and nobler qualities to them in comparison with others. Like people anywhere, they too were driven by selfish motives. They stretched their imperial power over to India in order to enslave the people and exploit her resources, and not with a philanthropic motive to deliver the Indians from the bondage of stagnation and irrational tradition. All this was an imperialist plan and there was nothing divine about it.

(B) Logical Conclusions

The conclusions that logically followed from the above assumptions were as follows: The selfish motive of material gain being the chief drive of the British Raj, it could not be expected to take a sympathetic attitude towards Indian demands and aspirations. The British government did not stop the export of foodgrains to England even during the worst famine in India. What did this indicate? Only that appealing to their conscience was futile. The British would not concede any thing that even slightly harmed their interest. Hence, pressure had to be used in support of one's demands. Mendicancy or praying and begging for benefits would lead us nowhere. Hence, the new ideology differed from the earlier one in almost every respect. Let us have a look at a few points:

Constitutional Versus Pressure Politics

Tilak rejected the efficacy of the constitutional method in the colonial Indian context. His argument in this regard is given below:

(i) He felt that constitutional methods had meaning only under a constitutional government. We had no constitution. An imperial bureaucracy was ruling India. What we had under the British Rule was only a Penal Code and not a constitution. Hence, there was no question of our adopting constitutional methods.

Secondly, his argument was that as the British would never concede anything that went against their interest, we needed to bring pressure on the alien bureaucracy in support of our demand. This could be done by involving people in the national movement. For this, they must be taken into confidence. Constitutional methods would not serve the purpose.

Thirdly, one of the ways of arousing the people emotionally was to base one's demands on the theory of 'natural rights.' The constitutional methods, on the other hand, appealed to the theory of legal rights under the constitution. Tilak felt that this was an ineffective and weak stand, incapable of arousing popular enthusiasm.

The liberals pleaded on the basis of British promises and on our rights as British nationals. On the contrary, Tilak demanded 'Swaraj' as a 'natural right' and not on the basis of British assurances.

(ii) Ends and Means

According to the liberals, purity of ends or aims was as important as purity of means. They justified the purity of means on theoretical as well as programmatic grounds. Theoretically, they held that noble means alone could yield fruit. Pragmatically, they feared that debasement of means would annoy the British rulers and spoil our cause.

Tilak too did not deny that purity of means was important and desirable. But, he felt that under certain circumstances this could not be a rigid rule. Means had to be adequate and appropriate according to circumstances. We should not abandon the goal only because it could not be achieved by fair means. If circumstances so demanded, we should not hesitate to use other or lesser means to achieve the desired goal. Such means too would be justified in the end. In such circumstances, we should be firm about the purity of the goal and not be fussy about the means. Tilak supported this theory by references to ancient Indian scriptures and epics like ***Gita*** and ***Mahabharata.***

(iii) Religion and Politics

In the western tradition, the liberals regarded politics as a secular affair and insisted on treating it as such. They kept religion away from politics. Tilak's view on this point was also totally different. He, no doubt, accepted the desirability of keeping politics separate from religion in general, but not in all circumstances. Religion always had a powerful emotional appeal and Tilak felt that this powerful appeal could and should be utilized in the service of politics, particularly under the circumstances prevailing in India in those days.

To Tilak, the ultimate goal of the national movement was Swaraj. In order to involve people in the movement, he interpreted the goal of Swaraj in religious terms and insisted that Swaraj is our religious necessity. The religion and the philosophy of Vedanta emphasize equal spiritual status and destiny of each individual. This is against bondage of any kind and Swaraj is therefore, not only a political but natural and spiritual necessity.

Tilak held that Swaraj was a moral and religious necessity for every man and group. For his moral fulfilment and for the performance of religious duties, man needs to be free. Without political freedom higher freedom is impossible. Thus Swaraj is our Dharma. To endeavour to attain it is our *Karma*- Yoga.

Q8. Write a note on Ambedkar's views on State Socialism.
Refer to Chapter-4, Q.No.-15

Q9. Briefly discuss Gandhiji's critique of modern civilization.
Refer to Q.No.-4 of this paper.

Q10. Write a note on the political ideas of Swami Dayanand Saraswati.
Refer to Chapter-4, Q.No.-4

Q11. Describe Abul Kalam Azad's political views during romantic phase of his ideas.
Refer to Q.No.-13 & Q.No.-14

Q12. Did Subhash Chandra Bose advocate Fascism? Answer with reasons.
Refer to Chapter-1, Q.No.-7

SECTION III

Q13. Write short notes on any two of the following. Each carries 6 marks:
(a) The Congress Socialist Party
Refer to Chapter-7, Q.No.-3

(b) Aligarh Movement
Ans. The War of Independence 1857 ended in a disaster for the Muslims. The British believed that the Muslims were responsible for the war of 1857 and therefore, they were subjected to ruthless punishment and merciless revenge. The British had always looked upon the Muslims as their enemies because they had ousted them from power. With the war of 1857 this feeling was intensified and every attempt was made to ruin and suppress the Muslims forever. Thus the Mughal rule came to an end and the sub- continent went directly under the British crown.

Aligarh Movement was the movement led by Sir Syed Ahmed Khan, to educate the Muslims of the Indian subcontinent after the defeat of the rebels in the Indian rebellion of 1857. It had enormous success and had a profound impact on the future of the subcontinent. Its most significant achievement was the establishment of Muhammadan Anglo-Oriental College at Aligarh, which later became Aligarh Muslim University.

Result of Aligarh Movement

The Aligarh Movement led to educational revival and reformation in the provinces of the Bengal, the Punjab, the Sindh and the North Western. Sir Syed Ahmad Khan through his articles in the magazines and the newspapers started religious movement for the reformation of the Muslims. The schools of modern education, were spreading, Sir Syed's social, moral and religious

Ideas. His ideas knitted the Muslims together in u string. Many muslims who were against his modern ideas became his friends with the passage of time, Aligarh became a centre of education for the Muslims of India, Sir Syed's ideas totally revolutionised the Indian Muslims. They were infused with new spirit and zeal. Sir Syed's Movement gave birth to scholars like Moulvi Chiragh Ali, Moulana Nazir Ahmad Dehlvi, Moulana Shibli Naghmani and Syed Amir Ali who did not accept his political theory. Sir Syed also left far-reaching effects on literature and poetry. Different forms of the English poetry and literature enlightened the Urdu poetry and literature and literary figures like Moulana Shibli Naghmani, Moulana Altaf Hussain Hali, Nawab Mohsin-ul-Mulik and Moulvi Chiragh got birth from the womb of this educational Movement. All these personalities infused among the Muslims of India a new life, energy and spirit. This Movement softened the hearts of the British and cleared many misunderstandings between the British and the Muslims. Different Societies established by Sir Syed brought the British and the Indian Muslims close to each other. The Government granted aids to the institutions opened by the Muslims. The Muslims got jobs in different departments of the Governments. Nawab Abdul Latif of Bengal accepted these ideas of Sir Syed Ahmad Khan. He pledged for the reformation of the Bengali Muslims. He established Muhammadan Literary Society in April 1863, in Calcutta for the welfare of the Bengali Muslims. In its weekly meetings, famous Muslims and Europeans delivered lectures on social, moral, and scientific aspects. This Society forced the Muslims of Bengal to get European education if they wanted to compete with the Hindus in life.

(c) Militant Nationalism

Refer to Chapter-3, Q.No.-1

(d) Colonial Impact on Trade and Industry

Refer to Page No.-15 [Impact on Trade and Industry]

EPS-03 : Modern Indian Political Thought
June-2011

Note:
(i) ***Section I***- *Answer* ***any two*** *out of four questions.*
(ii) ***Section II***- *Answer* ***any four*** *out of eight questions.*
(iii) ***Section III***- *Answer* ***any two*** *out of four questions.*

SECTION I

Answer any two of the following questions. Each question carries 20 marks:

Q1. Discuss the British colonial intervention in Indian economy.
Refer to Chapter-1, Q.No.-2 (iii)

Q2. Write an essay on Indian Nationalism in the 19th century.
Refer to Chapter-1, Q.No.-7

Q3. Discuss the political ideas of 19th century reformers.
Refer to Chapter-2, Q.No.-1 & Q.No.-3

Q4. Write a note on M.G. Ranade's interpretation of Indian history.
Refer to Chapter-2, Q.No.-9

SECTION II

Answer any four of the following questions. Each question carries 12 marks.

Q5. Comment on B.G. 'Tilak's perspective on social reforms.
Refer to Chapter-3, Q.No.-5

Q6. Describe the philosophical foundation of Sri Aurovindo's political though.
Refer to Chapter-3, Q.No.-8

Q7. Critically examine Dr. B.R. Ambedkar's concept of democracy.
Refer to Chapter-4, Q.No.-14

Q8. Write a note on the anti-colonial movement led by Birsa Munda.
Refer to Chapter-4, Q.No.-21

Q9. Briefly describe some aspects of the Hindu-Muslim problem in early colonial India.
Refer to Chapter-5, Q.No.-3

Q10. What were the political ideas of V.D Savarkar? Explain.
Refer to Chapter-5, Q.No.-9

Q11. Discuss M.K. Gandhi's critique of modern civilization.
Refer to Chapter-6, Q.No.-2

Q12. Briefly describe Gandhi's concept of Sarvodaya.
Refer to Chapter-6, Q.No.-8

SECTION III

Write short notes on any two of the following questions. Each question carries 6 marks.

Q13. Jaiprakash Narayan's concept of total revolution.

Ans. When Indira Gandhi was found guilty of violating electoral laws by the Allahabad High Court, Narayan called for Indira to resign, and advocated a program of social transformation which he termed Sampoorna Kranti [Total Revolution]. Instead she proclaimed a national Emergency on the midnight of June 25, 1975, immediately after Narayan had called for the PM's resignation and had asked the military and the police to disregard unconstitutional and immoral orders; JP, opposition leaders, and dissenting members of her own party ('the Young Turks') were arrested on that day.

Jayaprakash Narayan attracted a gathering of 100,000 people at the Ramlila Grounds and thunderously recited Rashtrakavi Ramdhari Singh 'Dinkar''s wonderfully evocative poetry: Singhasan KhaaliKaro Ke Janata Aaati hai.

Narayan was kept as detenu at Chandigarh even after he had asked for a month's parole for mobilizing relief in areas of Bihar gravely affected by flood. His health suddenly deteriorated on October 24, and he was released on November 12; diagnosis at Jaslok Hospital, Mumbai, revealed kidney failure; he would be on dialysis for the rest of his life.

After Indira revoked the emergency on January 18, 1977 and announced elections, it was under JP's guidance that the Janata Party (a vehicle for the broad spectrum of the anti- Indira Gandhi opposition) was formed. The Janata Party was voted into power, and became the first non-Congress party to form a government at the Centre. On the call of Narayan many youngsters joined the J P movement.

Q14. Ram Manohar Lohiya's strategy for change.
Refer to Chapter-7, Q.No.-4 (iv)

Q15. M.N. Roy and the Indian social reality.
Refer to Chapter-2, Q.No.-6

Q16. Indian Marxists on colonial rule.
Refer to Chapter-8, Q.No.-1

EPS-03: MODERN INDIAN POLITICAL THOUGHT
December-2011

Note:
(i) ***Section I***- *Answer* ***any two*** *out of four questions.*
(ii) ***Section II***- *Answer* ***any four*** *out of eight questions.*
(iii) ***Section III***- *Answer* ***any two*** *out of four questions.*

SECTION I

Answer any two of the following questions in about 500 words each. Each question carries 20 marks.

Q1. Write an essay on Marxist Political thought in India.

Q2. Discuss M.N.Roy's concept of Radical Humanism.

Q3. Describe the emergence and growth of socialist ideas in the 19th century.

Q4. Write a note on Subhash Chandra Bose's concept of socialism.

SECTION II

Answer any four of the following in about 250 words each. Each question carries 12 marks.

Q5. Explain the concept of Swaraj.

Q6. Discuss Gandhi's concept of Constructive Programme.

Q7. Examine M.A. Jinnah's views on Nationalism.

Q8. Critically examine Swami Vivekananda's concept of freedom.

Q9. Discuss Dr. B.R. Ambedkar's views on social change.

Q10. Describe Phule's concept of universal religion.

Q11. Write a note on Bhagat Singh's thoughts on social revolution.

Q12. Critically evaluate Sri Aurobindo's theory of nationalism.

SECTION III

Write short notes on any two of the following in about 100 words each. Each question carries 6 marks.

Q13. Formative influences on G.K. Gokhale.

Q14. Raja Rammohan Roy on the rights of an individual.

Q15. Congress Socialist Party.

Q16. Religious revivalism in 19th century India.

EPS-03: MODERN INDIAN POLITICAL THOUGHT
June, 2012

Note:
(i) ***Section I***- *Answer* ***any two*** *out of four questions.*
(ii) ***Section II***- *Answer* ***any four*** *out of eight questions.*
(iii) ***Section III***- *Answer* ***any two*** *out of four questions.*

SECTION I

Answer any two of the following questions in about 500 words each. Each question carries 20 marks.

Q1. Discuss the nature of colonial intervention in India.
Ans. Colonialism imparted different implications on our society. It is so because colonialism has been an important phase of Indian history. The word colonialism is often been understood to mean only political control by one country over another, but it means more than this. It is often used to mean our expression used for British rule in India. But it must be kept in mind that political control by one country over another, or British rule in India were only components of colonialism, but did not mean it totally. Colonialism infact is a larger phenomenon. It should be treated as a world phenomenon. It continued or affected various countries in many spheres. The countries of Asia, South Africa and Latin America were victims of this process, and the leading and economically powerful countries like France, Britain, Holland, Spain and Portugal were on the beneficiary sides. Colonialism fulfilled the interests of the latter ones. Colonialism should be treated as a structure which contains '*political control*'. When we say of colonialism, we mean the colonial interest (whatever the colonizing country may have); policies, state and its related institutions (judiciary, army, bureaucracy, legislature, etc.); culture and society. The wave of modernization including modern education and societal control, eradication of evil practices etc; idea and ideologies like the ideas introduced by Britishers and its personalities are to be seen functioning within the parameters of colonial structure. This structure can be defined by their interrelationship as a whole. So, we can understand the phenomena of colonialism as an integration of economy of the colony (like, India) with the economy of the metropolis (like, Britain) through trade, industry and business. This integration is concluded to serve the interests of the metropolitan economy and to the extent, it completely subordinates the economy of the colony to the economy of the metropolis. But this subordination does not confine to economy only, but also spreads to all the areas of society. And it is applied through various

stages. Historically, colonialism in India as well as other countries of Asia, Africa, and Latin America underwent three stages. Each stage represented a different pattern of subordination of colonial economy, society and polity and consequently different colonial policies, ideologies, impact and colonial peoples' response. The shift from one stage to another is infact the influence of change in the social, economic and political pattern of metropolis itself. Also, it is influenced by the broad changes in the positions of world economy and polity.

Q2. Describe the economic and social ideas of Gopal Krishna Gokhale.

Ans. As a leader of the Congress and as a member of the legislature Gokhale had to ponder over many socioeconomic issues of the time which, in turn, gave birth to his economic and social ideas. These ideas reflected his way of thinking which considerably influenced the process of social change of his time.

As far as his economic ideas are concerned Gokhale owes much to Justice M.G. Ranade and Prof. List, a German economist. Gokhale made a careful study of Indian finance from 1874 to 1909 dividing this period into four phases comparing the growth in expenditure with the growth of revenue. The results are given in the table below:

Average annual increase in Revenue and Expenditure		
Period	Increase in Revenue	Increase in Expenditure
1874 — 1884	1.25%	0.67%
1884 — 1894	1.5%	1.5%
1894 — 1901	1.5%	1.5%
1901 — 1909	2.5%	5.0%

On the basis of his study Gokhale concluded that the growth in expenditure tended to more than the growth in revenue, whereas in fact it was essential to keep the two in balance. Moreover, there was no point in having a surplus budget while the budget of the common man failed to balance itself. During a period of budgetary surplus, Gokhale recommended that the state adopt the following measures:

(i) a reduction in state demand on land by 25 to 30%,

(ii) the creation of a fund of million sterling to rescue the Indian agriculturists from the load of debt,

(iii) the activisation of co-operative credit societies through establishing agricultural banks on Egyptian model,

(iv) the promotion of industrial and technical education and the sanctioning of the increased expenditure for this purposes,

(v) free and compulsory primary education, and

(vi) improvement of the finances of the local bodies.

Gokhale saw that the agricultural industry in India was in a serious depression and the crop yield per acre was low. In such circumstances he resented the increase in the land revenue demanded by the state. He regarded land revenue and the indirect taxes as together placing an unbearable burden on the poor. He wanted the state to give importance to irrigation and scientific agriculture as measures for agricultural prosperity. He disapproved the excise duty on cotton textiles. Gokhale thought that such a duty further burdened the poor.

Following the German economist Prof. List, Gokhale pleaded protection for the new industries in India on the ground that she was an industrially backward country. Gokhale stood for the industrial development, advocated state initiative to further the process of industrialization, demanded protection for infant industries and thus paved the way for capitalist development.

Gokhale also advocated the cause of Swadeshi. To him the Swadeshi movement was both a patriotic and an economic movement. So far as its patriotic aspect is concerned it meant devotion to motherland but the movement on its material side was economic. It ensured a ready consumption of such articles as were produced in the country and furnished a perpetual stimulus to production by keeping up the demand for indigenous things.

To Gokhale the question of production was a question of capital, enterprise and skill and whoever could help in one of those fields could be called a worker in the Swadeshi cause. Gokhale did not mind even to seek governmental co-operation in the cause of Swadesh. Through this movement Gokhale sought to lay the foundations of indigenous capitalism.

In the sphere of social reforms Gokhale sided with Ranade. Like Ranade, Gokhale also believed that social reforms must go along with political reforms. He was of the opinion that the state must help the progressive elements in the society. He thus supported the motion on the Civil Marriage Bill.

Gokhale suggested free and compulsory elementary education for the masses. To him the elementary education meant the greater moral and economic efficiency of the individual. He also suggested prohibition of liquor and other measures of public health so as to remove hindrances and hardships from the path of the development of individual personality.

Gokhale's programme of social reforms reflects his liberal faith. Liberalism advocates the all-round development of the individual personality. Gokhale as a convinced liberal attached utmost importance to this aspect of human life. Caste barriers, racialism, communal disharmony, ignorance, religious fanaticism, subjugation of women, were all hindrances in the path of the development of individual personality and hence had to be removed immediately. Thus Gokhale's social reformism was also the child of his liberal outlook. His ideas of spiritualization of politics presupposed the moral purification of the individual along with that of his or her enlightenment which is implicit in his general programme of social reforms.

Q3. Discuss Mahatma Gandhi's Philosophy of Sarvodaya.
Refer to Chapter-6, Q.No.-8

Q4. Critically analyse the political ideology of Bhagat Singh.
Refer to Chapter-3, Q.No.-12

SECTION II

Answer any four of the following questions in about 250 words each. Each question carries 12 marks.

Q5. Examine E.V. Ramaswami Naicker as a thinker.

Ans. E.V.R. Naicker was the torch-bearer of new emerging forces in Tamil Nadu. He was a strong follower and supporter of Gandhian ideology in struggle against the colonial power. But on the question of communal representation and *Varanashram Dharma,* he differed from the Congress and Gandhiji and even left Congress. Initially he joined Congress for its lofty ideals and goals, one of which was the abolition of untouchability. E.V.R. was very condemning of *Varnasharma Dharma.* He considered that it could relegate the non-Brahmin caste Hindus to the position of *Shudra* in Tamil religion. He felt that if each caste were to follow its own *Dharma,* non-Brahmins would be forced to serve the Brahmins. He was so critical of Congress and Brahmins ideas that he even said that true freedom can be achieved only with the destruction of Indian National Congress, Hinduism and Brahmanism. His self-respect movement was a new development and was a revolt against the artificial division of society into *varnas.* It was a reform movement dedicated to the goal of providing non-Brahmins a sense of pride based on their Dravidianist past. The movement denied the superiority of the Brahmins and their implicit faith in the present system. One of its important point was a denial of the mythology of Hinduism by which it contended that, the unsuspecting were made victims of the Brahmins. He also convened a conference of self-respect on provincial ground at Chingleput on Feb. 17, 1929. E.V.R. also invoked people and especially women to fight against *"Hindi Imperialism".* He opposed the Congress policy to introduce 'Hindi' as compulsory language in schools in South. He believed that this was a way of overlooking the linguistic differences between the North and the South. Moreover, the Tamil opposition to Hindi came because the introduction of Hindi meant the revival of Sanskrit-a language that was traditionally opposed by them. He was of the opinion that the introduction of Hindi in the schools without making the mother-tongue also a compulsory subject was a deliberate attempt to relegate the Dravidian languages to the background. After 1949, E.V.R.'s role in the Tamil Nadu politics was less considerable. He carried sporadic agitations against C.Rajgopalachari's education policy in 1954. He came to support the Chief Minister of Tamil Nadu, Kamaraj as "*Pure Tamilian*", since he hailed from the backward community of Nadars. E.V.R. because of his past experience with the Congress which he considered as Brahmin dominated, opposed even liberal policies of C. Rajgopalachari.

Q6. Comment on the political philosophy of V.D. Savarkar.
Refer to Chapter-5, Q.No.-9

Q7. Write a note on political ideas of Mohammed Iqbal.
Refer to Chapter-5, Q.No.-11

Q8. Discuss the Bhoodan movement of Vinoba Bhave.
Refer to Chapter-6, Q.No.-9

Q9. What were the basic assumptions of Nehru's Foreign policy?
Ans. In the initial statements explaining India's foreign policy Nehru claimed that it had an independent foreign policy. Nehru developed an independent thinking in the area of foreign policy. He could understand the dynamics of global politics. There are basically two power blocks in international politics: Western Imperialist Block and Soviet Socialist Block. According to Nehru, India and other newly liberated countries should follow an independent line. They should not be a member of any block. Nehru states that, "we should approach these problems, whether domestic or international problems in our own way. If by any chance we align ourselves definitely with one power group, we may perhaps from one point of view do some good, but I have not the shadow of a doubt that from a larger point of view, not only India but of world peace, it will do haw." Nehru wanted that the non-aligned countries should function as a power block. They should share their wealth for their prosperity. Nehru was by no means for an India which would be isolated from the rest of the world. His independent foreign policy was not negative. He realised that India is a part of the world in regard to science, culture, economy and politics. He made the following observation making his views clear on this matter: "Our entire society is based on this more or less. This basis must go and be transformed into one of co-operation, not isolated which is impossible. If this is admitted and is found feasible then attempts should be made to realize, if not in terms of an economy which is cut off from the rest of the world, but rather one which co-operates. From the economic or political point of view, an isolated India may well be a vacuum".

Q10. Describe Dr. Ram Monohar Lohia's theory of history.
Refer to Chapter-7, Q.No.-12

Q11. Write a note on Subhash Chandra Bose's ideas of social transformation of India.
Refer to Chapter-8, Q.No.-10

Q12. Comment on Ranade as the prophet of Indian nationalism.
Refer to Chapter-2, Q.No.-11(iii)

SECTION III

Q13. Write short notes on any two of the following in about 100 words each. Each question carries 6 marks.

(a) M.N. Ray and Partyless democracy
Refer to Chapter-8, Q.No.-8

(b) Birsa Munda
Refer to Chapter-4, Q.No.-21(i)

(c) Tilak's views on Nationalism
Refer to Chapter-3, Q.No.-5

(d) Raja Ram Mohan Roy on women's rights
Refer to Chapter-2, Q.No.-6

EPS-03: MODERN INDIAN POLITICAL THOUGHT
December-2012

Note:
(i) ***Section I***- *Answer* ***any two*** *out of four questions.*
(ii) ***Section II***- *Answer* ***any four*** *out of eight questions.*
(iii) ***Section III***- *Answer* ***any two*** *parts of Q.no. 13.*

SECTION I

Answer any two of the following questions in about 500 words each. Each question carries 20 marks.

Q1. Critically analyse the various stages of colonialism in India.

Q2. Discuss the political ideas of 19th century Indian liberals.

Q3. Comment on Raja Rammohan Roy's interpretation of Hinduism.

Q4. Write a note on the political ideas of Tilak.

SECTION II

Answer any four of the following questions in about 250 words each. Each question carries 12 marks.

Q5. Describe some major tribal movements in India.

Q6. What did nationalism mean to Vivekananda? Explain.

Q7. Analyse the main trends of Muslim political thinking during the early phase of the twentieth century.

Q8. Describe Gandhi's concept of Hind Swaraj.

Q9. Write a note one JP's concept of total revolution.

Q10. Comment on the basic philosophy of socialism.

Q11. Write a brief note on the Marxist political thought in post independence India.

Q12. Discuss the socialist ideas of Acharya Narendra Dev.

SECTION III

Q13. Write short notes on any two of the following in about 100 words each. Each question carries 6 marks.

(a) Dr. Ambedkar on democracy.

(b) Bhagat Singh's views on terrorism.

(c) Prarthana Samaj of Ranade.

(d) Mohmmad Iqbal on Islamic democracy.

EPS-03: MODERN INDIAN POLITICAL THOUGHT
December-2013

Note:
(i) ***Section I****- Answer* ***any two*** *questions.*
(ii) ***Section II****- Answer* ***any four*** *questions.*
(iii) ***Section III****- Answer* ***any two*** *parts of Q.no. 13.*

SECTION I

Answer any two of the following questions in about 500 words each. Each question carries 20 marks.
Q1. Why are the social reformers of 19th century considered revivalists? Explain.
Q2. Critically examine Dr. B. R. Ambedkar's views on caste system.
Q3. Define Satyagraha. Describe the relationship between Ahimsa and Satyagraha.
Q4. Examine M.N. Roy's concept of Radical Humanism.

SECTION II

Answer any four of the following questions in about 250 words each. Each question carries 12 marks.
Q5. Explain the liberal strand of Indian nationalism against colonialism.
Q6. Analyse the different methods of social reform suggested by M.G. Ranade.
Q7. Examine Aurobindo's positive programme of Political Action.
Q8. Describe Naicker's views on Varnashram Dharma.
Q9. Analyse Mohammed Iqbal's views on nationalism.
Q10. Discuss the assumptions of Nehru's foreign policy.
Q11. How did Jaya Prakash Narayan interpret Marxism? Explain.
Q12. Distinguish between Indian Marxist and Instrumentalist Approach to the State.

SECTION III

Q13. Write short notes on any two of the following in about 100 words each. Each carries 6 marks:
(a) Raja Ram Mohan Roy's views on freedom of expression
(b) Jyotiba phule's views on caste
(c) Subhash Bose on socialism
(d) Bhoodan Movement

EPS-03: MODERN INDIAN POLITICAL THOUGHT
June-2014

Note:
(i) ***Section I***- *Answer **any two** out of four questions.*
(ii) ***Section II***- *Answer **any four** out of eight questions.*
(iii) ***Section III***- *Answer **any two** out of four questions.*

SECTION I

Answer any two of the following questions in about 500 words each. Each question carries 20 marks.

Q1. Discuss the liberal strand of Indian Nationalism.

Q2. Discuss the political thought of Bal Gangadhar Tilak.

Q3. What are the main functions of the State according to M.G. Ranade?

Q4. Discuss the role of the tribals in the Indian National Movement.

SECTION II

Answer any four of the following in about 250 words. Each question carries 12 marks.

Q5. Discuss Gandhi's critique of modern civilisation.

Q6. What was JP's contribution to the Bhoodan Movement?

Q7. Examine Abdul Kalam Azad's views on democracy.

Q8. Briefly analyse the main features of Muslim Separatist thought.

Q9. Discuss Jawaharlal Nehru's views on scientific temper.

Q10. Analyse the basic philosophy of Acharya Narendra Dev.

Q11. Describe Dr. Rammanohar Lohia's Theory of History.

Q12. Examine the Indian Left's response to the Second World War.

SECTION III

Write short notes on any two of the following in about 100 words each. Each question carries 6 marks.

Q13. Tribal Movement in Odisha

Q14. E.V. Ramaswami Naicker and the Self-respect Movement.

Q15. Mohammad Iqbal's idea of Islamic Democracy.

Q16. Gandhi and Ethics in politics.

EPS-03: MODERN INDIAN POLITICAL THOUGHT
December-2014

Note:
(i) ***Section I- Any two*** *questions to be answered.*
(ii) ***Section II- Any four*** *questions to be answered.*
(iii) ***Section III- Any two*** *questions to be answered.*

SECTION I

Answer any two of the following questions in about 500 words each. Each question carries 20 marks.

Q1. Discuss Raja Ram Mohan Roy as a social reformer.

Q2. Critically analyse the political ideas of M.G. Ranade.

Q3. What is the significance of Militant Nationalism in contemporary politics? Explain.

Q4. Discuss the philosophical foundations of Aurobindo's political thought.

SECTION II

Answer any four of the following questions in about 250 words each. Each question carries 12 marks.

Q5. Analyse the role of E.V. Ramaswami Naicker as a social reformer.

Q6. Discuss Dr. Ambedkar's views on democracy.

Q7. What are the salient features of the Tribal movements in India? Explain.

Q8. Discuss Swami Dayanand Saraswati's political ideas.

Q9. What was Swami Vivekanand's concept of freedom? Explain.

Q10. Discuss Mohammad Iqbal's views on nationalism.

Q11. Discuss Gandhi's theory of social change.

Q12. Discuss Jawaharlal Nehru's views on Socialism.

SECTION III

Write short notes on any two of the following in about 100 words each. Each question carries 6 marks.

Q13. Dr. Ram Manohar Lohia's views on Socialism

Q14. J.P.'s concept of Total Revolution

Q15. M.N. Roy's ideas on Partyless Democracy

Q16. The Lahore Conspiracy Case

EPS-03: MODERN INDIAN POLITICAL THOUGHT
June-2015

Note:
(i) ***Section I-*** *Answer* ***any two*** *out of four questions.*
(ii) ***Section II-*** *Answer* ***any four*** *questions.*
(iii) ***Section III-*** *Answer* ***any two*** *parts of Q.no. 13.*

SECTION I

Answer any two of the following questions in about 500 words each. Each question carries 20 marks.

Q1. Write an essay on British colonial intervention in India's polity.

Q2. Describe the different strands of socialism in India in the early 20th century.

Q3. Elaborate on the circumstances that led to the social reform movement in early 19th century India.

Q4. Discuss the salient features of Rammohan Roy's political liberalism.

SECTION II

Answer any four of the following questions in about 250 words each. Each question carries 12 marks.

Q5. Trace the influence of militant nationalism on the Indian National Congress.

Q6. Describe the salient features of Sri Aurobindo's positive programme of political action.

Q7. Examine Jyotiba Phule's critique of the British rule.

Q8. What were B.R. Ambedkar's views on state socialism? Elaborate.

Q9. Write a note on the main trends of Muslim political thought in the early 20th century.

Q10. Discuss the political ideas of Swami Dayanand Saraswati.

Q11. What is M.K. Gandhi's critique of modern civilisation? Explain.

Q12. Write a note on the Bhoodan movement.

SECTION III

Q13. Write short notes on any two of the following in about 100 words each. Each part carries 6 marks.

(a) Congress Socialist Party (CSP)
(b) JP on Total Revolution
(c) Assumptions of M.N. Roy's analytic famework
(d) Overview of Indian Communists (pre-independence)

EPS-03: MODERN INDIAN POLITICAL THOUGHT
December-2015

Note:
(i) ***Section I-*** *Answer* ***any two*** *questions.*
(ii) ***Section II-*** *Answer* ***any four*** *questions.*
(iii) ***Section III-*** *Answer* ***any two*** *parts of Q.no. 13.*

SECTION I

Answer any two of the following questions in about 500 words each. Each question carries 20 marks.

Q1. Write an essay on Marxist political thought in post-independent India.

Q2. Discuss M.N. Roy's concept of Radical Humanism.

Q3. What were Subhash Chandra Bose's views on Socialism? Explain.

Q4. Why did Ram Manohar Lohiya oppose both Capitalism and Communism? Elaborate.

SECTION II

Answer any four of the following questions in about 250 words each. Each question carries 12 marks.

Q5. Examine the critique of some of M.K. Gandhi's major ideas.

Q6. Comment on the centrality of the village panchayat in Gandhi's constructive programme.

Q7. Describe some important aspects of the Hindu-Muslim problem in early 20th century India.

Q8. What were Mohammad Iqbal's views on nationalism? Explain.

Q9. Write a note on the salient features of tribal movements in colonial India.

Q10. Explain the impact of colonialism on the Indian economy.

Q11. Write an essay on the economic ideas of B.G. Tilak.

Q12. Critically evaluate Sri Aurobindo's political thought.

SECTION III

Q13. Write short notes on any two of the following in about 100 words each. Each part carries 6 marks.

(a) Revival versus Reform
(b) Ram Mohan Roy on international coexistence
(c) Police in British Colonial India
(d) Congress Socialism

EPS-03: MODERN INDIAN POLITICAL THOUGHT
June-2016

Note:
(i) ***Section I***- *Answer* ***any two*** *questions.*
(ii) ***Section II***- *Answer* ***any four*** *questions.*
(iii) ***Section III***- *Answer* ***any two*** *parts of Q.no. 13.*

SECTION I

Answer any two of the following questions in about 500 words each. Each question carries 20 marks.

Q1. Discuss the impact of colonisation on Indian agriculture.
Refer to Chapter-1, Q.No.-2 (3)

Q2. Critically analyse the ideas of Bhagat Singh on terrorism.
Ans. The leaflet eloquently and succinctly explained the stand taken by the Revolutionaries. The futility of reforms, the mockery of parliamentary system, the need to prepare for a revolution and a justification of violence all of these found their place in the leaflet. The leaflet declared.

"It takes a loud voice to make the deaf hear, with these immortal words uttered on similar occasion by Valliant, a French anarchist martyr, do we strongly justify this action of ours.

"Without repeating the humiliating history of the past ten years of the working of the reforms (Montague-Chelmsford reforms) and without mentioning the insults hurled at the Indian nation though this house–the so called Indian Parliament–we want to point out that, while the people expecting some more crumbs of reforms from the Simon Commission, and are ever quarrelling over the distribution of the expected nones, the Government is thrusting upon us new repressive measures like the public safety and the trade Dispute Bill, while reserving the Press Sedition Bill for the next session. The indiscriminate arrests of labour leaders working in the open fields clearly indicate whither the wind blows.

"In these provocative circumstances, the Hindustan Socialist Republican Association, in all seriousness, realising their full responsibility, had decided and ordered its army to do this particular action, so that a stop be put to this humiliating force and to let the alien bureaucratic exploiters do what they wish, but they must be made to come before the public eye in their naked form.

"Let the representatives of the people return to their constituencies and prepare the masses for the coming revolution, and let the government know that while protesting against the public safety and Trade Dispute Bill and the callous murder of Lala Lajpat Rai, on behalf of the helpless Indian masses, we want to emphasize the lesson often repeated by history, that it is easy to kill individuals but your can not kill the ideas. Great empires crumbled while the ideas survived. Bourbons and Czars fell.

"Long live the Revolution."

The message was clear and was understood well by the British. The Revolutionaries were the greatest threat to the British Raj and hence should be crushed mercilessly. Once Bhagat Singh was arrested he was never let off. Even though public opinion and the leaders in Congress strongly favoured commutation of his death sentence, the Governor-General considered himself duty bound to see that to mercy was to be shown against the determined enemies of the British Raj.

In the process of trial Bhagat Singh made it clear that he did not believe in violence as an integral part of revolution. By revolution he understood a change in the social order based on justice. The Producers, whether labourers or peasants should get their rights restored. Inequalities and disparities must come to an end. Without reorganising the social structure any talk of ending war seemed to him absured. Universal peace under exploiting society was unimaginable and hypocritical. Such a society would necessarily be socialistic. He also considered revolution, like freedom, the birth right of people.

Though in their statement Bhagat Singh and Dutt had rejected any intention of killing any one in the Assembly and stated that nobody was hurt seriously because the bombs were of low intensity and meant as a warning, the judge found them guilty and sentenced them to life imprisonment.

Q3. Comment on Iqbal's views on nationalism.

Refer to Chapter-5, Q.No.-11

Q4. What is Bhoodan movement? Discuss J.P.'s contribution to it.

Refer to Chapter-6, Q.No.-9

Contribution of JP: Jaya Prakash Narain's joining with the Bhoodan Movement gave a momentum to it. J.P. was a hero of the 1942 movement who had an all India image because he was the leader of the Socialist Party. He did not get involved in power politics after independence. He was regarded as a saintly politician in the eyes of the public. J.P.'s popularity gave an impetus to the Bhoodan movement in Bihar. When the first annual Sarvodaya conference was held in the state at Chandil in 1953, J.P. gave a call for creating a Sarvodaya society by establishing a non-exploitive and just egalitarian socio-economic order. It is reported that many students from Allahabad and Calcutta who attended the conference quit universities and colleges to join the movement. Most of the land gift came from Bihar, the target to collect two and a half million acres of land gift within a year got transcended.

SECTION II

Answer any four of the following questions in about 250 words each. Each question carries 12 marks.

Q5. Identify the emerging characteristics of Indian political though in the early phase of colonialism.

Refer to Chapter-5, Q.No.-1

Q6. Summarise M.N. Roy's views on the State.

Refer to Chapter-8, Q.No.-4

Q7. How did Tilak justify the use of symbols in the National Movement? Explain.

Ans. Nationalism implies a psychological bond of unity. According to Tilak, symbols play a vital role in strengthening this bond. Secondly, symbols psychologically prepare men to rise above their self and identify with something higher and nobler like the nation.

According to Tilak, a feeling of oneness and solidarity among a people arising mainly from their common heritage was the vital force of nationalism. Knowledge of a common heritage and pride in it fosters psychological unity. It was to arouse this pride among the people that Tilak referred to Shivaji and Akbar in his speeches. Besides, he felt that by developing a feeling of common interest, a common destiny which can be realised by united political action, the feeling of nationalism could be strengthened.

The psychological bond of unity may at times be dormant. In such a situation people would have to be mobilized. Both real and mythical factors were to play an equally significant role in this process. Tilak believed that religion, which had powerful emotional appeal, should be harnessed for the dormant spirit of nationalism.

Tilak recognized the tremendous symbolic significance of historical and religious festivals, flags and slogans in arousing a spirit of nationalism. Tilak made very effective use of such symbols. He believed that these factors were more effective than economic factors when it came to mobilizing people. Thus, Tilak propagated the use of symbols in the form of the Ganpati and Shivaji festivals which subsequently acquired tremendous emotional appeal.

Q8. Briefly discuss the impact of British policies on tribals.

Refer to Chapter-4, Q.No.-19

Q9. What were the main political ideas of V.D. Savarkar? Describe.

Refer to Chapter-5, Q.No.-9

Q10. Write a note on Gandhi's perception of Satayagraha.
Refer to Chapter-6, Q.No.-5

Q11. Focus on the main features of Lohiya's theory of history.
Refer to Chapter-7, Q.No.-12

Q12. Discuss the formation of the Congress Socialist Party (CSP).
Refer to Chapter-8, Q.No.-5

SECTION III

Q13. Write short notes on any two of the following in about 100 words each. Each part carries 6 marks.

(a) Ambedkar's views on Conversion
Refer to Chapter-4, Q.No.-18

(b) Jawaharlal Nehru on Scientific Temper
Refer to Chapter-7, Q.No.-5

(c) Shir Aurobindo's theory of Spiritual Nationalism
Refer to Chapter-3, Q.No.-8

(d) Jyotiba Phule's critique of the British Rule
Refer to Chapter-4, Q.No.-5

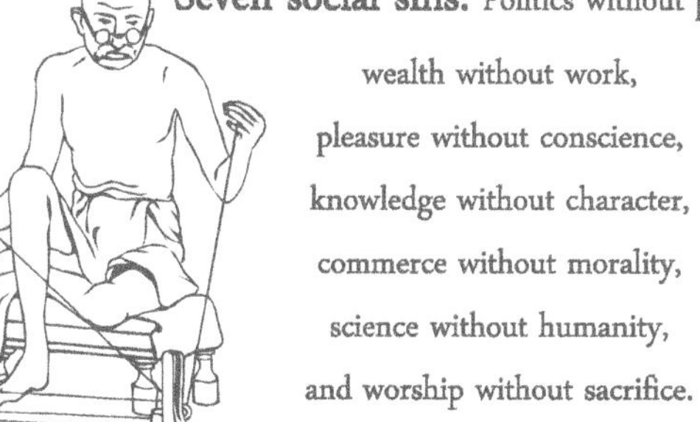

EPS-03: MODERN INDIAN POLITICAL THOUGHT
December-2016

Note:
(i) ***Section I - Any two*** *questions to be answered.*
(ii) ***Section II - Any four*** *questions to be answered.*
(iii) ***Section III - Any two*** *short notes to be written.*

SECTION I

Answer any two of the following questions in about 500 words each. Each question carries 20 marks.

Q1. How did religious revivalism help India's national awakening? Discuss.

Q2. Write a note on M.G. Ranade's views on economic transformation.

Q3. Discuss Bal Gangadhar Tilak's arguments against Factory Legislation.

Q4. Critically examine E.V. Ramasami Naicker's views on Varnashrama Dharma.

SECTION II

Answer any four of the following questions in about 250 words each. Each question carries 12 marks.

Q5. Write a note on M.A. Jinnah's two-nation theory.

Q6. Analyse M.K. Gandhi's critique of Western civilisation.

Q7. Describe Subhas Chandra Bose's views on Socialism.

Q8. Briefly discuss the characterisation of the Indian state by different Communist parties.

Q9. What were the differences between Nehru and other left wing groups? Discuss.

Q10. Discuss B.R. Ambedkar's ideas on caste and untouchability.

Q11. Critically examine the rise of Marxian Socialism in India.

Q12. Distinguish between revival and reform. In what way were the social reformers also revivalists?

SECTION III

Q13. Write short notes on any two of the following in about 100 words each. Each part carries 6 marks.

(a) J.P.'s Concept of Total Revolution

(b) Utopian Socialism

(c) Birsa Munda Revolt

(d) Bhagat Singh on Atheism

EPS-03: MODERN INDIAN POLITICAL THOUGHT
June-2017

Note:
(i) ***Section I - Any two*** *questions to be answered.*
(ii) ***Section II - Any four*** *questions to be answered.*
(iii) ***Section III - Any two*** *short notes to be written.*

SECTION I

Answer any two of the following questions in about 500 words each. Each question carries 20 marks.

Q1. Discuss the different strands of Indian Nationalism.
Refer to Chapter-1, Q.No.-6

Q2. Describe Gopal Krishna Gokhale's economic and social ideas.
Refer to June-2012, Q.No.-2

Q3. Evaluate Dr. B.R. Ambedkar's role in the drafting of the Indian Constitution.
Refer to Chapter-4, Q.No.-16

Q4. Discuss Gandhi's critique of Modern Civilisation.
Refer to Chapter-6, Q.No.-2

SECTION II

Answer any four of the following questions in about 250 words each. Each question carries 12 marks.

Q5. Briefly examine the impact of colonial intervention on India's agriculture.
Refer to Chapter-1, Q.No.-2 (iii)

Q6. What was Bal Gangadhar Tilak's theory of social reform? Elaborate.
Ans. Tilak was not opposed to social reforms. He agreed that with the passage of time social institutions and practices should and do change. In fact, in his own way he waged a battle against orthodoxy. His theory of social reforms, however, was different from that of the liberal reformers whom he opposed. He believed in organic, evolutionary and spontaneous reforms. He insisted

upon gradual reforms inspired by and rooted in the heritage of the people. He believed that the human society is always in a state of flux and can change only in a gradual manner. Never is there a sudden and total break with the past. If sudden and total break with the past is artificial, it is always rejected. This in turn creates disorder in society. Therefore, Tilak could not favour the idea of drastic change as contemplated by liberal reformers. He wanted social reforms to be introduced gradually. Tilak cautioned the reformers against wholesale rejection of the past. He urged the reformers to try and adapt (and preserve) the acceptable features of our tradition.

Further, Tilak opposed the reformer's thoughtless imitation of the west. Tilak never reconciled with the idea that all that is western is necessarily good. Tilak was open-minded and was prepared to accept whatever good the west had to offer. For instance, in his scheme of National Education he included western sciences and technology. His scheme of National Education was a fine blend of all that is good in the western and eastern traditions of knowledge, tradition and culture. It was a concrete expression of Tilak's own model of social reform.

Q7. Describe in brief, Sri Aurobindo's views on the nature of British rule.

Refer to Chapter-3, Q.No.-7

Q8. Discuss Jyotiba Phule's attack on the Varna and the Caste system.

Refer to Chapter-4, Q.No.-6

Q9. Elucidate the main trends of Muslim political thinking in the early 20th century.

Refer to Chapter-5, Q.No.-2

Q10. Briefly analyse Dr. Ram Manohar Lohia's idea of Socialism.

Refer to Chapter-7, Q.No.-4 (iv)

Q11. Comment on Nehru's scientific temperament.

Refer to Chapter-7, Q.No.-5

Q12. Examine the Indian Left's response to the Second World War.

Refer to Chapter-8, Q.No.-7

SECTION III

Q13. Write short notes on any two of the following in about 100 words each. Each part carries 6 marks.

(a) Revolutionary Socialism

Refer to June-2006, Q.No.-1

(b) Salient Features of Tribal Movements

Refer to Chapter-4, Q.No.-20

(c) M.N. Roy and Indian Social Reality

Refer to Chapter-2, Q.No.-6

(d) Jaiprakash Narayan's Concept of Total Revolution

Refer to Chapter-7, Q.No.-10

EPS-03: MODERN INDIAN POLITICAL THOUGHT
December-2017

Note:
(i) ***Section I - Any two*** *questions to be answered.*
(ii) ***Section II - Any four*** *questions to be answered.*
(iii) ***Section III - Any two*** *short notes to be written.*

SECTION I

Answer any two of the following questions in about 500 words each. Each question carries 20 marks.

Q1. Describe the condition of the lower castes in 18thcentury India.

Q2. Write an essay on the Self-Respect Movement launched by E.V. Ramaswami Naicker.

Q3. Discuss the measures suggested by Dr. B.R. Ambedkar for removal of untouchability.

Q4. Explain the Social Reconstruction Programme of Gandhiji.

SECTION II

Answer any four of the following questions in about 250 words each. Each question carries 12 marks.

Q5. Analyse in brief M.G. Ranade's ideas on Indian Administration.

Q6. Elucidate Sri Aurobindo's views on the nature of British Rule.

Q7. Examine in brief the political ideas V.D. Savarkar.

Q8. Explain Muhammad Ali Jinnah's Two-Nation Theory.

Q9. What were Nehru's assumptions of foreign policy? Elaborate.

Q10. What were the ways in which colonialism affected the caste system?

Q11. Discuss in brief Subhash Chandra Bose's views on Socialism.

Q12. Describe M.N. Roy's concept of Radical Humanism.

SECTION III

Q13. Write short notes on any two of the following in about 100 words each. Each part carries 6 marks.

(a) Raja Ram Mohan Roy on Liberty

(b) Jyotiba Phule on Equality Between Men and Women

(c) Congress Socialist Party

(d) Nehru on Fabian Socialism

EPS-03: MODERN INDIAN POLITICAL THOUGHT
June-2018

Note:
(i) ***Section I - Any two*** *questions to be answered.*
(ii) ***Section II - Any four*** *questions to be answered.*
(iii) ***Section III - Any two*** *short notes to be written.*

SECTION

Answer any two of the following questions in about 500 words each. Each question carries 20 marks.

Q1. Critically analyse the impacts of the British rule on the Indian economy.
Ans. Refer to Chapter-4, Q.No.-1 (Pg. No.-80)

Q2. Discuss the political ideas of Sir Syed Ahmed Khan.
Ans. Refer to Chapter-5, Q.No.-10 (Pg. No.-135)

Q3. Comment on M.N. Roy's concept of Radical Humanism.
Ans. Refer to Chapter-8, Q.No.-8 (Pg. No.-196)

Q4. Discuss the political philosophy of Subhash Chandra Bose.
Ans. Subhash interpreted Indian history and asserted that it has to be recorded not in decades or in centuries but in the thousands. India has passed through various vicissitudes of fortune. Neither the individual nor the nation can have an uninterrupted career or progress and prosperity. The same is true for India which has always been characterised by a very high level of culture and civilisation. Bose summarises his readings of Indian history as follows:
(1) A period of rise has been followed by a period of decline to be followed again by a upheaval.
(2) The decline is the result chiefly of physical and intellectual fatigue.
(3) Progress and fresh consolidation has been brought about by an influx of new ideas and sometimes an infusion of fresh blood.
(4) Every new epoch has been heralded by people possessing greater intellectual power and superior military skill.
(5) Throughout Indian history all foreign elements have always been gradually absorbed by Indian society. The British are the first and the only exception to this.
(6) In spite of change in the central government, the people have all along been accustomed to .a large measure of real liberty.
To regain lost glory Subhash wanted regeneration of energy in India.

SECTION II

Answer any four of the following questions in about 250 words each. Each question carries 12 marks.

Q5. Discuss Mahatma Gandhi's views on Satyagraha.

Ans. Refer to Chapter-6, Q.No.-5 (Pg. No.-151)

Q6. Discuss the economic and social ideas of Gokhale.

Ans. Refer to Chapter-2, Q.No.-12 and Q.No.-13 (Pg. No.-51, 54)

Q7. Analyse Aurobindo's views on Theory of Spiritual Nationalism.

Ans. Refer to Chapter-3, Q.No.-8 (Pg. No.-68)

Q8. Comment on the opinion of the Indian Marxists on Indian State and Ruling class.

Ans. Refer to Chapter-8, Q.No.-9(i) (Pg. No.-198)

Q9. What is the significance of Militant Nationalism in contemporary polities?

Ans. Refer to Chapter-3, Q.No.-2 (Pg. No.-59)

Q10. Discuss the main features of Hindu REvivalism.

Ans. Religious Revivalism

Religious revivalism was a trend within the reform movements which sought to reform religion, but differed in one important respect. It sought to reform by an appeal to the past-the Golden Age, a; it were. It sought to restore the glory of ancient religion. Mainly emerging from within the womb of Hindu Society, they tried to dexterously combine pristine religious purity with many modern values like individual liberty and democracy. Among the major religious reform movements of 19th ceatury India, like Brahmo Samaj, Prarthana Sarnaj, Arya Samaj and Ramakrishna Mission, it was the latter two that really represented this appeal to the past. The Arya Samaj with its slogan o: 'Hack to the Vedas' and the Ramakrishna Mission with its attempt to resurrect ved~antic Hinduism, though substantially different in their approaches to religion had the same essential purpose of reforming religion in terms with changing times. They sought to establish to some degree, the freedom of individual, break the stranglehold of Brahminism and reform the caste system which had birth as its solid determinant of status.

Thm, Arya Samaj and its chief architect Swami Dayanand Saraswati, repudiated the authority of the Brahmins and fought against the very idea of intermediaries between God and his devotees. To that extent, they freed the individual from

the tyranny of Hralimin priesthood. It opposed polytheism and associated meaningless rituals and superstitions which~plitth e people into innumerable sects. The Ramakrishna Mission which drew inspiration from saints like Chandidas and Chaitanya and was initiated by the rustic saint Ramakrishna, on the other haG' ~dealized Hinduism, its polytheism and idol worsl,ip. Swami Vivekananda, its chief propagandist, was chiefly concerned that Indian nationalism which he said must fight the corrupting 'materialist influences' of the west. Unification and reform of Hindu
society were a prerequisite to this end.

There was thus an essehtial unity in the religious revivalist movements, in terms of the objectives. The Arya Samaj fought against the rigid, hereditary caste system and argued for the inclusion of guna (character!, Karma (action) and Swabhava (nature) as criteria for the basis of caste. Even Shudras, according to it, could srudy the vedas. It was this appeal of religious revivalism that drew hundreds of nationalist towards it and it thus signalled a component of India's national awakening.

Q11. Critically examine Dr. Ambedkar's views on Democracy.
Ans. Refer to Chapter-4, Q.No.-14 (Pg. No.-104)

Q12. Comment on the Marxist political though in India.
Ans. Refer to Chapter-8, Q.No.-1 and Q.No.-2 (Pg. No.-186, 187)

SECTION III

Q13. Write short notes on any two of the following in about 100 words each. Each part carries 6 marks.
(a) Jinnah's Views on the Two-Nation Theory
Ans. Refer to Chapter-5, Q.No.-12 (Pg. No.-140)

(b) Political Ideas of Justice Ranade
Ans. Ranade is considered a prophet of modern India because he visualised the future, course of development in India. Ranade sought to enlighten the Indian masses about I the benefits of material progress which could be used as a means to ethical and desirable lives. Therefore, he expounded a political philosophy that aimed at spiritualisation of politics but oppossed the use of religion or spiritual authority in politics. He believed in liberalism but revised its basic tenets.

In the present section, we shall discuss:
(i) Ranade's ideas on liberalism,

(ii) on nature and functions of the state,
(iii) on Indian politics and
(iv) concept of Indian nationalism.

(c) Jyotiba Phule's Views on Caste System
Ans. Refer to Chapter-4, Q.No.-6 (Pg. No.-89)

(d) Assumptions of Jawaharlal Nehru's Foreign Policy
Ans. In the initial statements explaining India's foreign policy Nehru claimed that it was an independent foreign policy. Nehru developed an independent thinking in the area of foreign policy. He could understand the dynamics of global politics. There are basically two power blocks in international politics: Western Imperialist Block and Soviet Socialist Block. India and other newly liberated countries should follow an independent line. They should not be member of any block. Nehru states that, "we should approach these problems, whether domestic or international problems in our own way. If by any chance we align ourselves definitely with one power group, we may perhaps from one point of view do some good, but I have not the shadow of a doubt that from a larger point of view, not only India but of world peace, it will do haw." Nehru wanted that the non-aligned countries should function as a power block. They should share their wealth for their prosperity.
Nehru was by no means for an India which would be isolated from the rest of the world. His independent foreign policy was not negative. He realised that India is a paft of'the world in regard to science, culture, economy and politics. He made the following observation making his views clear on this matter: "Our entire society is based on this more or less. This basis must go and be transformed into one of co-operation, not isolated which is impossible. If this is admitted and is found feasible then attempts should be made to realize, if not in terms of an economy which is cut off from the rest of the world, but rather one which co-operates. From the economic or political point of view, an isolated India may well be a vacuum which increases the acquisitive tendencies of others and thus creates conflicts."

EPS-03: MODERN INDIAN POLITICAL THOUGHT
December-2018

Note:
(i) *Section I - Answer **any two** questions.*
(ii) ***Section II** - Answer **any four** questions*
(iii) ***Section III** - Write short notes on **any two** parts of question no. 13.*

SECTION I

Answer any two of the following questions in about 500 words each. Each question carries 20 marks.

Q1. Discuss the impact of colonial intervention on the social and cultural fields of India.

Q2. What was the role of the State as envisaged by Gopal Krishna Gokhale? Elaborate.

Q3. Analyse the influence of militant nationalism on the Indian National Congress and its significance for contemporary politics.

Q4. Discuss the political liberalism of Raja Ram Mohan Roy.

SECTION II

Answer any four of the following questions in about 250 words each. Each question carries 12 marks.

Q5. Discuss Aurobindo's concept of nation.

Q6. Analyse the philosophical foundations of Tilak's notion of Swaraj.

Q7. Examine Vivekananda's views on nationalism.

Q8. Discuss Gandhi's views on Hinduism.

Q9. Analyse the impact of British rule on the Indian economy.

Q10. Discuss the socialist philosophy of Narendra Dev.

Q11. Write a note on M.N. Roy's concept of radical humanism.

Q12. Critically analyse the basic philosophy of socialism.

SECTION III

Q13. Write short notes on any two of the following in about 100 words each. Each part carries 6 marks.

(a) Tilak and the Concept of National Education

(b) The Congress Socialist Party

(c) The Lahore Conspiracy Case

(d) Ranade and the Philosophy of Theism

EPS-03: MODERN INDIAN POLITICAL THOUGHT
June-2019

Note:
(i) ***Section I*** - *Answer* ***any two*** *questions.*
(ii) ***Section II*** - *Answer* ***any four*** *questions*
(iii) ***Section III*** - *Write short notes on* ***any two*** *parts of question no. 13.*

SECTION I

Answer any two of the following questions in about 500 words each. Each question carries 20 marks.

Q1. Critically examine the Tribal Movements in colonial India.
Ans. Refer to Chapter-4, Q.No.-3 (Pg. No.-84)

Q2. Discuss Jyotiba Phule's critique of the Varna and Caste system in India.
Ans. Refer to Chapter-4, Q.No.-6 (Pg. No.-89)

Q3. Examine the political ideas of Dayanand Saraswati.
Ans. Refer to Chapter-5, Q.No.-4 (Pg. No.-125)

Q4. Analyse Gandhi's views on the concept of Satyagraha.
Ans. Refer to Chapter-6, Q.No.-5 (Pg. No.-151)

SECTION II

Answer any four of the following questions in about 250 words each. Each question carries 12 marks.

Q5. Analyse the role of Raja Ram Mohan Roy as a religious reformer.
Ans. A review and revaluation of religion was Roy's primary concern. He was of the opinion that rationality and modernity needed to be introduced in the field of religion and that "irrational religion" was at the root of many social evils. The socio-political progress of this country, according to him, depended mainly on the successful revolution in the religious thought and behaviour. He was interested not only in reforming the Hindu religion, but also tried to remove the discrepancies among the various religions of the world. He undertook a serious study of comparative religions and realised in due course that true Hinduism, true Islam and true Christianity are not fundamentally different from each other. He hoped that the universal religion for mankind could be established by combining the best elements of all religions. This

concept of universal religion meant not merely religious tolerance, but also transcending all the sectarian barriers of separate religion. Roy, thus attempted a spiritual synthesis, stressing the unity of all religious experience. He became a confirmed monotheist. In 1828 he established the Brahmo Samaj. The Samaj acted as a forum for religious and philosophical contemplation and discussion. Roy's criticism of religious antagonised the priestly classes of all organised religions. Time has, however, proved beyond doubt the relevance or Roy's thoughts and deeds.

Influences that Shaped Him

Besides Bengali and Sanskrit, Roy had mastered Arabic, Persian, Hebrew, Greek, Latin and 17 other leading languages spoken in the world. Roy's familiarity with such diverse languages, exposed him to a variety of cultural, philosophical and religious experiences. He studied Islam thoroughly. The rationality and the logical consistency of Arabic literature in general and the mutajjil in particular impressed Roy greatly. The Sufi poets like Saddi and Haafiz made a deep impact on Roy's mind. The Quaranic concept of Tauhid or Unity of God fascinated Roy.

Thus, in this context, when Roy examined the Hindu religious texts and practices, he was greatly disturbed. He found polytheism, idolatory and irrational superstitions absolutely intolerable. He decided to fight against these age-old evils.

A Sanskrit scholar, Ram Mohan had studied the Hindu scriptures in depth and thus he got the inspiration to free the orthodox Hinduism from its obscurantist elements. Roy also had studied the teachings of the Buddha Dhamma. It is said that in the course of his travels he reached Tibet. There he was pained to see how the principles of Buddhism were blatantly violated and how idol-worship, which had no place in the Dhamma of Lord Buddha, had come to be accepted. He strongly criticised the practices.

As a Dewan in the revenue department, when the Raja was required to go to Rangpur, he got an opportunity to study the Tantrik literature as well as the Jaina's Kalpasutras and other scriptures. He also mastered the English language and acquainted himself with political developments and ideas like rationalism and liberation in England and Europe. The knowledge of English not only facilitated Roy's contacts with Englishmen but also opened up a whole new world to him. In Roy's own words, he now gave up his initial prejudices against the British and realized that it was better to seek help from these enlightened rulers in ameliorating the condition of the ignorant and superstitious masses. He became a strong advocate of English education and a supporter of British rule.

Roy admired the Bible as much as he did the Vedanta and the Quran. Many of his critics thought that two major features of Roy's Brahmo Samaj, namely, the opposition to idol-worship, and the practice of collective prayer were borrowed from Christianity. Roy was charged of Christianising Hindustan in a surreptitious manner. It is true that Roy advised Indians to imbibe Christ's ethical teachings. Roy himself admitted, "I found the doctrine of Christ more conductive to moral principles and better adopted for the use of rational beings than any other which have come to my knowledge." He also compiled "The Precepts of Jesus" with a view to proving how the teachings of Christ could be better adapted to rational man's use. At the same time it has to be noted that he was no blind admirer of the Christian faith. He rejected the doctrine of Christ's divinity (arguing that if Christ is divine, so is Rama) and the doctrine of Trinity preached by the missionaries.

From what has been said above, it should be clear that it is unfair to charge Roy with seeking to Christianise Hinduism. Rather it was Roy's ardent desire to revive Hinduism in its pristine, pure and universal form. He pleaded for an Advaita philosophy which rejected caste, idolatry and superstitious rites and rituals.

Thus, Roy was someone who had gone beyond narrow divisions of religious faiths. He embraced all that was the most valuable and the most inspiring in Hinduism, Christianity and Islam.

Reinterpreting Hinduism

Roy devoted all his energies to fighting sectarianism and other medieval tendencies prevailing in the Hindu society, such as polytheism, idolatory and superstitions. He was a firm believer of the Advaita philosophy which left no scope for such tendencies. Roy was quite sure that unless the Hindu society underwent a religious and social transformation, it would not become fit for political progress. According to him, the then prevailing religious system of the Hindus was ill-suited for the promotion of their political interests. The multitude of religious rites and ceremonies and the unnatural distinctions of caste and laws of purification, Roy argued, had deprived the Hindus of any kind of common political feeling. Hindus must accept some changes in their religion at least for the sake of their political advantage and social comfort. Reinterpretation of Hinduism, to Roy, was thus the starting point for the programme of socio-political reform. Roy sought to combine the deep experiences of spiritual life with the basic principle of social democracy. He denounced all superstitions and the evil practices based on them because he was convinced that these longstanding customary practices really did not form the core of their religious faith. They, in fact, had no place or support in the religious texts of the Hindus. Roy wanted to draw the attention of his countrymen to the ancient purity of their religion. To him, this purity was well reflected in the Vedas and the Upanishads.

In order to prove that blind faith and superstitious beliefs and practices had no basis in the pure Hindu religion, Roy undertook the difficult task of translating the Upanishads into English and Bengali. He gave elaborate notes and comments with these translations and distributed them free of cost amongst the people.

At the age of 16, Roy wrote a book challenging the validity of the practice of idol-worship, which according to him was the root cause of many other social evils. It led to the multiplication of deities and also a multitude of modes of worship. This, in turn, had resulted in dividing the society into innumerable castes and groups, each worshiping an idol different from others. The process of division and subdivision was unending. Roy considered idolatry to be opposed to reason and common sense. Besides, it had no sanction in the ancient religious texts. Roy preached monotheism and a collective prayer from the platform of the Brahmo Samaj.

Roy fought against the superstitions which had resulted in evolving many inhuman and cruel customs and traditions in Hindu society. He tried to convince the people that the superstitions had nothing to do with the teachings of original Hinduism. Roy not only preached but also practised what he preached. Travelling across the ocean was considered to be a sin by the orthodox Hindus. Roy was the first Hindu to break this superstition. He himself undertook overseas travel. This courage of conviction on his part made Roy's efforts more effective.

Q6. Discuss Muhammad Iqbal's concept of Islamic Democracy.
Ans. Refer to Chapter-5, Q.No.-11 (Pg. No.-136)

Q7. Examine the political ideas of V.D. Savarkar.
Ans. Refer to Chapter-5, Q.No.-9 (Pg. No.-133)

Q8. Discuss Dr. Ram Manohar Lohia's Theory of History.
Ans. Refer to Chapter-7, Q.No.-12 (Pg. No.-182)

Q9. Analyse Dr. Ambedkar's ideas of State Socialism.
Ans. Refer to Chapter-4, Q.No.-15 (Pg. No.-106)

Q10. Discuss economic and social ideals of Gokhale.
Ans. Refer to June-2012, Q.No.-2 (Pg. No.-237)

Q11. Discuss Vinobha Bhave's concept of Sarvodaya.

Ans. Vinoba Bhave developed Gandhi's economic thought in a more practical sense. Vinoba Bhave was concerned about creating a Sarvodaya society in rural India. This could not be based on unequal distribution of land. Concentration of land in the hands of few creates a basis for rural violence. Rural rich must participate in voluntary distribution of land. Bhoodan means land gift. According to Bhoodan's philosophy, the rich must be persuaded to participate in the process of land gift. Vinoba Bhave went on foot from village to village and propagated the Movement. He advised each rich man in the village to think of him as a son. In other words "if he has one son, then take him (Bhave) as the second son. If he has two sons, then take him as the third son". Vinoba pleaded with each landed man to share a portion of one's land as Bhoodan.

Q12. Analyse the social reform movement of India in the 19th century.

Ans. Refer to Chapter-2, Q.No.-1, Q.No.-2 and Q.No.-3 (Pg. No.-29, 31, 32)

SECTION III

Q13. Write short notes on any two of the following in about 100 words each. Each part carries 6 marks.

(a) The Kherwar Movement of the Santhals

Ans. This movement (1833) was motivated by the desire to return to an idealised past of tribal independence. The word "Kherwar" is said to be an ancient name of Santhals and in their opinion, it is linked to the Golden age of their history. At that time, the Santhals (Kherwars) were supposed to have enjoyed absolute independence. They had to pay tribute to their chief for the protection which he provided to them. This movement started under the charismatic leadership Bhagirath Majhi. He assumed the title of 'Babaji'. He announced that the world restore the Golden age of Santhals, if they returned to the worship of God and cleared themselves from their sins. He vowed to liberate them from the oppression of officials, landlords and money-lenders. He exhorted them to worship the Hindu God Ram, identifying him with Santhal "Caudo". He banned the Santhal's pigs and fowls. He assured them that their land would be recovered and given back to them. He explained their oppression as a divine punishment for not worshipping God and for turning to veneration of minor and evil spirits. He imposed on the Santhals the rules and behaviour which reflected the Hindu notion of purity and pollution. This movement took a more political turn later for driving the non-Santhals out of their habitat.

(b) Sir Syed Ahmed Khan and Aligarh Movement

Ans. Refer to June-2010, Q.No.-13(b) (Pg. No.-231)

(c) Jawaharlal Nehru and India's Foreign Policy

Ans. Refer to June-2012, Q.No.-9 (Pg. No.-240)

(d) The Prarthana Samaj of Ranade

Ans. The Prarathana Samaj was established in Bombay by Dr. Atma Ram Pandurang (1825-1898) in 1876 with the objective of rational worship and social reform. The two great members of this Samaj were shri R.C. Bhandarkar and Justice Mahadeve Govind Ranade. They devoted themselves to the work of the social reforms such as inter-caste dining, inter-caste marriage, widow remarriage and improvement of the lot of women and depressed classes. Mahavdev Govind Ranade (1842-1901) devoted his entire life to Prarathana Samaj.

The Brahmo Samaj established by Raja Ram Mohan Roy inspired Ranade to establish the Prarthana Samaj. However, Ranade decided from the beginning that the Prarthana Samaj would not follow the Brahmo Samaj in toto. He wanted the Prarthana Samaj to bring about changes from within, by remaining in the Hindu fold unlike the Brahmo Samaj which had disturbed, according to Ranade, the historical continuity of the community by going out of the fold. 'The Prarthana Samaj tried to take inspiration from the Indian sources, as it was believed in the orthodox quarters at that time that Brahmo Samaj was influenced by Christianity. Ranade claimed that he belonged to the long tradition of Marathi saints such as Jnyaneshvar, Namdeo, Eknath and Tukaram. In fact, the Samaj he claimed was continuation of the Bhakti movement. Thus, the sources of its inspiration were indigenous and its practices had local roots. Therefore, the Prarthana Samaj did not become a separate sect in Maharashtra and continued with its efforts to reform religion from within.

Thus, we see that although Ranade was a religious man who had great respect for the Hindu 'Philosophical and religious tradition, he wanted to reform Hinduism so that it could recapture its old essence.

EPS-03: MODERN INDIAN POLITICAL THOUGHT
December, 2019

Note:
(i) *Section I — Answer **any two** questions.*
(ii) *Section II — Answer **any four** questions.*
(iii) *Section III — Write **any two** short notes.*

SECTION I

Answer any two of the following questions in about 500 words each. Each question carries 20 marks.

Q1. Evaluate the role of the Tribal Movements during the British Rule in India.
Ans. Refer to Chapter-4, Q.No.-3 (Pg. No.-84)

Q2. Discuss the economic ideas of Bal Gangadhar Tilak.
Ans. Refer to Chapter-3, Q.No.-2 (Pg. No.-63)

Q3. Analyse the philosophical foundation of Aurobindo's political thought.
Ans. Refer to June-2010, Q.No.-2 (Pg. No.-226)

Q4. Comment on Dr. Abul Kalam Azad's views on democracy.
Ans. Refer to Chapter-5, Q.No.-14 (Pg. No.-143)

SECTION II

Answer any four of the following questions in about 250 words each. Each question carries 12 marks.

Q5. Discuss the rise of Marxian Socialism in India.
Ans. Refer to Chapter-8, Q.No.-1 (Pg. No.-186)

Q6. Discuss Acharya Narendra Dev's views on Socialism.
Ans. Refer to Chapter-7, Q.No.-9 (Pg. No.-175)

Q7. Analyse Swami Vivekanada's views on Nationalism.
Ans. Refer to Chapter-5, Q.No.-7 (Pg. No.-131)

Q8. Evaluate Indian Left's response to the Second World War.
Ans. Refer to Chapter-8, Q.No.-7 (Pg. No.-194)

Q9. Discuss Jawaharlal Nehru's views on Social Revolution.
Ans. Refer to Chapter-7, Q.No.-4 (Pg. No.-165)

Q10. Discuss Swami Dayanand Saraswati's political ideas.
Ans. Refer to Chapter-5, Q.No.-4 (Pg. No.-125)

Q11. Examine Naicker's views on Varnashrama Dharma.
Ans. Refer to June-2012, Q.No.-5 (Pg. No.-239)

Q12. Discuss Raja Ram Mohan Roy's views on Freedom of Expression.
Ans. Refer to Chapter-2, Q.No.-6, 7 (Pg. No.-38, 40)

Q13. Write short notes on any two of the following in about 100 words each. Each part carries 6 marks.
(a) Ranade and Prarthana Samaj
Ans. Refer to June-2019, Q.No.-13(d) (Pg. No.-268)

(b) Lahore Conspiracy Case
Ans. Refer to Chapter-3, Q.No.-11 (Pg. No.-74)

(c) Bhagat Singh's views on state Revolution
Ans. Refer to Chapter-3, Q.No.-12 (Pg. No.-75)

(d) Dr. Ambedhkar and the concept of State Socialism
Ans. Refer to Chapter-4, Q.No.-15 (Pg. No.-106)

www.ingramcontent.com/pod-product-compliance
Ingram Content Group UK Ltd.
Pitfield, Milton Keynes, MK11 3LW, UK
UKHW021706190726
13853UKWH00001B/436

9 789381 690215